What Happens to
Gods and Demons

What Happens to Gods and Demons

By
H. N. Verma, Amrit Verma

BLUEJAY BOOKS

An imprint of Srishti Publishers & Distributors
New Delhi & Calcutta

BLUEJAY BOOKS
An imprint of SRISHTI PUBLISHERS & DISTRIBUTORS
64-A, Adhchini
Sri Aurobindo Marg
New Delhi 110 017

First published in India by *BLUEJAY BOOKS* 2004

ISBN 81-88575-41-0

Printed and bound in India

Cover design by Sandip Sinha
Email: sundeepsinha@yahoo.co.in

CONTENTS

May the Lord Ganesha!
With his gigantic tusks, huge belly
And brilliance of billions of suns
Remove obstacles strewn
In my path of virtuous deeds.

Blessings to Malvika and Rishab

INTRODUCTION

Life is not a bed of roses but divine power can shape it so. Faith in gods and goddesses does help to make a devotee's life happy. That is what the devotees say.

A bed of roses may turn into a barren strip full of thorns, if a demon or demoness casts his/her devilish eye or in anger utters a curse on one who dared to cross his/her way. That is what faithfuls are apprehensive of and they advise their ilk to avert/prevent before it escapes the lips of the divinity.

Being on the right side of the super power which is invisible but omnipresent, omniscient and omnipotent, and seeking his blessings and guidance becomes the aim and endeavour of the devotees and faithfuls. Faith brightens their life and individually and collectively they earnestly do their utmost to please the deities and appease the evil forces. Deities and demons have become part of peoples' religio-social life. In temples, mosques, churches where those powers are housed and where the honest and dishonest, sincere and insincere congregate for religious purposes or devising collective action the customs continue and are acted upon sanctimoniously with greater vigour. The gurus say prayers and profess their experiences of peace in the divinity's presence and glibly talk to the gullibles of their communion with the super power whom they variously call Bhagwan, Allah, God. Some ring the bell and go round the sanctum sanctorum with symbolic authority of one who is Truth, Beneficent and Beautiful. They go on pilgrimages to holy places, high hills and take dip(s) in sacred waters to secure redemption. They are rid of sins, if any committed knowingly or unknowingly through thought, speech or action-faith says.

The resultant joy, happiness and peace on the positive side and sorrow and grief on the other grow and develop into myths which intermediaries interpret and interpolate and twist to serve their selfish ends. Pursuit of religion, philosophy and science consolidates their views on larger issues–of creation of universe and life and creator, and nature for some. Some equate God (Supreme Power) with nature. Different faiths offer different answers and paths to reach the goal.

Hindu scriptures opine that there are numerous paths to reach a goal. Nevertheless Truth is one, and that one is not only Truth but benevolent and beautiful also. Whether he is Being or not-being, He is elusive, a trouble shooter for spiritualists and mystics. Though unable to experiment in lab conditions on that elusive super power, some scientists confide that a stage is within reach and they can pin point that Tatekam of Upanishads. Have the scientists crossed the stage of Neti Neti which blocked the way of seekers? To us Einstein's finding appeals, frankly speaking. The eminent physicist said : God is like a clock maker who made the clock and left the place without leaving his address or giving any clues to his whereabouts. The clock continues functioning well and so long as it does so, the necessity of the clock-maker is not felt nor is there any curiosity about him. (God's case is different). Difficulty can arise only if or when something goes wrong with the working of the clock. A myth is like a clock – it is made but rarely one can say who the creator of the myth (myth-maker) is or where he has disappeared. None knows his whereabouts.

Myths, legends, folksongs, folklore, saga, adventure, loyalty – pertaining to deities and demons interest people – and they get expression through various media, including mass media. Worship of icons or congregation in vacant space evokes aesthetic feelings and emotions and provides occasion to pray for betterment of suffering humanity and for peace. Scriptures provide the grit. Vedas, Testaments, Quran (or Kuran), Jatakas – all are mythic in their approach. Hindus changed from Vedic to Brahmanic to Sanatan. Testaments separated and developed into old and new and the Quran and Hadith were interpreted to seek the Sunni-Shia-Ahmedia....requirements. The evolution of myths has kept pace with developments of all sorts.

Western scholars assign derivation of myth to 'Mythos', a Greek word. Our statistician friend, Dr. Jagdish Rustagi, though he disclaims being a philosopher, has settled on *Mithya*, commonly known as Shankarcharya's 'illusion'. Illusion is not a happy version. 'Jagdish' itself connotes Lord of the Universe, though we don't place him on that high pedestal. We appreciated his synonyms to myth – foibles, allegory, shibboleth. Finally, we are constrained to say myths are myths.

Myth has been defined in "A Dictionary of creative Myths" as a narrative of given culture groups' sense of sacred past and its significant relationship with the deeper power of surrounding world and universe, and Mythology has been equated with "a shadow of collective dream that threatens chaos and in the end becomes chaos, nothing becomes something." The cosmos had its beginning from a cosmic egg (Hiranyagarbha), primordial mound, deluge or other world, and the archetypal characters may be creator, trickster, first saved man with an urge for new beginning.

The physicists account the beginning of the universe to "Bang Bang". The first three chapters of this work are devoted to creation as viewed by Hindus, Greeks and Romans, and Science. Though myth is the predominant feature of this book, it examines the status from the point of view of Science and Philosophy.

The Vedic philosophy perceived coexistence of creator and nature as one. This was corroborated by Upanishads and the six systems of Indian philosophy.

The Indian and Greek are the oldest civilizations. The Greek civilization is now extinct. Fortunately their rich myths have great potentiality to inform, educate and entertain people. The Greek civilization appeared in the form of Roman civilization and the latter borrowed (or lifted) the entire mythology of the former – as also its literature and art – except names of some gods and goddesses whom they gave Roman names. The change was like the avatars of Vishnu in Hindu mythology. This work presents the myths of Indian (Hindu), Greek and Roman civilizations and hopefully it should entertain and educate readers about the significant aspects of those three civilizations. Once they catch attention the myths become fixtures of reader's mind.

The Indian Mythology is deprecated (or appreciated) for being an "extricable jungle of luxuriant growth" (*Encyclopedia of Myths*). Anyone who sets foot into it must face 'Aryanization of India', 'Evolution of Brahmanic Dharma with caste system tugged in its folds' and 'India That is Bharat'. No doubt initially the occupation based Dharma brought prosperity – because of the expertise and excellence gained by hereditary performance of manual work of caste-members, but its one unfortunate affect was looking down upon manual work and treating it as menial work. The Dwijas developed a superiority complex and treated the manual and menial works alike. Rites and hymns, wedging war and business were pure engagements and manual work impure and lowest in hierarchy. The latter day alien immigrants did not interfere in the affairs of Hindu community – the Muslim and Christian rulers adopted the Brahmanic Dwija trait that theirs was to rule. The Greek, the Roman and their successors, the Western civilization introduced a class of slaves from the vanquished enemy. One major difference which is noticeable is that whereas the 'Slavery' is extinct, the 'caste system' despite efforts of enlightened souls to repeal it has continued to survive in this land. The worse is that emigrant Hindus have taken with them the Varna Vyavastha which they practice and perpetuate in their adopted countries. The Upanishads and the Puranas play subsidiary roles in the faith.

The concepts of 'Sansar is Ishwarleela', 'Atma Parmatma', etc. have given birth to innumerable myths and characters full of virtues and vices. The work furnishes rudiments of such myths.

Myths are an admixture of facts and fiction, and not history. Not even prehistory. Innumerable myths were floated. Some disappeared. Some survived. The entertainment value of the myths is 'secular', despite their exaggerated garbs and norms, be they from any civilization. Death and liberation have no value for the dead and liberated. They have universal appeal. Recollection of the myths is its own reward.

Regarding creation, we posed to our Persian scholar friend, Mr. Rajinder Lal Mehra, "Is there a creator or the universe has evolved on its own" In reply he cited :

Hasti e ma Kharama e ma
Masti e ma nizam e ma
Zandagi e ma doam e ma
Minigaram me roam

(My existence, my movement, my inebriation, my constitution and my life – (each) is perpetual, I observe and pass by.)

Acknowledgements

We thank the following organizations whose resources we utilized as also our friends who took interest in the production of "What Happens to Gods and Demons Indian, Greek, Roman".

Surnyvale Public Library, San Jose Public Library, Standford University Law School, RCL Verma Library, Alampur (PIN 477 449), M.P., India and Ved Pratisthan, New Delhi

Ishan Kumar (Palm Dale), Bonie & Mark Bolwinkle, Minister of Church, John and Polly (Los Altos.), Arya Bhushan, Palo Alto, Nishi Mehra, Dr. L.C. Gupta., M.N. Deshpande, M.B. Lal, P. Sankar Sivadas, Niranjan Kapasi, A.C. Saxena, Som Sapru, G.P. Chaco – Press Enclave; Balasubramaniam, Bangalore; Amba Ramanathan, Virendra Varma (Sunnyvale), Molinder Singh Kohli (San Jose), Jal and Aloo Doctor, Deepika Mehra, Dr. Shri Kant Verma, K.L. Verma, Ravi Vyas, Mrs. Purang, Prabha Raina, Late Ram Dayal Mahte and Dr. Kamalesh.

Brahma's Statue at Batambang

BOOK I

1

CREATION, EVOLUTION –HINDU VIEW

How did the universe originate? How did life evolve? Is there a creator? If yes, why did he create it? Is there a soul? Questions like these have been teasing human minds, but so far no satisfactory solution has emerged. Religion, Philosophy and Science have made deep and extensive probes. Scientists now assure that they are inching towards the proximate resolution of the puzzles. A lookback at the stupendous efforts made by human kind would help understand the riddles and may guide us in correct direction.

It is said that religion began in the past with wonder and awe. It unfolded the creator (God or gods) as an omnipotent, omnipresent and omniscient idea. Efforts to define it gave birth to myths which inspired realization of someone who is perfect and ultimate. Some thinkers, especially mystic, conjectured that dragon within clamped man down and brought him in accord with inscrutable to recognize positive values. Success gave him an optimistic outlook. Knowledge gained through myths gave radiance, harmony and splendour to his personal as well as social life. Man's speculative and poetic expressions are scattered in scriptures, which though enjoyable offer no definite clue to the ultimate.

Religion also called faith, creed, sect, denomination and persuasion generally signifies a belief in and reverence for a supernatural power – a creator of the universe and life on it. Since people express their belief in diverse ways and their religion, each one claiming that it alone engenders harmony and peace and expects unto pursuants to live by a right conduct that makes life happy and, the world a peaceful place. He proclaims that abandoning right conduct has serious complications. Which means religion can have both beneficent and malevolent affects and sure enough there are both proponents and opponents of each religion. Even so, no human society can do without religion.

The first stepping stone of religion is ritual and since long man has been a engaged in rites and rituals. In the beginning he conducted rituals for the success of his hunting expedition and when he started living a settled life, he said prayers for sufficient rainfall for his field. He even went out visiting places of worship, bathed in rivers, made offerings and observed festivals to please his God. He tried to live by religion and inculcated among his children respect for customs and conventions. Strict discipline and observance brought in rigidities which bolstered intolerance, jingoism, misunderstanding and friction. Human history is full of crusades and recently jihad has been twisted to cause immense suffering to human beings all over the world.

Religion concerns with issues like creation (of universe and life) and observance of ethical values aiming at human happiness. People, as a mark of their religious involvement, participate in cultural activities and performances. But such activities divide societies and have deleterious affects on mankind.

The mythic accounts of creation are man's symbolic engagement in non-worldly affairs. His simple life gets vitiated and becomes complicated by stresses and strains. He suspects Vishnu's veracity. How could he rest on the hood of Sheshnag and at the same time be engaged in creation of the next world? The august presence of the Lord may appeal to the faithful but his engagement is not convincing. A rational being blames superstitution and blind faith. However, he need not discard myths because by doing so their value as repositories of the past will be lost. Myths are man's heritage.

Philosophy also deals with subjects like creation, creator, nature, self but at a higher, speculative level. It probes being and non-being in the context of nature. So far it has not succeeded in finding any ultimate truth (*sat*). The six schools of thought also provide a panoramic view of the creator's play with nature.

Religion explains creation in terms of its creator, God and primordial matter (Prakriti) – and in the scheme of things God sustains the cosmos. He is one and one alone, gives bounties to man while all nature's bounties merge and become one in time. Also, Prithvi is the abode of man who alone was considered worthy of revelation. While the entire cosmos is the realm of effulgence, beyond it is the expanding universe – Swaragalok or SVA.

Puranas are the store house of Hindu myths, myths relating to gods and goddesses, men and women and animal. Myths have been shaped into folktales, folklore, legends, sagas etc. Local color and revision for media adaptation are forgotten because of their topical value. Some become irrevelent. Some relate to distress when man creates more myths and tells stories. He prays to God to remove obstacles strewn in his path. There are myths about every matter. Man is embroiled in myths.

Science searches for perfect solutions. The Greek thought influenced western thinkers and after two millennia, Einstein revolutionized the concepts of time and space, and with it human life has totally changed. May be sometime in the near future we reach the elusive reality which the Brahmanic speculation tried to understand and may be we solve the mystery of the universe, life, creator and nature, etc. in the near future. We give below a gist of Hindu scriptures that provide the religious and philosophical background to Hindu myths. These go back to more than 3500 years.

A. Hindu Scriptures:

Hindus regard their scriptures as the source of all knowledge. These are sacred and were revealed to man by a divine power which is omnipresent, omnipotent and omniscient. The scriptures have been categorized as Shrutis and Smritis. A Shruti is that which was 'directly heard' or revealed; it includes the entire Vedic literature viz the Vedas, the Vedanta and the six systems of Indian philosophy. A Smriti is that which is remembered. Smritis include all religious literature such as Epics, Puranas and Dharmashastras. Entire scriptural literature is full of myths.

The word Veda is derived from Vid to know, and it stands for revealed and inspired knowledge. There are four Vedas, namely Rig, Yajur, Sam, and Atharva. In the prayers (known as Suktas), they deal with matters of moral and religious importance, including man's relationship with God. The Suktas were shaped by Rishis and recited by Brahmins, the interpreters. (Hindus revere the Vedas as the fountainhead of their knowledge, like the Christians do the Bible and the Kuran is revered by the Muslims). However, Hinduism is liberal and permits its adherents freedom to believe or not in the Vedas. The Shruti is not Shastra, that it is not a text of systematized knowledge; nevertheless it has the potentiality of becoming a Shastra. The Vedas, according to their contents, are classified under three heads - knowledge (Gyan), code of conduct (Karma) and worship (Upasana). The Rig stands for knowledge, Yajur for karma, Sam for devotion. Atharva is a definer and clue to God. Thus Rig deals with spiritual and mundane knowledge, Yajur with Karmakand, and Sam with prayers and (chants). The first three Vedas are the limbs of the Lord. Rig is his form, Sam his head, Yajur his belly, Yonder is Brahman the great seer-Om.

The Vedas donot demarcate between empirical and spiritual existence. To appreciate and understand the nature of Shrutis, ancient Indians evolved Vedangas and Upavedas. The Vedangas are Shiksha (orthography), Vyakaran (grammar), Nighantu (lexicon), Jyotish (astronomy), Chhand (prosody), Kalpa (system of rituals and ceremonies).

The Upavedas are – Ayurveda (medical science), Gandharva (Aesthetics), Dhanur (defense sciences), and Artha (system of economics and finance). The Vedangas have been divided into three parts – Shrauta, Grihya and Dharma. Shrauta provides instructions about fire sacrifice and Vedic rituals. Grihyashastra defines religious ceremonies, customs and Sanskara Vidhi. The origin of Dharamashastra lies in cosmic order (i.e. Rita). Dharma derived from Sanskrit – root Dhri means wear. Among the Dharamashastras, Manusmriti and Yajnavalkyasmriti command the greatest respect. We have mentioned the 'disciplines' in detail because each one of them has its own myths.

The Upanishads elaborate Vedic concepts and contain speculations. The word literally means come and sit near – which is an advice by a guru (teacher) to his shishyas (disciples). Though the Upanishads number 108, only 13 are considered as major philosophical works. These 13 are : Aitreya, Brihadaranyaka, Chhandogya, Isha, Kaushitaki, Kath, Ken, Maitri, Mandukya, Mundaka, Prashna, Shvetashvetar, Taittariya. Of these three - Mandukya, Maitra and Shvetashvetar - are named after the sages the rest 10 are titled after the first word of the work. Besides, there are minor Yogic works, namely, Yog Tattva, Dhyan Bindu and Nada Bindu. The Dhyan Bindu deals with Om. The Upanishadic speculations revolve around Brahman and Atma.

The six systems of Indian philosophy are : Nyaya (propounder Gautam), Vaisheshik (Kanad), Samkhya (Kapil), Yoga (Patanjali), Purva Minansa (Jaimini) and Uttar Mimansa (Vyasa Vadarayana). (All these schools accept the authority of the Vedas. Majority of the Hindus regard the authority of the Vedas as supreme. Those who accept the authority are Astiks (theists). Those who donot are Nastiks. (In Vedic term an Astik is one who believes in the existence of supreme self as the first cause of creation, sustenance and destruction.)

Vedas and Upanishads

Rig Veda :According to the Vedas, all knowledge emanated from Brahma in the form of scriptures. The Vedas and Upanishads provided Rita, that is social order. The Vedas consist of four literary compositions : Rig, Yajur, Soma and Atharva, each is divided into 3 parts – Samhita, Brahman and Aranyaka. The Rig-Samhita a collection of hymns is in praise of gods. It consists of 1028 Suktas (hymns), these are grouped in 10 Mandals (or Ashtakas). These were composed some 3500 to 3000 years ago. The hymns were recited by Hotri and transmitted orally from teachers to pupils. Subject-wise and author-wise particulars of these Mandalas are :

Mandala		
I	:	*Old Hymns*
II to VII	:	*Families of four Rishis*
VIII	:	*Kanva, Angiras*
IX	:	*Soma*
X	:	*New Hymns*

The Yajur veda contains sacrificial prayers recited by Adhvaryu priests engaged in manual work. The Yajur-Samhita has two texts – Krishna and Shveta. Krishna is preserved in Taittariya – Maittarayani, and Kathak recensions, and Shveta in Vajasaneyi Samhita.

The Rig Veda (Nasadiya Sukta) describes the stages of Revolution. In the beginning there was nothing except time. There was neither Sat nor Asat; there was no realm of air or sky or water, nor was there death or immortality. The breathless breathed by the force of nature. Then there was Tamas – chaos, void – all formless. From Tamas was born Tatekam – that Single One. From it rose Kam, force (Shakti) and Prayati (energy). None knows wherefrom the world came.

Tatekam, a multiple of attributes, is engaged in multifarious functions – matters of being and becoming, origination, presentation and destruction. As originator or creator, scriptures describe him as absolute, eternal and embodiment of cosmic phenomena. In brief, Nature is the revelation of Tatekam – God. None originated him. He created the primordial matter. The creator sustained the cosmos.

The Vedas define the Bhagwan - as the one and one alone who gives men bounties while nature's bounties merge and become one in Him. The world is made of substances that were created and already existed.

The Rig-Veda solves the problem of multiplicity (plurality) of the divine power by calling it by different names. What is the nature of that Ekam? The question is - if God is the creator, who created the God? Even a pedestrian poses: "Which came first egg or hen?" Another riddle he poses, "If you say God created man, may be man's mind created God." The concept of Hiranyagarbha (golden egg) is one of that sort. The Rig Veda says the universe emerged from a golden egg. The golden egg owed its existence (or birth) to the union of Mother Earth and Father Sky. And, this led to emergence of being in series, including Being and Non-being.

In the early Vedic period there were four prominent gods - Indra, Varuna, Vayu and Surya. Each one of them was a mighty natural power. Indra, the king of Gods maintained Riṭa (that is order) in the universe; Varuna was the god of rains, Vayu the god of air (vital for inspiration), and Surya, the provider of heat and energy. These gods suckered the universe, including mankind. Later, to these four some more names were added – Agni, Brihaspati, Soma. Then more were added and the number swelled to 33. Of these 8 were Vasus, 11 Rudras, 12 Adityas, Indra and Shiva – all manifestations of the Supreme God.

These were Soma, Indra-Vishni, Indra-Parvat, Agni, Indra, Soma, Varuna, Mitra, Savita, Vishnu, Pushan, Ribhava, Usha, Maruts, Gravan, Vishvedeva, Rudra, Vayu, Ashvins, Aapah, Sarasvati, Adityan, Rudrah, Vasana, Brihaspati, Brahmanaspati, Aryaman, Indrani, Apasara, Mitra-Varuna, Indrayni, Indra. Subsequently the number was streamlined to three –the Trinity – Brahma, Vishnu and Shiva. The Trinity was responsible for everything concerning the universe. Brahma was its creator, Vishnu sustainer, and Shiva the preserver and destroyer. Each one of them had his consort. They were not mere decorative pieces but shared the responsibilities of their spouses also. Brahma's ally, Saraswati was the goddess of learning, Vishnu's consort Lakshmi was the goddess of wealth and Shiva's consort Parvati advised him. Lakshmi and Parvati incarnated whenever their consorts came to earth or occasion demanded their presence. Saraswati is eternal. Parvati and her incarnates slayed demons who were disturbing social order and harmony. Devi and her children – Ganesha and Subramanyam (Kumar Skandha) - participated in Shiva's work. Eight Lokpals and Gram Devatas (village deities) were also worshipped.

Vishnu is pleased with devotion, Shiva by ascetic practices. Creation has been described in the Purusha Sukta of the Satpath Brahman of Rig Veda. According to it Prajapati organized a sacrifice in which devatas also participated. The Agni (fire) excited passion in Heaven and Earth, which resulted in the creation of Being. The Devatas became jealous of the Heaven. But sage Angiras mediated between them (Heaven and gods) and reconciliation was brought about, and happy at this, gods distributed gifts. Besides Agni, other Devatas - water and air, played important role in creation. Their process of creation was different.

Gods also organized a sacrifice. From which emerged the universe. This was enveloped by the Purusha who had 1000 heads and an equal number of limbs. Then Purusha also began creation. His three quarters became the world. His mouth (that uttered words) became the Brahmin, his arms became Kshatriya, thighs became Vaishya and feet Shudra. Also from the Purusha, emerged beasts, plants, words, rituals, hymns, the Vedas. From the mind came moon, from head the sky, from feet the earth, from navel the atmostphere. It gave birth to Rita, that is the order of the cosmos. The creation was not yet over. Its completion required opposites because there could be no being without non-being, no sky without air, no darkness without light, no life without death. However, there was one that breathed deep in the void – that which was heat and became desire and spirit. Then non-being and being became one and chaos turned into order. But none knows what happened; had that order come from God? Only the Creator knows and may be he too knows nothing about it.

Water is another primordial element that was associated with creation. The only element that wished to reproduce, water became heated and produced the golden egg (Hiranyagarbha). This was the first creation – it contained all life – all cosmos. The Hiranyagarbha floated on water for sometime, from it emerged Prajapati. After resting for a year he tried to speak. From the sound of his breath emerged earth, the next sound became sky and subsequent sounds became seasons. Prajapati stood in the egg-shell for one year. In this posture he could see his life for the coming one thousand years. He bestowed on himself the power of reproduction and created Agni out of himself. Besides, he created Devas (gods) and Due (light). His breath downward gave brith to Asuras (demons) and darkness whom he overpowered. And, then came Day and Night. He created the Beings and thereby he created time also. Agni, water, wind, earth and sky played role in creation.

The Atharva Samhita contains information on preservation and maintenance. It is a collection of songs, spells (magic) and incantations for healing of diseases, restoration of harmony and excorcism of evil spirits. The Sama Veda deals with music.

As against the Samhitas, the Brahmanas are treatises of prayers and sacrificial ceremony. They also contain cosmogenic myths, legends, gathas and exploits of royalty. The Aranyakas (Forest Books) contain instructions for hermits. In short, the Vedas cover instructions regarding various human activities, purposefulness and attainments.

According to the Vedas, God is Truth and Truth is God. The God is not only Truth, He is Benediction and Beauty also. He is a composite whole of Truth, Benediction and Beauty (Satyam-Shivam-Sundaram).

When the structure of the universe and life was laid, the evolutionary process slowed down. Also, the evolving concepts and designs got beyond common man's understanding. As a result Brahma's work gradually began fading out and it was taken over by Vishnu and Shiva. That was the Brahmanical arrangement. Perhaps there was jealousy among gods who too are prone to weaknesses. Brahma protested and fought for retaining his work and consequent power, like today's politicians using character assassination of adversaries/competitors as weapons. Efforts to assassinate Brahma's character were made by targeting his association with his mind-born daughter, Saraswati. Brahma was unceremoniously dropped out. After this Brahma lost his right of worship. May be at a later date there was a tussle between the devotees of Vishnu and Shiva also. The tussle continued for centuries until thanks to the saint-poets and their followers, they patched up their differences and the places of their worship were thrown open for devotees of both. This facilitated Vishnu's nine incarnations in Brahmanic stories.

The first Avatar was Matsya of marine world. The next two were Tortoise and Boar (Kurma and Varaha) – creatures of land. The next avatar was Nrasimha (man-lion), the fifth one was Waman (Dwarf – mixed breed of small statured beings struggling for existence), the sixth was Parasuram, a Brahmin who detested threat of Kshatriyas to get better of Brahmins and he exterminated them 13 times from the face of the earth. The 7th and 8th avatars are Rama and Krishna who were respectful to Brahmins. The 9th avatar of Buddha was accepted by Brahmins to avoid his nuisance value to Brahmanism. The 10th KALKI avatar is awaited.

The Upanishads elaborated the concepts of reproduction, heat, primeval waters, Prajapati, Golden Egg, Brahman and Atman. Prajapati of the Vedas became Brahma in the Upanishads. A non-being developed inside an egg. After a year it broke into two parts of gold and silver – which became sky and earth – Akash and Prithvi - and from them emerged the universe and life. In the Antariksha were mountains, rivers, clouds and Sun. Everything moved towards Sun.

But why this creation? It is for His sake. 'Ishavasya' – the world is pervaded by the supreme reality – it is charged with the existence of the highest self. It does not suffer from any time-space limiation. The entire creation exists within him and he is beyond creation. While most of the myths are purposefully created, their motives are not selfless.

A few extracts from Hindu scriptures – Vedas, Upanishads, Puranas, Epics (Mahabharata and Ramayana), Manusmriti and other sources are given below:

ON GOD :

Who knows and who can tell
Wherefrom it all came,
And how creation took place
The gods came after creation
So who knows truly when creation happened
When did all creation originate
Whether he fashioned it or he did not
He surveys it all from heaven
He knows – or may be even he does not know

Rig-Veda

ATMAN :

First there was Atman. It was alone. Then it created water. Then it wanted to create gods,. It created man. The man was given a mouth. Out of mouth came speech and god of fire. It gave man nostrils out of which came breath, the god of air. Then it gave men limbs out of which came many other gods. Finally Atman entered the man at the parting of the head and (it) became the 'I'. *-Aitreya Upanishad*

BHAV :

To secure an offspring, Brahma practiced penance which generated heat. From heat were born fire, sun, moon, wind and dawn and (Usha). On Brahma's advice they all, except Usha who took the form of a nymph, practiced asceticism. Her presence agitated minds of others, and their seed flowed. Lest it go waste, it was collected in a bowl made by Prajapati. From this seed was born Sahashra Bahu (man with one thousand arms). Prajapti blessed him – "Bhav" – exist. Kaushitaki Brahman

BRAHMAN :

When one breathes, one knows him as breath
When one speaks, one knows him as speech
When one sees, one knows him as the eye
When one hears, one knows him as the ear.
When one thinks, one knows him as the mind.

-Chhandogyopanishad

BRAHMAN & ATMAN :

Pondering over multiple gods, the Upanishads conclude that there is only one God and that is Breath. God is Brahman. The ultimate soul; the atman is only a reflection of the Brahman. Everything is Brahman. Everything has name, form and activity. The absolute unmanifest is the manifestation of these three aspects to whom the man prays.

Lead me from the unreal to the real
Lead me from darkness to light
Lead me from death to immortality.

BEING :

Originally there was only Being, out of it manifested the universe. (This was Brahman). Everything came from Brahman, and it will, as it breathes, dissolve into him. It further says Brahman is the ultimate factor; sense organs work because of Brahman. He who knows Brahman does not know Brahman, for knowing it is to lose one's identity in the Brahman *-Kenopanishad*

The world is a Being. Were it not so, how could the world have emerged from non-Being? Wanting to reproduce itself, the Being gave off heat, which gave off water. The water procreated itself and gave off flood. *-Chhandogya*

Chhandogyopanishad throws light on merger of Atman with Brahman. There developed the idea of grace of guru by which man gains knowledge and revelation. Guru stands between the Brahman and the Vedas.

The Brahman should not be confused with Brahmin or Brahma. Brahman is inside the Atman. Brahma, Brahman are indescribable. Brahman is the spirit that awakens the mind; it originates life and makes us speak in words. It is the spirit behind seeing and hearing. It is the ear of the ear, the eye of the eye, word of words, mind of mind, and the life of life. Brahman cannot be spoken to. The spirit behind the possibility of speaking is Brahma(n). *-Kenopanishad*

(It is) Yoga (that) leads to merger of Atman with Brahma under guru's guidance. A yogi practices yoga. He gradually withdraws from empirical individuality until his absorption in Purusha (Mahayogi). *-Kathopanishad*

SRASHTI :

Atman the cause of Srashti (creation) : In the beginning there was nothing but Atman – in the form of Purusha. Finding himself alone, he said, "I am alone " and he became two – a male and a female. They came together and a child was born. Frightened at the sight of the newborn, she hid and turned herself into a cow. Then the man became a bull and from the two cattle were born. Then she became a mare and he a stallion. So it went on and many forms of animals were born. In a sense Atman was the cause of creation. Anyone who understands this becomes a creator. But know that you cannot see the seer of all things. You cannot hear the hearer of all things. You cannot think of thinker of all things. You cannot understand the knower of all things. That which is beyond all comprehension is the self within you. *–Brihadaranyak*

An inquisitive person questions – who created me, who created the natural phenomena – the earth, the Sun, the Moon and all this variety in the universe. The motive to creation was simple – He wanted to unravel his mysteries. Man knew he was made by his father and mother. So were the natural phenomena made. The clue was – whatever was on earth or in sky or water, it was a product of the world's creator. May be the Earth was the mother and the sky the father. Then their thoughts went further. May be one time they were one, then they separated and whatever originated between them – in the Antariksha were their products. Even so, who made them? There must be a Supreme Being – Brahman – who must be responsible for all that exists. From the thoughts arose doubts about existence from perpetuity.

Hindu scriptures inform about movement of people also. But most of the studies of Hindu scriptures are based on presumptions and suppositions. For instance, western historians drew inferences from their preset view that Aryans migrated from a central place in different directions. Unreal inferences were drawn to prove the preset idea and a great deal of confusion has been created. Even the views of Indian scholars e.g. Dayananda, Tilak and Aurbindo are at divergence. Aurobindo comments on Dayanada, "Vedas are a planetary revelation of religious, ethical and scientific truth. Its religious teaching is monotheistic. The Vedic gods are descriptive names of one deity, they are at the same time indicative of his powers as we see them working in Nature and by a true understanding of the sense of Vedas we could arrive at all scientific truths which have been discovered by modern research." Tilak's "*Arctic Home in the Vedas*" states that Aryans descended from the Arctic Region in glacial period. This was contradicted by A.C. Das in *Rig Vedic India* and he showed that Punjab and adjoining area was Aryan's cradle home. T. Parasuram Aiyer considers the whole of Rig Veda as a figurative representation of the geological phenomenon belonging to the birth of our planet. His explanation of Ahivrata and release of seven rivers is novel. Anyway, it is too hasty to pronounce that the Vedas are all myths.

PURANAS

The discourses of Upanishads were too terse for people. They wanted to hear the discourse in a simple language and fictional form. The Vipras evolved Puranas which were full of fiction and their recitation in an imaginative way had dramatic affect. (A Vipra is any ordinary human being who has been given Upanayan and after this he becomes eligible to learn Vedas. Devoted to Vishnu, a Vipra becomes Vaishnava). Puranas are myths, legends and moral precepts. They whet the listener's appetite to hear more. The stories were developed by experts with vested interests in social control. The recitation of Katha by the Vachakas (singers) with musical interest was liked by people.

Puranas were compiled and shaped over hundreds of years and they reexamined the identity of Brahma in various forms and replaced him by Brahman who was without any beginning or end. When Brahman woke up he was lying beneath waters. The Earth floated as a vessel on the surface of waters. The Brahman as avatar of Brahma created the world. Each creation follows dissolution of world. He gives form to power and substances within it to be created. This episode follows at the end of each Kalpa.

There is a large number of Puranas, devoted to each deity of Trinity and to Devi. The Mahapuranas devoted to Brahma are – Markandeya, Bhavishya, Waman, Brahma, Brahmananda, Brahma-Vaivarta/Vaivasvat. Those devoted to Vishnu are : Vishnu Purana, Srimad

Bhagvat, Garuda, Padma, Varaha. Puranas devoted to Shiva are : Matsya, Kurma, Linga, Vayu, Skandha, Agni. Devi Bhagvat, Harivansha Purana are devoted to the Devi.

Besides Puranas there are Uppuranas. To name a few: Aditya, Ashraya, Ausavas, Bhaskar (Surya), Devi, Shaiva, Durvasa, Kalika, Kalki, Kapil, Maheshvar, Manav, Marichi, Nandikeshvar, Narad, Nrasimha, Parasar, Sambha, Santakumar, Shivadharma, Surya, Sutasamhita, Sthanas, Varuna, Yug, Vayu, Brihat.

Each Purana consists of :

1. Sarga (creation of universal process with 5 great elements and sex).
2. Viraga (creation of several orders of living beings by Brahma).
3. Sthana (greatness of Bhagwan shown by destruction of enemies).
4. Poshana (protection of created world).
5. Uti : tendency created in men to procure fruits for their actions.
6. Manavantara Katha : stories of Manu who held sway.
7. Ishwarkatha : Stories of Bhagwan and his devotees.
8. Nirodha : The dissolution of the world.
9. Mukti : Release of Atma from bondage of Karma and attainment of true nature.
10. Ashraya Bhagwan : Praise of divine power that supports the world.

Some of the Puranas are deities to specific devotees and are popular amongst the devotees of that deity. Of late the rigidity of sects has almost disappeared. A Hindu has no bias and he can now read any Purana he wants.

Bhagvat Purana's melodious rendering and an assurance of improving lot of audience in this and the other world have a charm of their own and make it the most popular, Purana. It begins with the statement that Saunaka and many other Vipras assembled in Naimisharanya to perform a sacrifice.

The Suta was offered a seat. Sukhdeo, son of Vyasa, was present. The audience was free to pose questions or seek clarifications such as why had Krishna to incarnate? If chanting of Krishna's name and presence of realized souls can solve the problem, why then, should the Lord incarnate? Krishna is the master of mystic powers and a store house of religious principles. Prayers and hymns sung in his name please him. The audience is reminded that their Dharma is to offer unmotivated, uninterrupted, devotional service to the Lord, for this helps the devotee to acquire knowledge and detachment from the world. Man should not desire sense gratification. Vyasa laid stress on Varnashram.

In the beginning of creation, Vasudeva by his own internal energy created energies of cause and effect. After creating the material substance, the Lord expands himself and enters into it. And although he is with the material modes of nature and appears to be one of created beings, he is always enlightened in his position.

The Lord, as universal soul, pervades all things, just as fire permeates wood, and he appears to be of many varieties, though he is unique and absolute. The universal soul enters into the bodies of the created who are influenced by the modes of material and causes the subtle mind enjoy. Thus the Lord maintains all planets inhabited by demigods, men and animals. In his incarnations, he performs leela (postures) to reclaim the pure and good.

Krishna is the source of all incarnations. In the beginning of the creation the Lord incarnated himself to the form of Purusha and matter from which emerged the 16 principles of material action.

Shankaracharya in *Shankar Vedanta Sutra* treats creation as Bhagwan Leela in terms of time and dissolution. According to it the universe consists of 14 lokas – Bhulok, Bhuvalok, eclipse, planet, magic, demons, winds, swarga, dhruva (with regions of Shukra, Brahaspati, Budha, Shani, Bhaum, Saptarshi), Mahar (or Kritaka – Akritaka), Janas, Tapas, Satya, Vishnupad, Avarna. Three of these Lokas - Bhu Bhuvah and Swarga - are called Kritaka. Janas, Tapas and Satya lokas are called Akritakas. There are seven lokas below the earth-viz. Atal, Patal, Sutal, Talatal, Mahatal, Rasatal, Patal. Mayasura held sway in Atal. He created 96 Mayas in three of which live beautiful damsels who give sensory enjoyment to whosever enters Atal loka. In Vital, Rudra is in the company of Bhavani. He is surrounded by Bhutas. Bali resides in Sutal. (Bali was son of Prahlada. Bhagwan incarnated as Vaman and took away the three worlds from Bali. During his world conquest Ravana came to the island but he was denied entry by the guard who was Bhagwan himself.)

Mayasura lives in Mahatal. He built three cities for Asuras which were destroyed by Rudra. In reverence Maya fell on Rudra's feet. The deity forgave him and allowed Maya to live in Mahatal where he lives in fear of Vishnu. Snakes, including Kadru's sons, live in Rasatal. Vasuki and Nagas live in Patala. They are fond of gems which dispel the darkness. Below them is Bhagwan in the form of Sankarshana, who is a 100 - headed sepent.

The world system consists of seven islands with a center. The island is surrounded by salt water. Six islands are surrounded by ocean. Beyond this are mountains and world's end consisting of nine positions. In each of these Bhagwan is worshipped in particular forms of Vishnu. Of the nine continents, Bharat is one.

Time :

Like man's limited life span, the universe, including Bhulok, has a limited life span. The Bhulok's duration is Chaturyugas consisting of Krita, Treta, Dwapar and Kali. Their durations are : Krita –4800 divine years, Treta 3600, Dwapar 2400 and Kali 1200 years. The beginning and end of a Yuga is called Sandhya. One hundred Chaturyugas form one day of Brahma, which is known as Kalpa. His night is of the same duration and his life span is 100 years. The present Kalpa is Svetararah kalpa. In its beginning Bhagwan appeared as Varah and brought up the world from the lower world where the Asuras had taken it. The present Kalpa is Padma (Lotus) Kalpa.

Fourteen Manus hold sway in a Kalpa. Each has a duration of 71 Chaturyugas. Six Manus have held sway so far and now seventh Manu is ruling. Each Manavantar has a separate Manu, Indra and seven rishis. Bhagwan takes avatar. The next Manu will be Savarni and Bali will be next Indra.

The myth is quite complicated and it is difficult to say how the various figures have been arrived at. Of the number 71 is the most astounding; it is indivisible. To complete the story, a manvantar holds sway over three worlds. After each Kaliyuga the Vedas are spoiled and seven Rishis reproduce these by tapasya. In Kritayuga men are pure, in Treta men worship Bhagwan or organize Yajnas. Manu rules over the earth and propagates the human race. He also compiles rules scattered in Vedas and reproduces them as laws of manu. Towards its end, the yuga is divided in four parts, each of which is divided in many parts and each is entrusted to a person known as Vyasa.

Dissolution :

When the purpose of evolution is complete, Pralaya occurs and the material world dissolves into elements. The Pralaya could be natural; it follows a set course. For one hundred years, there are no rains and all water evaporates. A huge fire reduces the world into ashes. This is followed by torrential rains over a period of one hundred years. All compounds dissolve into elements. The earth is reabsorbed into water, water in fire, fire in air, air in ether, ether in inert consciousness. Mind, sense of perception, and action are absorbed in sattvic consciousness and all consciousness is reabsorbed in Mahat and Mahat (is reabsorbed) in Prakriti.

The dissolution may be of another type. According to it three lokas – Bhu, Bhuva and Swarga – are destroyed as the Kalpa ends and the night of Brahman begins. Rest of the process viz absence of rain is repeated but only three worlds are affected. The Rishis of Mahar loka move to Janaloka.

The functions could be separated. Fundamental substances, mind and instruments of soul are Bhagwan's works. He sustains the world and to serve this purpose he comes down in different forms – of animals, men and devas. Brahma creates differences of Sattva, Rajas and Tamasa. Bhagwan dissolves the world in forms of time, fire and Rudra.

Bhagwan's interest in creation, sustenance and dissolution is to help the Atma (self) rest in the universe. Unaware of their nature, the creatures regard their bodies as Atma (soul) and seek the gratification of their senses because of ignorance. They indulge in various types of Karma and are connected with one body after another. This is Sansar. Therefore (in Sansar) Bhagwan gives them bodies and souls and informs them through the Vedas what they ought to do and refrain. He expects Atma (soul) to realize its own nature, kill its hankering for self enjoyment, develop love for Bhagwan, identify himself with him in the end and secure him for himself. This is man's true goal.

Is Bhagwan the universe or is he Brahmand consisting of Prakriti and Atmans?

EPICS

Ramayana and Mahabharat

The Ramayana and the Mahabharat are two great popular epics. They have played a unique role in the country's integration.

The Ramayana is the work of the great Sanskrit poet Valmiki. Around his personality many myths have developed. The story of Ram with many dramatic events and Ram-Ravana War is a massive work of 24000 shlokas. It is a store of history and sociology of ancient India. It is claimed that episodes of Ramayana occurred 87,000 years ago.

Mahabharat is a much older work than Ramayana, though Ram belonged to a period prior to that of Pandavas. After war at Kurukshetra, the city of Hastinapur and Indraprashta met the same fate as the Cnossos and Phaestus and Anatolia Hittites met. They were totally destroyed. Mahabharat has about 100,000 shlokas. From the language used customs observed and other matters, it has been surmised that Mahabharat was written by Vyasa Vadaryana on a date prior to Ramayana's.

Mahabharat treats Brahma as Prajapati. Brahma had his weaknesses. Prajapati created such women as generated desire and anger in man who could become neither God nor immortal. Mahabharat is full of legends, myths and moral precepts which have become folklore. Brahmins incorporated many doctrinal, mythological and theological passages in the versions of royal bards.

About Vyas Vadarayana it is said that he was son of Satyavati, a fisher woman and Parasar a learned Brahmin. She bore a child, who would grow up to be Vyasa. Vyasa was assigned to write the history of

Kaurvas-Pandavas. He was so fast in dictating the matter that no ordinary man could cope. Lord Ganesha finally agreed and wrote with his tusk that had accidentally broken.

Valmiki had an interesting life. From a bandit he turned into a great poet. The first verse that he uttered was full of pathos. A hunter had killed a male bird (Kraunch) whose death was mourned by his female companion. He cursed the hunter "You will never achieve your honour".

GURU AND DESCIPLE

In ancient India when children entered adolescence, they were sent by parents to guru's ashram for learning. For a few years they stayed in the Ashram and after the guru found they had received education in the Vedas etc. and were capable of leading a Grihastha's life, they were sent back by the guru to their parents' home. But before they left, they received a valedictory address from the teacher. The address showed the keen interest the guru took in his pupils' formative life. One such address is reproduced :

"Always speak the truth, follow the righteous path and donot give up further studies. You would compensate your teacher adequately if you enter life, have a family, provide security to your family, be good to fellow beings, and donot open your mouth carelessly, as and when you impart instructions to others. Consider your mother a goddess, your father a god, treat your teacher and guest respectfully. Your action should command appreciation. Your attributes should reflect worthy conduct and not weaknesses" (Taittariyropanishad 1.11.1-2).

SATYAKAM JABALI

We give below the story of Satyakam Jabali relevant to the teacher – taught relationship : A young boy named Satyakam asked his mother: Who is my father? He had decided to learn from a teacher and thought the teacher might ask him about his father. The mother replied "Son, I do not know who your father is. All I remember is that when I was young, I worked here and there and conceived you from whom, I donot recollect. But if your guru asks, tell him that your name was Satyakam Jabali".

Satyakam went to a teacher named Harindramata Gautama who posed that very question. He replied as his mother had advised. The teacher was pleased with the boy's honesty and admitted him in his Ashram. Gautama ascribed the boy's truthfulness to his birth in a Brahmin family, for who else would relate such an unpleasant truth? he thought. After performing the pupils' initiation ceremony, he asked Satyakam to take four hundred cows and come back when the number of cows given him increased to one thousand.

Satyakam proceeded with cows to a jungle and stayed there for many years. He became so sensitive over the years to environment that he thought creation was manifestation of God, and cows too were part of that creation, and of the same inner self. The creatures too were revelation of nature, he felt. Then after sometime the cattle increased to more than one thousand and remembering his guru's advice, he returned to the teacher's ashram. Pleased with his pupil's behavior and conduct, the guru told him, "Satyakam your face shines like a person's who has realized the truth, the Brahman, who was your teacher." Satyakam requested him "Please teach me the knowledge imparted by the guru to the disciples about the supreme god." "The guru knew that the disciple was ripe for spiritual knowledge and with a touch he blessed Satyakam.

A comparable later day story relates to Ramakrishna Paramahansa. The saint was addressing an audience about devotion, that 'Nam Jap' was the simplest form of devotion. A man in the audience, who was surgeon by profession, stood up and interrupted. He said that he saw no point in repeatedly saying one word, Jai Ram, Ram. What good does it do? Is n't it too brief to have an effect. Ramakrishna told the man to shut up. The surgeon lost his composure. Paramhansa told him, "I asked you only once to shut up and you are affected by this brief admonition. What makes you think Nam Jap of God will have no affect"? The point was made. The surgeon became silent.

SVETAKETU:

The story of another learner tells that the process of learning is arduous and unending. More than two millennia ago there was a great scholar named Uddalak Aruni. He sent his son, Svetaketu to a teacher's ashram for learning. The child learnt the Vedas from the teacher for 12 years and when the learning was complete; Svetaketu went home and reported to his father.

Aruni appreciated the sincerity of the son in learning and the pains the teacher had taken in guiding his disciple. However he questioned son Svetaketu about the spiritual knowledge he had gained and found him deficient in it. He asked whether the son had asked the guru about spiritual knowledge – by knowing which all is known. The son was perplexed and he respectfully asked, "Father! What is that knowledge?"

Father Uddalak Aruni replied, "When you understand the nature of clay, you know about things made of clay and that the difference among things is of name and form. When you know the essential nature of gold, you know about things made of gold, the difference is only a name and form. Similar is knowledge, knowing which we know all. Then know the essence of things, which underlies all names and forms. He further elucidated, "In the beginning there was the Pure Being, one without a second. Some say there was non-existence out of which Brahmand was born. How could existence he born of non-existence?

No, in the beginning there was non-existence alone – one only, without a second. He, the one thought let there be many. This way he projected the universe out of himself and having done so, he entered into every being and every thing. All that is has its self in him alone. He is the truth. He is the subtle essence of all. He is the self of all. And, that thou art, Svetaketu".

Svetaketu asked, "Father, what happens when man sleeps?" Uddalak replied, "As bees make honey from juice of many plants and trees, and the honey is one and knows not from which flowers its parts came, similarly when men are merged in one existence, whether in deep sleep or death, they know nothing of their past or present state. Because of ignorance they know not that they merged in him and from him they came. Whatever the creatures they have their self in him alone. He is the truth. He is the self. And, that thou art, O Satyaketu". When the son protested that he cannot see the self, Uddalak replied, Salt crystals are not seen in water, so is the self in Brahman".

The religio-philosophic views of Hindus about creation are provocative but they are left in lurch-so as suit the Brahmanic order.

Vishnu with Brahma and Shiva. Vishnu is the supreme Cosmic Principle

2

WESTERN VIEW

Evolution :

The explanation of Science regarding origin of universe and life is also unconvincing. However, science has proved more successful in solving some of the problems in unorthodox ways. That nature could substitute God or the two could be treated as synonyms is not totally absurd. But the two donot take us far. Like the man of God who cannot provide a satisfactory answer as to who created God, the man of science too is at a loss to satisfactorily account for the pinhead wherefrom the universe originated or how the chaos shaped the cosmos. In either case– creation or evolution–the riddle of the first cause remains unsolved. Therefore, the mythology of creation is looked upon with doubt, though not disdain.

The religious legends divide the universe in three parts – Akash (sky), Antariksha (horizon) and Prithvi (earth). The evolution of mother earth we live on and which suckles all life took billions of years.

Life evolved on earth in millions of years. The biologist figures out that life is made of millions of cells. The primates, the distant ancestors of human kind, first appeared on earth about fifty million years ago. Then they looked like squirrels. Over millions of years they changed with the environment, they learned new skills, slowly developed into apes and from apes into Australopithecus (who lived about three million years ago) to hominid (homohibilis, the first tool maker who lived about two million years ago) and Human (homo sapiens sapiens), male and female developed around two hundred thousand years ago. The Neanderthals – the short and stocky human with low, ridged brows - lived around two hundred thousand to 35,000 years ago.

The human kind could not develop fast because of unstable climatic conditions prevailing during the Ice Age. Each time culture appeared rooting, inclement weather conditions destabilized it. Climatologists assert that culture should have taken wings much before had the climatic conditions been congenial for development. But it turned out that several times when it was needed most, at that very moment climate withdrew its support and the development fizzled out. But it was to man's good luck that the much wanted sun shone on his fortune and the inter-glacial period of the preceding 12000 years provided the mother earth with a perfect condition for agriculture at that moment, the human civilization took off. Until then man had led a life of hunter-gatherer in search of food. He was tired of such a life. A stele erected by King Asurbanipal summarizes the ferocity of beasts. "Andrameda was saved from being sea monster's snacks, Minotaur was killed and Greek youths saved for minding Heracles took a zoo of lions, hydras, wolves and witches were to be beware of." The agricultural prospects brought a boom, and he did not let the opportunity slip. Anticipating a bright future, he searched for suitable sites for cultivation and settlement in the proximity of water to meet and satisfy his own needs as also the needs of his animals and agriculture. Searches took men to the plains in the vicinity of Indian Ocean and Mediterranean Sea and they selected the valleys of Indus, Tigris-Euphrates, Nile and other great rivers where they brought their tools, implements and animals. They organized settlements, which gave them relief, prosperity and joy. They had the fortitude to face adversity and move on, in case need arose. They built small single mud houses in villages close to streams and ponds. Trade routes influenced their culture, religion, politics. As they prospered, they thought of creation and creator. Sometime their thoughts synchronized, but at other times their views and interests clashed. The civilizations were born.

Growth of agricultural seeds and weeds, trade and crops, and urbanization brought all round prosperity. Towns like Mohenjodaro and Harappa in valleys of Indus and its tributaries, Jerico in Jordan and Huyuk in Turkey came up. These were the first towns of the world. Ideological stratification and political formations kept pace with larger community interests. Adjustment, cooperation and conciliation brought the people together and bound them in families, castes, tribes and kingdoms. Survival instincts and congenial surroundings helped them to regulate their customs and practices. Natural powers also helped them. From this arose the concepts of gods and goddesses and one Super God. Talents among the people ushered in momentous innovations in art, religion, technology, etc. They assimilated powerful features of their ancestors and discarded all that was superfluous. They undertook long journeys, proceeded on adventures and expressed their varied rich experiences in symbolic forms. They thought of themselves as gods and their adversaries as demons who were powerful but evil spirited.

In Middle East by 2000 BCE people in Crete, Minoa and Mycenea led settled life. But developments made them move away from these islands to other places to which they took their culture. They evolved gods and goddesses who lived on Mount Olympus and there grew corpus of myths with divinities, humans and creatures who were half-man, half animal, people with three eyes, monsters and mysterious fellows. This happened after the decline of Minoan power in 1400 BCE and the Myceneans took over as masters of the sea. The Mycenean power collapsed in 1100 BCE. For the next three centuries poverty and illiteracy were rampant. Then life stories passed on from generation to generation. The evolution of writing differentiated prehistory from history. The origin of the Greek myths lies in obscure prehistory. From Greece the myths travelled far and wide. Homer described the Greek-Mycenean civilization in Iliad and Odyssey.

The powers of gods and demons were symbolized according to their capacity to help or harm. They could have more heads and limbs than a human being in proof of their power. A multi-headed god faced a multi-headed demon. In some cases a demon with more heads than a victorious god showed that god was more powerful. If pleased with the prayer of a devotee, God could bless him with some special power or weapons. Many factual and imaginary myths developed and their compilation shaped history. Experimentation and their results opened the path of security. The process differed from that of religion and philosophy.

Myths are plastic like. They can be distorted, altered and spread, according to need or demand of the occasion. These (myths) could be propagated through scriptures and religious literature. The creators of the myths were intelligent. (Mostly Brahmins had worked on Hindu myths with some motive.)

Myths helped civilizations to stagger on. Cultures crystallized. Sometime they made path easy and transactions smooth. On the other hand they caused superstition. A question lingers on. Who invented these myths? What made people believe in myths?

In the initial stage of development mankind believed in multiple gods. Priests tried to please divinities by worship and food, gifts, incense, animal sacrifice. Then they realized that being infinite – and unknowable – God had no use for offerings. No one had ever seen God. Only scriptures had theorized. The Vedas and Upanishads of the Hindus, the Testaments of the Hebrews and Christians and the Kuran of the Muslims and other scriptures offered various theories of creation/evolution.

Most myths are related to Greek gods. Zeus was their king. He established an empire known as Olympian, after Mt. Olympus in Greece. He lived with goddess Mnemosyne (meaning Memory). The two had nine talented daughters known as Muse. They were experts in arts like singing, acting, writing, poetry. Zeus ruled in an authoritarian manner and maintained order among the temperamental gods. With Zeus begins the Greek mythology and pre-Greek history, which forms the background of the Western Civilization.

During the Neolithic age, the culture of the Southern and East-Central Europe was goddess-centered. (Goddesses were the focal point of people's religions).

They gave no credence to the biological role of male in impregnation and believed that goddesses and heroines gave birth parenthetically (i.e. women became pregnant automatically without fertilization by a man or god). Women had marginal power of fertility. Later, they worshipped deities in an organized manner as is evidenced by their rituals, pottery, figurine graffiti found in caves etc. The Mother Earth was responsible for human beings as well as animals. This was depicted in icons in human-animal, animal-human hybrid and snake women figures.

The Greek poet Hesiod thought God created the universe from chaos. First came earth and then in succession came gods, heaven, underworld, ocean, day and night. In the Greek pantheon gods had human form and lived on Mount Olympus, ruled by Zeus and his wife Hera. The Greeks had city states, each city had its deity – protector but God was their real ruler-protector. (Later the god of the empire was their supreme god). If people suffered any loss it was either due to his fate or his past evil deeds. In the scheme of things angels and archangels (like Gabriel, Raphael) also played a role. Pluto thought the world was created by demiurge and man by lower gods. Human beings had material bodies which attracted souls. The human bodies were weighed down by sin but souls born from upper world were immune from sin. Gods suffered human weaknesses. They ate, drank, quarrelled, indulged in sex, bore children.

Everything had its deity. There were deities of wind, rain, crop, hunting, war, peace, city, kingdom. But in the early stages there were no demons or devils. There were spirits only. Underworld was presided by Leviathan.

The concepts of monotheism developed fast in the middle east, the Jews were the first to develop the idea. At the same time other civilizations were also developing. Sumeria, Assyria, Babylon developed their own cultures. Proximity to water played important role in development. The area surrounding the confluence of Tigris and Euphrates flourished with all round growth.

In 3000 BC Sumer was divided in city states. Each city had its patron deity and the city and the deity had their legends. Shara was the deity of Umm city, Zahala of Kish, Sin of Ur, and Sun of Siffa and Larsa. Sumer had three deities viz. Anu of sky, Enlin of wind and earth and Ea of water. Marduk, one of the deities, became Enlin, the high god of Sumer. His story is narrated in Gilgamesh.

Marduk was replaced in Assyria by Ashur who has been described as the head of Assyria in an inscription of Sargun II.

In Persia Zorostrianism developed the idea of one god and demonized all other gods. It brought the idea of good and evil divine forces, each with its own pantheon. In 6th century BCE when Persia conquerred Isreal, monotheism followed in its wake. From Isreal the idea travelled to Greece and Rome. Christianity later travelled from Palestine to Roman world. Lord Issiah II claimed to be the exclusive lord. Isreal wrote, "I am the Lord and there is no other, besides me there is no other God". Some of the followers of Christ had developed the concept of Trinitarianism. There then prevailed the idea that a dome covered the earth and seven lights. Earth was considered spherical and the idea of its being a disk was given up. They thought earth was a circle floating on water in the spheres of planets and concluded that God could not be human material, but then they could not say of what stuff the God was made. The Bible in Genesis provided another clue. God made universe from water and darkness, and by mere word he produced many things. He made Adam out of clay.

The idea was considered in terms of creation in Egypt. The Egyptians thought creation began with the rise of a hill named Atum (or soul) which rose from water. (Atum sounds like the Indian term Atma – Atman – which stands for soul.) Then came earth, sky, sun, moon, stars, air. God Ptah created Khanum by word and formed human beings from clay on wheel. During the reign of Akhenton in the 14th century BCE, the Sun took the place of God. Empedocles theorized four basic elements. Aristotle thought planets were made of ether, that was how they could remain/stand suspended.

In the Middle East Mesopotamia was a leading centre of thought. From there developed the western civilization. From Ahish (that is Chaos) which was alive, came out water, heaven and earth; they were followed by gods in pair (like male river, female river; male heaven, female heaven). Water gods clashed with other gods (Marduk killed Tiamat). They thought earth was a disk surrounded by mountains floating on water. The universe was a three storeyed structure – of heaven, earth and oceans. The world rose from material world from which came up first gods who were different from olden gods. Next came primeval beings who were personified natural world.

The olden gods gave birth to gods of nature who gave place to gods of civilization, such as Zeus (3rd generation god), and Marduk (5th generation god). According to them both gods and humans were material beings – both had bodies. They though heaven was a dome above the earth. Gods dwelt in their homes in heaven on high mountains. (Greek gods lived on Olympus).

The new ideology rejected the idea that there were men of matter. (He should be spiritual). He could not emerge from water or any other substance for he was enormous and infinite, hidden behind the eighth sphere. He(God) should be Monad, for Monad alone could exist, and Chaos should have come later. He Who is, should have created many – out of nothingness. He created diversity in cosmos.

From scientific view Monad was different from a heavy element. The olden creator gods were made of the same stuff as cosmos, and from Chaos, they with their hands formed the material world. Alternatively, they could have birthed it or spoken it into form of existence.

In the new conception of the Monad as geocentric universe, both material and darkness were opposed to it (i.e. to Monad). So some mediator could be the cause of the universe, with or without His (God's) will. Could it be that, Monad was a god of light. If so, then how could the cosmos be dark?

In the creation by Monad, wisdom (Sophia) is the lowest created member. The myth was that Sophia gave birth to a monster and out of shame she threw it out in darkness. Darkness congeals in materiality which forms a veil between itself and the world of light. Below the veil the Monster deems itself as God and creates lower geometrical cosmos filled with wicked spirit, to rule over the seven spirits and earth below. The Monster says "I am the Lord, beside me there is no other". In his new work, "*The River of God, a New History of Christin Origin*" (2001), Gregory J. Riley makes two points. Creation of new, good Christian world owes much to Zorostrianism according to which devil defiled the good world but as destined it was destroyed and replaced by a new world. Two, as for God's responsibility for creation though none has seen Him and He is invisible and unknowable, He can be perceived through the process of one becoming diverse. The mediator Logos became incarnate as the Son of God.

Snake is associated with the myth of creation of universe and mankind. In Europe snake figures were found in shrines and on pottery. Creation pottery had serpiform legs and human female figures. The earliest forms of divine snakes were found in Egypt. Sumerian seals depicted snakes alongside deities. The Delphi had shrine of Temis guarded by Python. (Apollo slayed Python). The Greek icons and myths used snakes and birds. In the Baltic states snakes were fed with milk. (In India they are worshiped even today on Nag Panchami). In the Vedas there are references to Danu, female serpent and her son Vrattra who were killed by Indra. She was consort of Mitra and Varuna. Yahwah, a Western deity was enemy of snakes. Shiva puts on a serpent like a garland. The Krishna legend of overpowering the Naga King in Jamuna water is similar.

In Greek and Roman mythology many goddesses had wings. The Mesopotamian cultures worshipped goddess Ninhursag (Great Mother). The Egyptian Great Mother was called Ugraik, Hather, Anat. In Accadia she was known as Ishtar. (It sounds like Stree, a Sanskrit word for woman.)

The present day Indo-European languages (Greek, Roman, Indian languages, Persian (Iranian), German, Russian, Armemian, Latin,

Lithuanian and English British (commonwealth countires) and USA have some common words. The Indo-Europeans had tripartite social classes law givers, warriors, and nurturers. (To this, Hindus added 'Shudra' based on birth,) In course of time Greek thought developed into western civilization and they abandoned such classification because experience taught that humanity was one. But then they made the weak people their slaves.

To return to the myth of Zeus. He delegated the task of creating races to Prometheus (i.e. forethought) and Epimetheus (afterthought). The latter gave the animals choicest traits like swiftness, strength, fur wings, bells, leaving little to human beings for their survival in a hostile world. Prometheus tried to rectify the imbalance by fashioning some humans from mind with sparks of life leftover from chaos and gave them the physical form of gods. He wanted to enable them to struggle against wild beasts and inclement weather. But Zeus turned down this idea. Despite this, Prometheus gave them fire which made their life cosier. He taught men the uses of fire, calender, writing, healing and arms.

When Zeus came to know of this indiscretion of Prometheus, he was angry and introduced changes in creation. Seeing only males, he devised a female gender to cause trouble and grief to male. He asked Hephaestos to make woman from clay, and moulded an immortal goddess, Pandora whom gods and goddesses gave gifts. Athene clothed her and taught her spinning. Aphrodite filled her with grace. Hermes put fine speech in her mouth and trickery in her mind. Zeus sent her to earth with Hermes and gave her a sealed box as dowry which she was not to open. He gave Pandora to Epimetheus who accepted her as his wife. Pandora's curiosity got better of her and she opened the sealed box. The moment she opened it, a swirling torment of evils – pettiness, worries, diseases rushed out and much though Pandora tried to put them back in the box, she failed.

Zeus had not forgiven Prometheus. At his instance Hephaestos bound Prometheus to a huge rock on the summit of a mountain where every day a vulture gnawed his liver. Not satisfied even with this severity, Zeus wanted to destroy humanity and he threatned to flood the earth. Prometheus had the foresight and he warned his son Deucalion, who with his wife Pyrrah, climbed to the top of Mt. Parnassus, near Delphi, and escaped the rising waters. The couple gathered small stones, veiled their heads and walked along coast, casting stones behind them. The stones turned into men and women and thus the earth was repopulated. (The story resembles to Manu's escape). Ever since Zeus created female, she has played various roles in different phases of life. A virgin woman was thought of as a store house of energy which continued to be charged. In her next phase, that of matron, she could impart/transfer energy into man.

A virgin was considered perpetually young. Goddesses giving energy to others were beneficent and those who did not distribute energy to others were maleficent.

Aphrodite, the Greek goddess of love, was like an unwedded maiden inexperienced in love. When she mated with Achilles, the union resulted into the birth of Aeneas, the hero of Trojan War. Like Aphrodite, there were two other virigins – Artemis and Athene. Athene was both pure and autonomous. She was born from the head of Zeus – it was an andregenous birth. (Saraswati, the Hindu goddess of learning was the manasputri - born from thought – of Brahma). Athene became pregnant of Metis (wisdom) who emerged with arms signifying warrior function. These goddesses were assimilated in Greek culture but they were given subordinate status.

The Greek goddesses of love had to be virgin. They maintained fire in the hearth, and were called Vesta. As a rule a Vesta girl had to remain virgin and violation of the rule resulted in live inhumation. When Rhea Silma, a vesta, bore a child she was spared when she explained that God Mars was the farther of her child, and cohabitation with a god did not involve depletion of energy.

Among Romans the rule of virginity was irrevocable. Because, it was thought if a woman was neither virgin nor married, she could become a threat to patriarchal arrangement as she had become autonomous. Any woman who took control of her own sexuality, was condemned as well as feared by the society. (Lithuanians gave a great deal of importance to virginity). A virgin was preferred for sacrifice to a deity. For a carnal sin vestal virgins were buried. A true virgin was buried as a religious necessity and honour and not as a punishment. In this perspective, Aphrodite's virginity was an attribute to her and she was the epitome of desirable feminity. Aphrodite was sacralized. She is Qurania, Areia and Hetaira, all combined into one.

The credit for launching the Greek myth of creation goes to the Greek poet Hesiod. According to a myth, in the beginning there was chaos (void/hollow) in which seeds and elements of different things swirled en masse. From it were born Night and Erabus, both black, sober and unending. The light brought by chaos pierced the darkness and gradually order emerged. While the heavier elements settled down and turned into earth, the lighter parts drifted upwards and became the sky. The area under the Earth was known as Tartarus. While the Sun, Moon and Stars shone above in heaven, they separated Earth from land and sea. Rivers flowed from land to sea and trees and plants appeared on the land.

Zeu's ancestry goes back to Uranus that is Father Heaven (or Sky) and Mother Gaea (or Earth).

Uranus:

While the Mother Earth was endowed with the personality of Gaea, Uranus personified the spirit of Father Heaven. Gaea and Uranus had many children, who were in fact creatures and not human. They had strength of volcano, earthquake and hurricanes. Three creatures were born first each with 50 heads, 100 hands and an eye in the middle of the forehead. (They were called Cyclopes i.e. wheel eyed). The three were named cottos, Gyas and Bralreas. Later she gave birth to 12 children who looked human but were unusually huge and strong. Six of them were called *Giants*. They were named Oceanus, and Tethys (in-charge of sea), Hyperion and Thea (Sun and Moon), Rhea (great mother) and Cronous, the remaining six were called *Monsters*.

CRONOUS vs. URANUS

Mother Gaea loved all her children, but Uranus did not, rather he hated the Monsters. To save them, Gaea hid them beneath the earth's surface. Though they were safe, their life beneath the earth was miserable and this distressed her. With Cronous, the youngest but the strongest of her children, Gaea conspired to remove Uranus from the scene and bring the Monsters in open. In a conflict that ensued Uranus was wounded and drops of blood from his body fell in the sea and on the earth. From the blood drops in the sea, Aphrodite was born. Aphrodite is Roman Venus. She is the goddess of love. From the drops on land spawned Giants with animal skins, and Furies who tormented humans and shed their blood. In the end Uranus lost the battle and Cronous imprisoned him under Tartarus. The Monsters too were sent to prison.

With Uranus far from the scene, Cronous assumed the kingship of heavens. He married fellow Titan Rhea. The couple begot children but Cronous feared the children might rebel, as he himself had done against his father. He decided that he would not let the children live – he would swallow them. And, this is what he did. He swallowed the children soon after their birth one by one and stored them in his body. When Rhea saw he had swallowed five children, she decided to put down her foot and stop the grisly practice. So when the sixth child was born she named him Zeus and had him hidden in a cave in Crete. She dressed up a stone that looked like a child and gave it to Cronous. Then one day Rhea gave Cronous a large doze of medicine. He felt nauseous and started vomiting. He threw up five children and the stone that was wrapped up like a child and he had swallowed under the impression that it was a new born child of Rhea. The first one to come out was the stone, which was followed by others named Hestia, Demeter, Hera, Hades and Poseidon. Of these Hera was the only female, the rest were male.

The brothers and sister, who were thus saved, waged a war on Cronous and Titans. The war went on for ten years but neither side got upper hand. Titan Prometheus advised Cronous to release his Monster brethren from Tartalus as they would fight on their side against Zeus. But Cronous declined to release them. Annoyed at this attitude of Cronous, Prometheus and Epimetheus went to Zeus's side. They advised Zeus to release brother Cyclopes also and Zeus acting on their advice immediately released the brother Cylopes. Won over by Zeus's generosity, the Cyclopes presented their benefactor, Zeus, with powerful weapons like thunder, lightening, thunderbolt. They gave to Hades a special cap. As and when Hades wore it, he turned invisible. To Poscidon, they gave a trident which became his symbol. (Poseidon's trident resembles Shiva's Trishul).

The two sides now fought ferociously. In the end Zeus won and wrested control over the world from Titans and sent them to prison in the dark Tartarus (something like hell, bounded by Styx river).

Zeus and companions who lived at Olympus came to be known as Olympians. They divided the kingdom amongst themselves, under the overlordship of Zeus. Zeus took Hera as his wife. Zeus's lust for women was unsatiated. Hera was annoyed at this and took revenge from erring women. She punished them. She became the guardian of marriage. She considered cow and peacock as sacred. The Greeks visualized her as a lady with a wedding veil. (Hindus also consider cow sacred.)

The brothers and sisters of Zeus had their own realms. Poseidon held control of the sea and earthquakes. He gave mankind the first horse and was known as the god of horses. Hades became the ruler of the underworld. He found Demeter's beautiful daughter Persephone irresistible and abducted her. She patronized the myrtle tree and the dove, the latter was her pet bird. Hestia remained a virgin. She was a protector of health. Demeter saw agriculture. Later she left Olympus and stayed on earth. The Greeks built a temple in her honour at Elusis. As mentioned above, Zeus had earned notoriety for his extramarital affairs. But in one respect he was good. He accepted and owned the children from such women as his own. From Cemel he had a son Dionysus who was fond of wine and fertility and was for the same reasson known as Bacchus.. (The myth is he visited India).

Ancient Greece gave the world many works of great literary worth. Homer's *Iliad* and *Odyssey* (8th BCE) recite episodes as fantasies. Hesiod (author of *Theogany*), Aechylus, Sophocles and Euripides were other eminent writers. Herodotus and Lucien wrote on Greece-Persia wars. Poets - Ovid and Vigil – gave great works – *Metamorphosis* and *Aeneid*, resepectively. In ancient Greece people had polygamous relations. Men and women mixed freely.

Tree of Greek Gods (Uranus to Zeus)

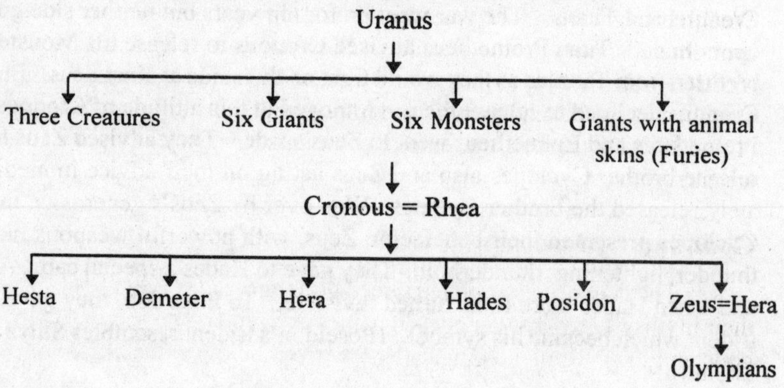

Greek Life :

After reaching zenith, the Greek civilization began to decline. The Greeks worshipped and said prayers before gods and goddesses in temples. One of the ancient temples, the Parthenon (447-438 BCE), was dedicated to goddess Athene.

The Greeks organized Olympic sports and competitions like Pentathelon (running, wrestling, long jump, discus, javelin) and horse and chariot racing. The events concluded with music, poetry and dramatic performances. These were mainly open for males but once every four years these were open to women also.

The Greeks fought battles on land and sea. Their ships were long and narrow and moved fast. These were equipped with arrows with a sharp battering ram and powered by 170 oarsmen each. These were equipped with huge square sails. The battle ships smashed into enemy ships or sailed close enough for sailors to jump across and fight on deck with swords and spears. After many battles in which they were defeated, Greeks succeeded in defeating Persian invaders in wars between 490 and 479 BCE. In 338 BCE Greece lost to Macedonians and with this Greek power came to an end.

The Greeks thought poorly of others and called opponents Barbarians. They made coins of silver and gold, with city symbols having portraits of heroes and heroines. They sacrificed animals. Priests gave visitors *prasad* of roasted meet from the altar, sparing fat and bones for the gods.

Roman Life :

Greece had influence in the Mediterranean city states. The Greek colony of Etrusia was instrumental in founding Rome in 753 BC. In 509 BC Rome became a republic, after removing King Taraqain, and emerged as a great power. In 272 BC Rome controlled whole of Italy. Their centrally controlled army and military efficiency led to Roman prosperity. Wealth brought from foreign countries and slaves from conquerred states brought prosperity to the people. (They conquered Carthage, Britain (55 BCE), and Egypt (31 BCE). By AD 117 Emperor Trajan's empire stretched from Scotland to Syria and Iraq. A wall built by Emperor Hadrian (117-138 AD) marked the empire's boundary. The empire collapsed around 500 AD.

Gods and Goddesses :

The Romans assimilated Greek gods and goddesses and absorbed their myths with minor changes in names or events. The names of Greek gods and their Roman equivalents, are given below:

Greek	Roman	Greek	Roman
Cronous	Saturn	Hades	Pluto
Aphrodite	Venus	Poseidon	Neptune
Zeus	Jupiter (Jove)	Ares	Mars
Odysseus	Ulysses	Athena	Minerva
Artemis	Diana	Apollo	Apollo
Hesta	Vosta	Hermes	Mercury
Hera	Juno	Hephaestos	Vulcan

Cebele is an unusual instance. Cebele, meaning Great Goddess, was brought from Mount Ida in Anatolia in 204 BC in the shape of stone and was installed with great pomp. Later a festival – Megalosia – was named after her.

Cebele had lion as vehicle for ride. She is shown flanked by two lions. From the vehicle she resembles goddess Durga. The Romans had a triad of goddesses namely Juno, Minerva and Venus. The Roman poets contributed to the growth of myths. They immortalized Roman families for perpetuating moral values. Isis, Egyptian goddess was also adopted. Later when Christianity reached Rome, Isis was assimilated as Virgin Mary.

Romans borrowed iconography froni Greece. Hygeia, the Greek goddess of Health conferred prophylactic powers on Hercules. Athene and Hera, Greek goddesses, were represented iconographically as serpents, and mythologically as birds. Apollo was represented as both bird (swan and goose) and snake. (The Hindus also had triad of goddesses Saraswati, Lakshmi and Parvati, consorts of the three gods – Brahma, Vishnu and Shiva). General Hannival of Carthage attacked Rome through Spain and Alps.

According to legend, the state of Rome was founded by twin brothers Ramulus and Remus, said to be descendants of god Mars and princess Rhea Silvia. Thrown in river Tiber by their wicked uncle, they were washed ashore and saved by a she-wolf. A shepherd brought them up and they were united with their grandfather King Numitor. When they became adult they founded Rome. But they quarrelled as to who should rule Rome. The clan of Ramulus came to be known as Latins (Latinum-Roman district).

The Roman society was well structured. At 25, young men learned trade or joined army. Women devoted themselves to make a family stable. Writing was encouraged in political circles and among wealthy people. As for the army, Roman citizeus became legionary (regular) soldiers, men from other nations were enrolled as auxiliary (helping) troops. Roman soldiers·wore armor of metal strips over a tunic, leather sandles, a cloak, a hamlet and short pants. They served for 25 years and on retirement were given a lump sum. Roman Centurions were senior officers.

Romans lived a luxurious life. They learnt architecture from Greeks, particularly making semi-circular arches. Their houses contained an atrium which made it very impressive. Their large houses had pumped water supply as also a hypocaust – under floor central heating. Their central point was called forum. The society was divided in two parts – citizens and non-citizens (proverbial) who had few rights; the slaves had no rights at all.

The Romans had a common coinage for trade between member nations. The Romans were either very rich or very poor and led an oppressive life. Romans in general were fond of drinks and used olives and garlics in plenty. Bacchus was the Roman God of wine and fertility. Entertainment was an essential part of Roman life. They regularly visited theatre or arena to watch sporting events, including blood sports. Music accompanied most of their religious ceremonies. Slaves and religious martyrs pitted against animals. Condemned criminals fought against each other until death. They enjoyed chariot races and built a coliseum that could accommodate 50000 specutators.

The Romans adopted Greek architectural styles. They developed semi-circular arch and added Puzzalona to straighten building material. They used polished marble, fine mozaics and paintings. They invented the dome and decorated floors with mosaic. They constructed a network of roads for supplies and movement of soldiers.

Roman house wives were familiar with herbs and spices. Their food consisted of fruits and vegetables, bread, milk and milk products. They used common material imported from India and silk from China. Purple was their preferred colour. Many women covered their faces and applied chalk dust for face powder. They used costume jewellry. Toga was their natural tie. Man sported long hair and curly beards. By the end of the Roman era, clean shave was a fashion. Brooches and pins were used to hold loose clothes together.

Roman villas were decorated with murals. They built fortifications in the form of strong walls or forts for protection of legions. Most towns had public water fountains, bath houses and toilets. But their knowledge of medicine was poor. They were superstitious and believed that diseases were a curse inflicted by gods. They sought cures by super natural means and visits to shrines and carried Talisman to ward off evil spirits. They used herbal medicines. They removed arrows struck in body by operation/surgery, resulting sometime into amputation or death.

Bacchus, like the Greek Dionyssus, was Roman's god of fertility. Goddess Vesta blessed the ceremonies. While male priests could marry, female priestesses had to remain virgin throughout life. Women were expected to be dutiful wives and mothers. Marriages were arranged by parents and girls married at an early age even at 13. Dowry was given by girls' parents. A wedding ring was placed on the third finger of the left hand because it was thought that the nerve directly ran therefrom to the heart. The bride wore a white toga with a coloured veil and a feast was held at her father's house. A wedding cake was served to the guests. There were animal sacrifices also.

Women experienced prejudice and were treated as second class citizen. Girls were educated to a basic standard and worked in the fields, in addition to carrying out domestic chores. Or they became servants in a house. Will of girls could secure them jobs in a shop or they worked as hairdressers and only a lucky one could become priestess. Boys played with lead soldiers and girls with rag dolls. Juno was women' patron goddess. (Juno was Jupiters' consort.). Minerva was another goddess of women. Originally Juno was the goddess of Moon, the queen of heaven. Romans adopted a goddess, named Isis who was associated with the cycle of life. Child mortality was high. Only half of the children could reach 20.

Many of the Roman gods were borrowed from the Greek mythology. But Romans were more superstitious. They were afraid of gods and averse to accommodate gods of the conquered people, even though the conquered people adopted Roman customs. Only later the Romans adopted Christianity and worshipped Christian God along with their own. By 337 AD Christianity had become the main religion of the Roman empire. Romans adopted the Greek god of Sun and retained the same name (Apollo). Mithun, the Persian god of light, was identified with Sun. They slayed a bull for sacrifice.

Juleus Caesar (100-44BC) was a prominent politician of Rome. He defeated General Anthony and Cleopatra, the queen of Egypt. Caesar was assassinated by fellow senators. Caesar's son Augustus declared Rome a Republic.

Senators were very powerful. They made laws but the system was abused and laws were repealed to appease the public. Magistrate courts punished offenders for crimes but it took a form of compensation rather than retribution. Sentences were sometime commuted to slavery. Senates were open to corruption by businessmen. Each city had an elected council of 100 men who held office for life. Crucifixion was a common form of execution but it is wrong to think that it was reserved only for religious victims. Death was caused by asphyxiation. Death was slow but excruciatingly painful. Criminals carried death by sword, while people who lost battle were executed by strangulation.

Romans emulated Greek style of art and architecture but made some innovations. Modern Europe owes much to Rome for roads, architecture, language, literature, military strategy and laws. In 395 the western Europe was divided into two states – East and West. By 476 Western Europe fell to invaders and became Christianized. The Eastern part, known as Byzentine lasted for 1000 years. Germanic tribes overran Rhine border in 406, Rome in 416 and Britain in 476. The Huns invaded and captured territory from Rhine to China. Atilla defeated Rome emperor Theodosius. The break up was responsible for the formation of modern Europe. Francis settled in France and Saxons invaded England.

BIBLICAL ACCOUNT :

The Floods are a divine displeasure. Myths and anecdotes make primordial history more interesting. They tell how the humanity originated and how it multiplied, diversified and dispersed. The myths explain the mystical, cosmological, sociological and pedagogical functions of human life and its origin. The Holy Bible consists of an ancient popular myth relating to the 'Genesis'- creation of universe and life in a short span of six days. The Creator blessed the Seventh Day as the Day of Sabbath.

Day 1. God created the heavens and the Earth. Earth was then a formless void. Darkeness covered the face of the deep sea while a wind swept over the face of the waters. Then god created the light and separated it from darkness. He named the Light Day and Darkness the night. Then came morning and evening.

Day 2: God made a dome called sky in the midst of waters, and separated water under the dome from water above the dome.

Day 3: God brought together the water under the dome; then dry land appeared which he called earth. Then he desired that Earth put forth vegetation, plants yielding seeds, and fruit trees with seed in fruits.

Day 4: He wished and there were lights in the sky to separate day from night, there were signs for days, seasons and years. The sky gave light to the earth. The brighter light ruled the day, the lesser light the night.

Day 5: He created sea monsters, moving living creatures, creeping things, cattle and wild animals on the earth. He blessed them to multiply and fill the waters in the sea and birds and living creatures on earth.

Day 6: He created in his image human male and female and let them have dominion over fish, cattle, animals, creeping things in water and earth. He told them to eat seeds of plants, fruits from trees, and beasts of earth, birds of air or everything with breath of life.

Day 7: He rested and blessed the 7th Day as the Day of Sabbath.

On the day God made the earth and heaven, He planted trees laden with fruits in a garden in Eden. Four rivers, two of which were Tigris and Euphrates, watered the garden and its trees. From the dust of its ground, he formed man and breathed life into his nostrils. He also created a tree of life and another tree of knowledge of good and evil. Seeing man alone, he took off a rib of his, closed it with flesh and from the rib made a woman. The man was named Adam and the woman Eve. Then he made animals, birds and trees and gave them name.

As Eve was created from Adam's rib he clang to her and for her sake left his parents. That is how man and woman became one person, one flesh. In the beginning they were both naked and had no feeling of shame. Nor had they any temptation for fruit. But a serpent happened to be there. It was crafty and told the woman, "Did God tell you not to eat any fruits from the garden?" The woman said, "We may eat of the fruit of the trees in the garden, God said, but you shall not eat of the fruit of the trees in the garden, middle of the garden, nor shall you touch it, or you shall die." The serpent persisted and told the woman, "You will not die, for God knows that when you eat fruit of it your eyes will open, and you will be like God, knowing good and evil. " So the woman took a fruit from the tree and ate it, and gave some to her husband and he ate it. Then the eyes of both of them were opened and they knew they were naked and they covered fig leaves together and made loin clothes for themselves. They heard a sound that evening and hearing the sound of the Lord walking in the garden, they hid themselves. When God questioned, the man and the woman told him that they were tricked by serpent into eating the fruit. The God cursed the snake, "Upon your belly you shall go and dust you shall eat all the days of your life and there will be enmity between the snake and woman and then between their off springs. Man will strike snake's head and snakes will strike his heel".

God cursed the woman that her pangs in child-bearing will increase and she shall have desire for her husband to rule over her. Eve was so named because she was the mother of all living. God made garments of skin for them and said, "The man has became like one of us, knows good and evil and now he might reach out his hand and take also from the tree of life and eat and live forever. At the Garden gate, he placed a cherubin and a flaming sword, and turned him to guard the way to the tree of life.

When Adam had lived 130 years, Eve conceived, Adam became father. He and his progeny had long life spans as below:

Adam 930 years → Seth 912 years → Enosh 905 years
Kenan 910 → Mahalelal 910 → Jared 895
Jared 962 → Methuselah 365 → Lamech 777
(Leemah became father at the age of 182, and Noah at 500)
Noah → Sham, Ham, Japeth (age of fathering came down to 30) → Abraham etc.

The God saw humankind's wickedness with his flesh and felt sorry for making them. So He said, "I will blot out from the earth the human beings I have created." But Noah who had walked with God found favour with him. God made a covenant with Noah that flesh will not be cut off by the waters of a flood that destroys the earth. Noah and his sons and people escaped. Noah planted the vineyard. His three sons had many children to crowd the earth.

The whole earth had one language and the same words. Humankinds settled down, built houses and a city with tower, to be called Tower of Babel and from there the Lord scattered them over the earth. After this, the age of fathering children came down to 30 years. And, here started Abraham's story.

The theory of evolution has revolutionized the complexion. Scientists donot agree with the Biblical rejection of Nature's role in creation. They treat the whole planet as an organism. At the same time the idea of growth is not acceptable to all. In the Bible eternity withdraws and nature is corrupt. Moreover, in the Biblical thinking we live in exile. From the Bible we donot know how to apply religious ideas to contemporary life and to human beings. This shows how religion is proving a failure to meet the demands of the modern world. We need a myth to identify the individual with the planet, not alone with his local group.

But it is far fetched to think that loss of myths and their memories can lead to society's disintegration. Myths offer models but these should be appropriate to the time because many virtues lose their value and many turn to be vice. Take the case of Eve and the serpent which is symbol of the truth. So are birds. The serpent is symbolic of bondage to earth (and bird of release of spirit). Man shows his growth from the union of father and mother. A tribe has a God, who is their saviour. He becomes world's God, world's savior. But each of the three Middle Eastern religions strikes up with its own myth that it is a chosen group and that their God is with them in clashes and protects them. Clashes between civilizations become clashes between gods. Metaphors have made the difference. Of Kuran's version of Jihad and Bible's birth of Jesus and resurrection and salvation there are many critics.

3

AS SCIENCE VIEWS

The universe is self created and self sustained, that is what Science says about the origin of the universe. Science takes this view so as to deny that it has been created by some one. Science accepts a thing only after its reality is established by experimentation in lab. That what man understands is God cannot be produced in lab, and therefore the reality of a creator of the universe cannot be established. Or, in other words God's (i.e. Creator's) existence or absence is hypothetical. Science affirms to a process of evolution as the cause of universe and life. After evolution of human life, it became a challenge. He interpretes that there is no Creator, a super power to whose idea he was led to form by the analogy of a father.

Man in gratitude to his creation developed ritual; he said prayers in praise of the creator and asked for his blessing by offering sacrifice, which would also appease his anger if he had unknowingly done a wrong. Who he was? He was inexplicable – an awe- inspiring mythological figure. But science does not surrender to this idea.

Philosophy also does not believe in a power that created the universe. The Mahapurana says, "Some foolish man declared that a creator made the world. If god created the world, where was he before creation? How could God have made the world without some materials? If you say he made this first and then the world, you are faced with endless regression. Know then the world is uncreated, as time itself is without a beginning or end."

Some people throw up hands and say that they do not comprehend the mystery of the universe and life, because man himself is a product of accidental mutation, propagated and supported by the laws of genetics.

Scientists state that some 15 billion years ago a primordial fireball (or pinball according to some) containing all the matter of the universe in the form of compressed gas and under pressure of four forces (gravitation at macro level, a strong nuclear force and electromagnetism at micro level), interacted for a fraction of a second and released energy by primordial cataclysm. This caused a deafening sound – "Bang Bang". The sound announced the birth of the universe. But why had there to be Bang

Bang? What was the purpose? Who motivated it? What was the source? No satisfactory responses in reply to these questions have come up. They continue to tease man's mind.

The Bang bang was pure energy released by a gigantic explosion that resulted in an undifferentiated soup of matter and radiation with particles in rapid collision with each other with super speeds in all directions. This started filling space. Its velocity caused temperature to go up to an eruption, at 100,000 million K which fell in three seconds to 100,000 K since the matter expanded in opaque density, in the process giving birth to new particles, actuated both by force of gravitation as well as interaction of the cataclysmic elements in cosmic soup.

After billions of years of this the dense particles of gas got compressed under their own gravity and formed a core which ultimately ignited by compression heat and gave birth to stars and galaxies including our Sun, which are still receding from the thrust of the original explosion. This caused collapse of big stars ending in supernova. The universe was born. The stars that depleted energy became white Dwarf. Pulsars, Black Holes. The Black Holes gurgled into spongy, foam like structure.

The fast expanding matter went into turmoil, and the hot matter started cooling and attained its own identity. The competing natural forces produced enormous energy, inducing 30^{10} increase in the size of the universe. Since the universe cooled down below a thousand degree Kelvin, the photons of light could not convert into matter and anti matter pairs. To the contrary they annihilated each other and the energy returned to photons. The energy was in slight excess of anti-matter. The roving nuclear in the mean time snatched loose electrons and made hydrogen, helium and lithium. (It was 75% hydrogen and 25% helium.) This fusion formed heavier elements. The magnetic field transported energy away from the cloud core which disabled the centrifugal forces from dominating over the pull of gravitational field. It settled down into a stable life. Its magnetic activity gradually subsided. Planets condensed out of the glowing gas. For the first time the universe became visible to light and was free from flying photons in the background of the cosmic microwave. Then after expanding for a million years, as matter gravitated into the massive concentration of galleries, it cooled. Between 50 to 1000 billions of galaxies, each containing hundreds of billions of stars undergoing thermonuclear fusion in their cores were formed. Those stars had ten times of more mass than the Sun and they achieved sufficient pressure and temperature in their cores to manufacture dozens of elements heavier than hydrogen, including elements that compose planets and life thereon. Those elements would have been useless if they were to remain locked inside the stars. But high mass stars fortuitously exploded, scattering their electrically enriched guts throughout the galaxy.

SOLAR SYSTEM :

Time passed on. Then about ten billion years ago, the first storms formed in the disc of Milky way. One of the starts was our Sun. It was born as the Orion Arm of the Milky Way in the outskirts of Virgo super cluster from the gas cloud that spun a disc 4.5 billion years ago. There was sufficient supply of heavy elements to spawn a system of nine planets, thousands of asteroids and billions of comets. During the formation of solar system, matter condensed and accerted out of parent gas cloud while it was circling the Sun. Nine planets circled around the Sun. These were Mercury, Venus, Earth, Mars, Jupiter, Saturn, Uranus, Neptune and Pluto. Sol in Latin, means Sun and Solar System means the Sun System. Uranus, Neptune and Pluto are very dim and can be seen with the help of a telescope. He needs no telescope to see Mars, Jupiter or Saturn, as they glow, though they are not stars. Mercury also can be seen without telescope but only early in the evening, just after sunset. Moon, another part of solar system is easily seen. Moon goes around the earth. Moon is Earth's satellite. Most planets have their own satellites. Asteroids, comets and meteoroids too are parts of the solar system. (Asteroids are big chunks of rock that go around the Sun. Comets are collections of ice, gas and dust. The center of the comets may be only a few miles across. The tail of gases may be millions of miles long. Meteroids are bits of rocks and metals, mostly small, but some may be as large as boulders. They look like shocking stars.

The high velocity comets and other debris have persistently impacted for millions of years. As a result the surface of rocky planets melted and was rendered sterile. As the surface of planets cooled, the star system decreased. Under these circumstances the earth was formed in a gaze around the sun whose oceans remained in liquid form – unfrozen. The Earth was at an ideal distance from the Sun and the Earth orbits around it (that is around the Sun) at a distance of 150 millions kms. and it completes its journey in a year. The Earth provided a good ground for molecules and life began to emerge from a small bacteria (anaerobic), as it emerged in the chemically liquid oceans. The bacteria gave the Earth Carbon dioxide, rich atmosphere with sufficient oxygen (OZ) atoms combined with Ozone (O_3).

Explosions in the stars scattered elements throughout the cosmos, giving birth to new solar systems and planets. Clusters of matter, stars and galaxies can be seen with the help of a telescope. Our Milky Way circles closer to Andromeda galaxy. The solar system has many parts – the Sun, 9 planets and their satellites, asteroids, comets and meteoroids. Seven of the planets have one or more satellites. Four of them have rings. They 9 planets move around the Sun in paths called orbit. When the Sun was young and everywhere there was cosmic debris, the planets took a billion years to evolve. They formed from grains, retained, ice, frozen methane and solid ammonia. Gravity attracted very light gases, hydrogen and helium that were blown away from the inner solar system. The outer planets were made of gas and they have small rocky cores.

The solar system formed of some dusty substance in the disc's edge orbits around the disc at a speed of 250 kms per second and it takes 225 million cosmic years to complete one orbit.

The spinal arms of the Milky Way coil outwards and are revealed by the radio emissions from the oxygen gas clouds. They are lined by massive stars running their life cycles. They explode and set out blasts that squeeze neighboring gas and dust clouds. When these clouds collapse, the dust storms form in groups, first in an open cluster. In the distance of 8000 light years the Sun has 700 clusters that are not held by any gravity amongst themselves as they orbit around the galaxy.

All bright stars shine because of the heat they generate in their interior through the process of nuclear fusions. They are visible because they reflect the light from the Sun and wobble in the sky.

PLANETS

Mercury : Mercury is the planet close to (but millions of miles from) the Sun. It's diameter is one third of Earth's diameter. Mercury rotates on its axis once every 58.64 (of our) days. It has no atmosphere. Its temperature reaches 600°F and ranges from 190° in the glare of sun to 180 in the night. It has a diameter of 4880 km and its size is intermediate between Earth and Moon. Its mass is 5% of the Earth's mass. It takes 88 days to go once around the Sun. (A rocket flying at the speed of 50000 miles an hour would take 4 weeks from Mercury to Sun and 8 years from Pluto to Sun.)

Venus : Venus is the physical twin of Earth. It is the second nearest planet from the Sun and has 82% of Earth's mass. It is similar to Earth in size, mass, age and distance from the Sun. It is a desert and its temperature reach 475°C (860 F). Its diameter at the equator is 12104 km and it is covered by clouds. Its atmospheric pressure is upto 90 times of the surface of Earth. High and acidic rain fall from clouds is swept along by fierce winds. Its atmosphere is 98% carbon dioxide and 2% nitrogen. Mercury and Venus are the hottest planets. Plants and animals would burn in Mercury or Venus. They would freeze on Neptune or Pluto. Jupiter, Saturn, Uranus and Neptune are bigger than Earth.

Earth : Earth is rich because of the atmosphere that shields it from Sun's radiation and water which covers 71% of its surface. Earth is the only planet on which people live. Mercury, Venus, Mars and Pluto are smaller than Earth.

Mars : Mars comes nearest to 5.6 million km to the Earth. It orbits around the Sun once every 686.98 (of our) day. The day on Mars lasts 24 hours 37 minutes 23 seconds. Its diameter is 6795 km (i.e. about half of Earth's. Its surface is scared by crates. Its mass is about $1/10^{th}$ of Earth's mass. Mars is un-Earth, un-Venus like. Its surface is almost primordial. Its largest volcano – Olympus Mon rises 23 km about surrounding plains and has a diameter of 500 km. (The Earth's largest volcano, Mauna Leo in Hawai, US, rises 9 km above sea floor and has a diameter of 200 km). Between the orbits of Mars and Jupiter there are asteroids, rocky lumps of debris, 2500 of which mostly a km across, have been identified. They take three to six years to orbit the Sun. The debris could not stick because of constant disturbances caused by gravitational pull of Jupiter. Mars is 50 million miles farther from Sun than Earth. Earth is the only planet on which people live.

Jupiter : Jupiter is the largest planet in the solar system. It is composed of gas and its mass is 1900 times of the mass of Earth. It has a diameter of 143,000 km. It takes Jupiter 11.86 years to complete one orbit of Sun. Jupiter has its own family of moons which were discovered by Galileo and are named Io, Europa, Ganymede and Calliste. IO is red. While Europa and Ganymede are covered by ice, Calliste is covered by fresh ice.

Saturn : It is second largest planet - smaller than Jupiter; its diameter is 9.4 times of Earth's diameter and 95 of Mars' diameter. It orbits the Sun every 29.46 years. It is ten times far from Sun than Earth. Saturn is famous for its rings. Saturn and Jupiter are very cold.

Moon : The Earth-Moon system is unique. It is one-fourth of Earth size. It has a diameter of 3476 km and orbits the Earth at a distance of 384000 km. The Moon resembles Mercury. Mercury and Venus have no moon but Mars has two tiny moons – Phobos and Deimos which are asteroids. The Moon was ripped out of Earth by the impact of an object as big as Mars some four billion years ago. Because of this Earth spins rapidly on its axis in 24 hours, there is annual cycle of seasons and cycles of ice ages. (Sanskrit terms for the planets are : Soma (Moon), Bhaum (Mangal), Budha (Mercury), Brihaspati (Jupiter), Shukra (Venus), Shani (Saturn), Surya or Ravi (Sun). A cluster is called Saptarshi.)

Uranus : Beyond Saturn there are two more giants – Uranus and Neptune. Uranus orbits the Sun once every 84.01 years. Its temperature is 150^0 C. It rotates counter clock wise and is ringed with icy black particles.

Neptune : Neptune orbits the Sun once every 164.79 years. The distance between Neptune and the Sun is 4.2 light years. It is twin of Uranus in temperature and rotation, and experiences continual ferocious storms, equal to Earth's surface. (Neptune and Pluto are the coldest planets).

Pluto : Pluto is the most distant and smallest planet. It is a large piece of debris, more like comets and asteroids. It is at a distance of 40 AV from the Sun. Its mass is 0.3% of Earth's mass, and its diameter is 2320 Km. It is two-thirds of Moon's size. (Pluto and Charon are made of water ice and frozen matter with less than two-thirds of water density. Its surface has temperative of 220^0 C and it takes around 248 years to orbit around the Sun. It may be added that beyond orbit of Jupiter there are cosmic icebergs and icy bumps (comets). When the Earth passes through a comet trail, the sky is lit up by the streaks of meteors. The comets are on the fringes of meteors.

Why do planets differ from each other? The explanation is that as the solar system condensed out of a collapsy's cloud of dust and gas, the nature of individual planets was determined first by rotation then by heat being radiated by the Sun. The cloud of material rotates and cannot be stationary. As the cloud collapsed inwards, it rotated faster due to the angular momentum. Most of the mass in the cloud that condensed to form the solar system settled into a ball at the Center-Sun. The Sun got most of the mass but the disc got most of the angular momentum. The planets and moons formed in the swirling disc and preserved its angular momentum.

We have mentioned the solar system in brief. Besides, stars at large (fantastic) distances also deserve attention. Cygni is eleven light years away, and Alpha Lyrae 27 light years away from Sun.

Star formation is a continuous process. It involves recycling material from clouds of gas and dust in the space. The nearest star system to the Sun is 7000 times further away than the average distance of Pluto from the Sun. The starts in the disc of milky way form a spiral pattern. A star like the Sun begins to operate as a nuclear fusion reactor when the temperature in its core rises to 15 million degrees. Then as long as the hydrogen fuel is available in the core to turn into helium, the nuclear reactions stop the star from collapsing any further and getting away hotter inside. The life time of a star depends on the mass. The Sun will be a main sequence star for 10000 million years. Is not all this account mysterious? No, it is not myth.

A conservative Hindu believes in the effectiveness of Gayatri Mantra. To them it is a miracle, and not mystery. Solar System is a miracle as well as mystery that has to be unravelled. Once Einstein commented, "The eternal mystery of the world is its comprehensibility."

The fact that a complexity becomes comprehensible is a miracle. The Gayatri Mantra has either been kept secret or so much adulated that it has become a mystery. Should we ponder over it, it becomes comprehensible and simple. Let not its repetitiveness turn the mantra into a mystery. The fact about Gayatri has to be realized that the Sun is the cause of all life and prosperity and affluence. It also unravels the secret of evolution of life. Thanks to Darwin, Mendall, Wallace and Malthus who contributed to this. Let the enlightened world appreciate that the Mantra knows no distinction of sex, religion, wealth, etc. To deny its reach to female, as has been the sanction by teachers of Hindu religion, is improper. Part knowledge, dispenser's knowledge enhances.

The solar systems are escorted by families of moons orbiting around them. The Sun is the most dominant member of the solar system. It contains 99.86 of the mass of the system and holds everything in orbit in its gravitational grip. The mass of the Sun, which has 1.4 million km. diameter, is 330,000 times of Earth's mass. Sun's diameter is 109 times of Earth's diameter. It is 100,000 light years across and 2000 light years thick. The Sun's density is 1.4 times of water's density, the density of Sun's heart is 12 times of solid lead and its temperature is 15 million ^{0}C. In this condition electrons are stripped from their atoms and leave bare nuclei of hydrogen and helium. The core of the Sun acts like a perfect gas. The central region of the Sun which is only 1.5% of its volume contains half of its mass. The energy in its core is in the form of high energy proteins. The temperature of the bright visible surface of the Sun is 550^{0}C and atoms there release energy in the form of photons of light. It takes only 8.3 minutes to cross 150 millions to reach Earth. All the light we see from the Sun comes from its 0.1% layer. It is only 500 km deep. However, the Sun's influence extends further into space in chromosphere which blends into corona (a region) and extends to millions of Kms into space.

The Sun generates energy at a steady rate, while the planets wheel around it, develop in their own way and help develop life. The planets orbit around in the same direction. The Sun also rotates once every 25.3 days in the same direction. Earth's surface is protected form the Sun's molecules hostile ultra violent photons. The diversity of life on Earth owes much to the cosmic abundance of carbon and molecules.

What is in store for the Earth, mankind and Sun. We end at a dismal note. The Earth's eco-system has suffered havocs from encounters with large left over meteors. A disaster occurred some 65 million years ago when a ten trillion ton asteroid hit Yucatan Peninsula and obliterated 70% of Earth's flora and fauna, including Dinosaurs. But it did good also in a different way. Dinosaurs did not let small animals to grow. Now in its absence earth's small surviving mammals filled freshly vacated niches. The big brained primates evolved a genus and species to a level of intelligence that enabled them to invent methods and tools of science. Thus began the human life which is surviving.

The Sun does so much good to human life. In fact all life on Earth owes it existence to the Sun. The Solar system has maleficent affects also. Solar stars can leap from the Sun and unleash a cascade of events. On reaching earth they can plunge people into darkness, rob them of their freedom to communicate which may be misunderstood as divine wrath.

There are many myths about the Sun. The Greek myth has 7-horse driven chariot, an Indian myth relates to Kunti begetting son Karna from Sun who gives Kundals which worn by Karna made him unconquerable. An American Indian myth (of Navahos) relates to two sons going together to Sun to procure weapons for protection from monsters. An Aztec myth makes two of their men offering human sacrifice to Sun God so that he keeps on moving and saves the universe from falling down.

The Sun has been orbiting the galaxy and has completed 20 orbits so far. The solar system was made of 75% hydrogen and 25% helium. It was laced with 1% of heavier elements manufactured inside stars and scattered through space after they died. When the interstellar cloud collapsed and its heart shrank ak 15 million ^{0}C, it became hot and the hydrogen nuclear began to convert into helium and released energy. It required conversion of 5 million tons of mass into pure energy to stop its further collapse. So far the Sun has used 4% of its initial supply of hydrogen, and the little loss it suffered turned into radiation. The mass of energy radiated by the Sun is hundred times of the mass of the Earth. Even if the Sun used all of its hydrogen in another five million years, it will have plenty of hydrogen in its outer layer with the heart of entire helium. The Sun's core will sink and get hotter and the nuclear fusion reactions will convert helium into carbon nuclear at 100 million ^{0}C temperature. The extra heat generated into the core will make the outer layers of the Sun swell up and it will turn into Red Giant and engulf Mercury. Eventually after a billion years the Sun will exhaust its helium and it will cease to generate energy inside and then fade away to become a cooling cinder, a white dwarf, bigger than the Earth.

In the next 4.5 billion years, the Sun's magnetic activity will continue to subside, while its size and brightness will slightly increase. Then it may run out of hydrogen that fill in its core the fusion reactor. It will swell to a giant orange size and find new ways of nuclear fusion. The surface gravity will weaken and its connective bubbles that spawn about 1000 km will become larger. During the next few million years the Sun will grow up into a large red giant and as the connective flows out, its undulating surface will be covered by huge connective cells. It will look distorted from its spherical state. In this state intense radiation will cook the Earth that might be engulfed by the Sun. This will herald the end of the Earth. After this the Sun will shrink to the size of Earth and it will eventually fade out.

Distance of Planets from the Sun

Planet	Miles
Mercury	35,898,000
Venus	67,084,000
Earth	92,752,000
Mars	141,298,000
Saturn	884,740,000
Uranus	1,779,152,000
Neptune	2,787,892,000
Pluto	3,658,000,000

In the USA a struggle continues between evolutionists and creationists – whether evolution or creation or both should be taught in schools, because the anomalies in both religions and science may confuse students and harm them rather than doing good.

Evolution of Life

The sound "Bang Bang" was too loud. Billions of years passed but nothing happened. Then gradually the universe began taking shape and even today it is expanding and changing. During the interval innumerable heavy particles surrounding gases fell on seas and formed amino acids. The chains of amino acids construed protein molecules and cells that built human body. The Sun's radiation produces nucleotides which help build a macro molecule (i.e. genes) in innumerable number.

The genes are attached to chromosome, and each gene carries a unit of information about heredity, known as replication. (The DNA is shaped like helis – a long thread, a molecule of two intertwined chains of nuclear acids. Mutation helps in evolving new organs and species. Chemical forces and environment help in the continuity of species. Thus man is a product of genes and mutations – and it is not ordained by a divine power; it cannot go beyond the genetic code and DNA replication.

The genes form segments of DNA strand. The duplex (of the genes) automatically separate and the two components reconstitute. Each of the two molecule nuclei contains the strand of the new pairing. Thus they are identical to each other as also to parent molecule. They also guarantee continuation of that species of life on land and in water and air.

Each protein contains a large number of amino acids in different proportions and in different sequences. Any change in the protein can cause mutations which occur accidentally in the sequence of nucleotide or/and amino acids or in the wrong pairing of nucleotide.

The DNA system was unlocked half a century ago on April 25, 1955, and this solved the riddle of transfer of hereditary traits from parents to sons and daughters. Jim Watson and a colleague figured out that

DNA was a molecule of gravity. It contained a code of sex in sequence. A couple of 3 billion genome was found that completed human genome and made Molecule diagnostic therapy possible.

There are billions of interconnections between neurons fixed memories. This invention has proved that the brain functions in the body so long as other organs function and human life is there. Through its neuron network it perceives the outside world. What happens to brain after death? Is death the end of brain also. Some people think that after death the body dies, not the soul, which survives. They think that soul is a part of the brain.

The brain functions through its billions of cells. It becomes aware by sensory perceptions and responds to these perceptions. Some organs like heart, kidney, liver stomach function automatically and continuously. They take and give inputs and outputs. (The genes by their biological processes transfer part knowledge. They implant, etch or fix in the second generation of brain for the next generation.) There are billions of interconnections between neurons in different parts of the brain. They act in groups and their response is integrated by reference to images of past events or to the value systems.

These developments have made human genome possible. Darwin's theory of natural selection 'has been overrun by scientific advances'. Similarly survival of the fittest is outdated, and scientists are capable of manipulating life itself. They have decoded the entire humane genome and may soon be able to repair DNA, and may improve the human species – or they may redesign it. Man may modify his body parts through trans species cloning with animals.

BOOK II

4

GODS AND GODDESSES

BRAHMA

The concept of one Supreme God is the basic structure of Hinduism. It was amplified by the Upanishads, later simplified by Puranas and epics. Scriptures say God is absolute, infinite, Anadi (without beginning), Ananta (without end), impermeable, all pervasive; tiny of the tiniest. They call him Brahma (Brahman) who reveals himself to different people at different times, in different places, in different ways. They worship him in various forms, icons or even without form. But how to reconcile the contradiction? How can he be one and many at the same time? Is it then an illusion (Maya), enigma or myth? How is this divergence reconciled?

The Hindu tradition considers all knowledge as revealed by God in the form of the Vedas. The Satpath Brahman has revelations. Should these be regarded as divine or myths? Some myths relate to Brahma who is known as Vishwakarma (world-maker), Prajapati. To Hindu cosmology Brahma is known as Hiranyagarbha also. From Brahma originated not only the world, but also space, time, causation which in concert with three gunas of Sattva, Rajas and Tamas construed the phenomenal world. Before we distinguish between Brahman and Brahmin, we narrate a few myths relating to Brahma :

One: Brahma sprang from the lotus that originated from the navel of Vishnu while he was resting in Amrit Sagar (sea of nector). Brahma was called Narayana. (Only later the appellation 'Narayana' was applied to Vishnu.)

Two: Brahma once incarnated as Varah (Boar) and raised the earth from beneath the waters and created the world. Later, this creation was transferred to Vishnu.

Three: Brahma acted as the chief priest at the wedding of Shiva-Parvati.

Four: Once Brahma willed and created a Manasaputri (mind-born) daughter Saraswati. She was a very beautiful and charming girl. Brahma was attracted by her. To avoid him, Saraswati flew away in the sky but to keep an eye on her, Brahma created an eye on his head. He flew to her. Brahma represents the Vedas and Saraswati the spirit.

Five : According to one version all creatures were born from the union of Brahma and Saraswati.

Six: Brahma invented music, dance and stagecraft.

Seven: The myth is that Brahma was censored for his relations with Saraswati; the 'reservoir of reverence' of gods was lost and they approached Rudra and proposed that Brahma should be punished for doing 'what is not done'. Rudra then hurled on arrow at Brahma and his seed fell down on the earth. The deities were worried about the loss of precious seed and felt that it must be preserved. So they took it by turn to Rishi Bhaga, Pushan and Brahaspati. But it was so potent that Bhag lost his sight the moment he saw it, Pushan lost his teeth the moment his teeth tonched it, and Brahaspati proved totally ineffective. After this they took it to Savitra who used it for the gift of life. (It is interesting that Pushan lost his teeth and cannot accept any gift that is hard. He is therefore given ground rice in Ahuti).

Eight : Because of his involvement in a bad deed, Brahma lost his right to Ahuti in worship. In India there are many temples where Shiva or Vishnu (his avatars of Rama and Krishna) are worshipped. But there is only one temple where Brahma is worshipped. That is at Ajmer. The functions and rights of Brahma have been taken over by Shiva and Vishnu.

Nine : Brahma was called Panchanan (i.e. deity with five faces). In a fight with Shiva (Rudra), Brahma lost one head and since then he is depicted as having only four faces. Brahma's icon of four faces represents four Vedas, four Varnas and four arms. Brahma's image has an Akshamala (garland) in neck, and Kurcha, Shrukla, Shruva (spoon), kamandala and Pustak (book) for prayer.

Ten : Brahma had three mind-born sons (Manasputras), named Marichi, Atri and Angiras. Manu was Brahma's great grandson. Brahma's vehicle was Garuda.

All this may sound mythical. After all, a thin wedge demarcates mythology from history. Whereas mythology is an admixture of facts and imagination, history is based on and is also substantiated by facts.

BRAHMINS

The words Brahma and Brahman are synonymous. A third word 'Brahmin' has been coined by suffixing 'n' to Brahma which has several meanings and performs several functions and has been cause of confusion. A Brahmin could mean :

I. A community – Brahmin community

II. A member of a specific community or caste.

III. A priest possessing perfect knowledge of Yajna and its rites.

IV. One of the three Dvijavarnas (viz. Brahmin, Kshatriya and Vaishya). Dvija means twice born; one birth given by mother, the second follows upanayan (thread) ceremony which entitles a dvija to conduct sacrificial rites, to impart vedic knowledge and to tender advice to rulers. While Dvijas can part knowledge of Vedas to those eligible, it is not to be imparted to Shudras and women. Efforts have been made by elightened souls during the last three millennia to correct this indiginity thrust on women and Shudras, but without any result.

V. Brahma's job was creation and its philosophic equivalent is 'Absolute' – Purna or Ishwar. The Brahma (or Brahmana), in the sense of absolute, imposes a Brahmanic ordeal on society. He helps maintain social order and 'Dharma'. Only one born of a Brahmin parents can be a Brahmin; no one born of a non-Brahmin parents can be a Brahmin. Practical difficulties have arisen in this regard. (What would be the caste of a Brahmin boy married to a non-Brahmin Dvija girl – say Kshatriya or Vaishya?) What would be the repercussions of a Brahmin boy marrying a Shudra girl? Similar questions could be posed in respect of marital relations of boys of Kshatriya, Vaishya and Shudra castes with Brahmin girls? These caste barriers are breaking, but slowly, and those who break face difficulties. Relations of Hindus with Christian and Muslim girls also is a moot point.

VI. Brahmin has relevance to Shrutis and Smritis. Shrutis consist of Samhitas, Brahmanas, Aranyakas and Upanishads. The Brahmanas consist of sacerdotal practices and theological reflections around vedic sacrifice. Brahmana (as a book) differs from Brahmin.

VII. Brahman can be identified with 'Purusha' who is mentioned in the Satpath Brahmin. The sacrifice of Purusha gives birth to four varnas; each member of each varna is to adhere and should carry out assigned duties (functions) in the larger interest of social order and Dharma. Abandoning the assigned duties or transgressing into functions of other Varnas is adharma (an irreligious act, against the code of conduct) which could result into chaotic social conditions. The code breaker may have to undergo rebirth and re-death. Brahmins were responsible (or they assumed responsibility?) for the socio-economic order that resulted from reciprocity between God and men.

The Brahmanic system evolved and set a life pattern, that was divided into four stages of life and four goals for life. The four stages of life were : I) Brahmacharya (celibacy) to undergo initiation and attaining Vedic knowledge; ii) Grihastashram (house holder's life- to raise family), iii) Vanaprasthashram (moving to forest), and iv) Sanyas (renunciation) for pursuit of liberation (Moksha).

The four goals of life for a Hindu are : I) Artha (to earn wealth), ii) Dharma (duty), iii) Kama (desire), and iv) Moksha. Moksha means liberation from an entity and merger with the Brahman. A goal should be pursued by an individual no doubt in his own interest, but it should not be to the detriment of others. Maintenance of socio-economic order is essential for the good of the society. The Arthashastra, Kamashastra and Neetishastra describe in detail the goals and the means to attain the goal(s) and whatever goals are set and means adopted/resorted, they must be ethically sound. If not so, disasters could occur. The Shastras prescribe that it is the Brahmins' (Brahmin community's) dharma to see that the totality of the cosmic order is observed and maintained by the Kshatriya rulers and others.

Brahmins were true seekers of knowledge about Brahma (Ishwar) and they devoted their energies, unlike other Savarnas or Shudras; to the learning goddess Saraswati, because learning was their source of livelihood. But then they monopolized it and made it hereditary, denying others to enter the exclusive club they had established. The knowledge came handy to induce, compel, terrorize people that any deviation to their dicta and its interpretation would spoil their this world and the world after life. This is what drew others' ire. However, credit should be given to them (the Brahmins) that they preserved the ancient wisdom (to which they interpolated also) to serve their clannish purposes. But who won't? The Papacy and the Sheikhs, Maulanas are in no way different from Brahmins. And, the present day politicians who believe in sharing of wisdom and power have imbibed the Brahminic culture and wisdom.

When the Vedic Dharma started deterriorating the Bhagvat Gita arrested the decay of the orthodox socio-religious tradition and rejuvenated the Brahminc religion and reshaped the concepts of absolute sacrifice. (Sonak's Brahaddevata – 40 Legends of Rishis)

Upanishads were terse. The Puranas tried to reach the message to the general public.

THREE STORIES

(i) Self Respect

Once a farmer did a good turn to a king. The King had lost his way while on a hunt in forest. The king told the farmer' "If you ever need anything please come to me. I will be glad to help you". After some time the farmer had a problem and went to seek the king's help. The king welcomed him graciously. After he had said his prayer, the king raised his hands asking for a number of gifts from God. The farmer also heard, the king asked God to help him in solving the many difficulties that he faced. The king asked the farmer if he needed his help. The farmer answered, "Sir, I will beg from the same source, God, you were just now begging from. For now I know that you too are a poor beggar. And it would be a disgrace for me to beg of a beggar."

(ii) Dronacharya and Ekalavya

Dronacharya was a great martial arts teacher. He taught and trained the Kaurava and Pandava princes. Many others flocked. Once a low caste Nishad boy named Ekalavya came but he was not accepted.

Ekalvya went to the forest and set up up a clay-image of Dronacharya and started practicing archery. Because of his keen desire to learn he became very proficient in archery. One day a hunting dog of the princes strayed near Ekalavya's hut and started barking. Ekalavya did not want to harm it but at the same time wanted its barking to stop. So he sent seven arrows that shut the dog's mouth. When the princes returned they were amazed to see the dog and searched for the man who was expert in archery. They found and took Ekalvya to their Guru who too was surprised.

Dranacharya asked him who Ekalavya's teacher was. The Nishad boy told everything. The guru appreciated his devotion. The story was at some stage revised. Ekalavya is asked for guru Dakshina (fee), which is thumb of the right arm. Which Ekalavya gives. Yet the boy was not disabled for archery as he used his feet for the purpose that was served by the thumb.

iii) Maitreyi and Immortality :

Yajnavalkya had two wives, named Maitreyi and Katyayani. The great sage on reaching old age decided to renounce the world and gave Katyayani the house hold share. But Maitreyi was a seeker and posed a question to him, "Would I attain immortality if not merely the share in the property but the whole world belonged to me?". "No, " said Yajnavalkya but "your life would be comfortable. But riches can't make a person immortal". Maitreyi asked, "What is the spiritual knowledge that could help achieve immortality". The sage said the husband is dear not for the sake of being husband but for the sake of self. Nor is wife, nor children, not even self dear for itself. They are dear for the sake of inner self which is the motive for love of things. That innerself is to be perceived through sources. The knowledge of the innerself makes every thing known. Where there is consciousness of self, individuality is no more there.

Yajnavalkya elaborated his statement. "As long as there is duality, one sees the other, one thinks of the other, one smells the other, one speaks to the other, one thinks of the other, one knows the other, but for the illumined soul when everything is dissolved in the self, who is there to be seen and by whom, who is there to be spoken, and by whom, who is there to be known, by whom? The intelligence reveals all, but by what is intelligence revealed? By whom will the knower be known? The self is described as Neti Neti- not this not that. It is incomprehensible, for it cannot be comprehended. It is undecaying, for it never decays; it is unattached for it never attaches itself. By whom shall the knower be known? This is the truth of immortality. That is the highest knowledge. Meditate that, realize that (the self)." *-Brihadaranyaka Upanishad*

5

BRAHMA'S ASSOCIATES

SARASWATI

Saraswati is the name of two important functionaries in Indian mythology. One is the creation (Manasputri) consort of Brahma, the goddess of learning; and the other is the name of one of the three sacred rivers (Triveni) mentioned in the Rig Veda, that was believed to flow underground to join the two other sacred rivers – Ganga and Yamuna, at the confluence at Prayag (Allahabad). She is closely connected with the Vedic cult.

Saraswati as the goddess of learning is popular and worshipped by people. She is also prayed for bringing fertility to earth and prosperity, vitality and health. She is called bountiful (subhaga) and is invoked with Ida and Bharati, Mahi and Hotra. She is a purifying presence. She became a goddess of inspiration. The Brahmins identify her with the Vedic goddess Vac (speech). Many Richas in Rig-Veda pray her for boons. Goddess Saraswati's vehicle is Hansa, the bird renowned for its sense of discrimination between water and milk. The Hansa drinks milk and ignores water mixed with it. Some Puranas identify her vehicle with peacock. Her other names are Sharada, Vageshvari, Brahmi, Mahavidya.

The following melodious verse is recited as the Saraswati Vandana at functions connected with education : May the Goddess Saraswati whose face is round like moon, who wears white necklace and white dress, holds Veena in her hands, is seated on lotus, and is always praised by Brahma, Vishnu, Shiva and other gods, protect me from incivilities.

Saraswati means watery or flowing with water. As a river, it gives fertility to the earth. With geological changes, the course of the Sarawati river changed and she disappeared in the deserts.

Saraswati was also called mother of the Vedas and credited with inventing the Sanskrit (Devanagari) alphabets. Beautiful, she was sometime depicted with four arms and seated on either swan or peacock or lotus. She is also goddess of music. In Buddhism Saraswati is a companion of the Bodhisattva Manjushri.

INDRA

Indra is the most glorified god. His glory surpasses the glory of all gods; he is the supreme lord and the greatest seer. He possesses power to tear the enemies and honours the saccrifices. He is the infinitesimal soul in the body. He is the eldest among Maruts, Vayu (master of *prana*) and Agni. He has shining weapons, golden armaments and resplendent chariots. He sends rains and creates light. Indra is friend and brother of Agastya and the latter participated in some of Indra's activities. His wife was Indrani and Chandragupta was his son.

Indra is associated with Soma, that is Sun, Ananda, enlightenment and elixir of life. He is Shatakratu – deity of hundred actions. He smote Vrittra who had hidden the clouds and covered ignorance. The myth is that the flow of Sapta-Sindhavah was sealed by the python who had coiled across their fountains. By a good storke of his Vajra Indra smote the Python and released the outflow of the rivers. He is the god of war and fertility. He had the courage and intemperance of a Kshatriya. This swashbuckler swilled ambrosia, not to live but 'to get drunk'. The largest number of hymns (25) in Rigveda are addressed to Indra. Armed with arrows and a thunderbolt (vajra) he rides a chariot.

Indra resembles a character of Greek legends – Zeus, and is depicted with two or four arms. He is the Lord of Heaven and lives on Mount Meru, to the north of the Himalayas. He was also known as Mahendra and Shakra.

There is an interesting myth relating to Indra's character. Because of his being extremely powerful, Indra was not liked by some gods and humans. One such human was Tvashtri. He had a three headed son who, with one head read Vedas, with second took his food and with the third he observed the horizon. His ardour of asceticism and pious humility of heart made Indra uneasy and he decided to intervene. He sent seductive nymphs to tempt the young ascetic, but in vain. He smote his thunderbolt that killed him but even in death the body radiated so much light that Indra's fears were not calmed. He ordered a passer by woodcutter to cut off the dead man's head. At that instant doves and other birds flew from the dead man's heads.

To avenge the young man's death Tvashtri brought to life a huge demon named Vrittra. In the battle that ensued, Vrittra, gobbled Indra. The terrified gods gagged the demon and Indra jumped through the demon's gaping jaws and fled. At Vishnu's advice Indra made peace with the demon but one evening when he got a chance he hurled the foam of the sea that blinded Vrittra. Indra killed Vrittra. Every one rejoiced but Indra felt guilty that he carried the burden of sin of slaying a Brahmin.

AGNI

In Veda Agni is the supreme lord, divine power, all knowledge omniscient and adorable. It is the first to be involved. It is Jatavedas. It knows all manifestations or phenomena; possesses all divine forms and activities. It is the energy with which men work; it is symbolized by the Yagya.

Agni as the divine will inspired by divine wisdom. It is the effective power of truth-consciousness. Agni is Satya. It is associated with significant attributes and aspects. It is accompanied with lesser divine powers–Mayas, felicity, Bhadra and Suvit (blessings and righteousness) as opposed to Durit, Dukha, Durguna (i.e. obstacle, sorrow and vices). Agni is Agrani, leader, honest and sincere in dealings of any group, society or state organization.

Agni may be simple fire produced by attrition or solar heat and light, cosmic energy, intelligence, spirituality or Ish himself. (The discovery of man-made fire is attributed to Rishi Angiras). Rig Veda refers to seven Angiras-rishis who discovered light and made the Sun to shine and finally ascended to the heaven of truth. (Agni in the material realm is the master of tejas, one of the keshas, material principles).

The first verse of the first Mandal (Book) of the Rig-Veda Samhita is devoted to worship of Agni. It reads :

We worship the Adorable God, the high priest of cosmic activities, the divine, the one who works through the eternal laws, and who feeds and sustains all that is divine and luminous.

May the Adorable God, eternally adorned by the seers of time, past and present, be a source of inspiration to wise men of all ages.

May the inspiration derived from the Adorable God be a source of ever-increasing affluence, vitality and prosperity.

O Lord! You are the protector of the unobstructed cosmic sacrifice of creation. May the blessings from all sides assuredly reach the seeker of truth.

The Adorable God, the source of vitality and knowledge, the giver and acceptor, is truth personified and divine unparalleled. May He be a source of inspiration to the aspirants.

O Adorable Lord! Vital, living and energetic, may you bestow on your devotees all that is good in you. This, verily, in its turn, would be dedicated to your service by them.

Day and night, we approach you, Lord, with reverential homage through sublime thoughts and noble deeds.

We approach you, Lord, the radiant, the sustainer of the cosmos, the constant illuminator of truth, with humility to appreciate the glory ever-increasingly manifested in your own creation.

Lord, be unto us easy of access, as a father is to his son. May you be ever-present with us for our sake.

अग्निमीळे पुरोहितं यज्ञस्य देवमृत्विजम्। होतारं रत्नधातमम् ।।१।।
अग्निः पूर्वेभिर्ऋषिभिरीड्यो नूतनैरुत। स देवाँ एह वक्षति ।।२।।
अग्निना रयिमश्नवत्पोषमेव दिवेदिवे। यशसं वीरवत्तमम् ।।३।।
अग्ने यं यज्ञमध्वरं विश्वतः परिभूरसि। स इद्देवेषु गच्छति ।।४।।
अग्निर्होता कविक्रतुः सत्यश्चित्रश्रवस्तमः। देवो देवेभिरा गमत् ।।५।।
यदङ्ग दाशुषे त्वमग्ने भद्रं करिष्यसि। तवेत्तत्सत्यमङ्गिरः ।।६।।
उप त्वाग्ने दिवेदिवे दोषावस्तर्धिया वयम्। नमो भरन्त एमसि ।।७।।
राजन्तमध्वराणां गोपामृतस्य दीदिविम्। वर्धमानं स्वे दमे ।।८।।
स नः पितेव सूनवेऽग्ने सूपायनो भव। सचस्वा नः स्वस्तये ।।९।।

Agni born from the friction of two pieces of wood (aronis), has miraculous growth. It also dwells in the water and in the sky as lightning and tears as under the cloud and flames the heart of the Sun. He made the Sun and filled the night with stars. He is messenger for gods as well as mankind. He despises none, as he is guest of every hearth,. He is protector of home, and protects him from enemies. Agni is requested to rewarm with his flames the immortal being which subsists in the dead man and to lead him to the world of just.

Agni is son of Brahma (elsewhere he is described as Kashyap or Angiras) and Aditi. He is the husband of Svaha and father of three sons – Pavak, Pavaman and Suchi. He is a three legged red man with seven arms, and black eyes and hair. He rides on ram and wears a upanayan and a garland of fruits. Flames spark from his mouth and his body sends forth rays of light. His attributes are the axe, wood, the bellows, torch and sacrificial spoon.

Rituals direct burning fire as of three kinds – Ahwaniya to the east, Dakshina for Manes (cult) and Garhapatya for cook to the west. The Bhrigus, aerial gods of storms unite heaven and earth, and they with Matariswan (the wind representative) receive and transmit the fire of heaven.

An interesting legend relates to Agni and sage Bhrigu. What happened was that a woman named Puloma was bethrotted to a demon. Seeing the beautiful girl Bhrigu fell in love with her and married her according to the Vedic rites. The demon abducted her and brought her to his house. The sage was furious and cursed Agni. (Agrni had given information about Puloma's whereabout to the demon.) Bhrigu told the Agni, "Henceforth thou shalt eat of all things". Agni demanded the reason for the curse. He said, "I too can hurl curses. But I respect Brahmin and control my anger". Bhrigu thought over and agreed to change his curse and said, "As the sun purifies all nature with its light and heat, so Agni shall purify everything which enters his flames".

VARUNA-MITRA

A verse in Rig Veda (1.2) refers to Varuna and Mitra. Varuna is associated with Mitra (pure vigour). Varuna and Mitra bestow water on earth.

According to Aurbindo, Indra, Agni, varuna and Mitra, these four gods, represent working of truth in the human mind and temperament. Mitra is judge of love and joy and Varuna is destroyer of enemies. Impure discerment and breach of harmony interfere in intellect's search for truth. Vayu, the fluid in mid-region, is purifier.

God is one, and all virtues unite in God. A Yajna for God unites Sat-Chita-Ananda –truth, mind and joy. Varuna is associated with vastness and purity, and Mitra with all that is shining and harmony. The god pours out knowledge, inner light and immortality in man by the movement of Mitra-Varuna, light and purity, harmony and infinity, which makes it the home of God.

Mitra and Varuna, the sons of Aditi, form a dyad and maintain rita (universal order). Varuna and Mitra appear like Iranian's Ahur-Mazda. Some scholars identify Varuna with Uranus, the Greek God of rain water, and some link him with Som. He rides Makar and bears the title of King of Dead. As Lord of waters, he is called Prasetas. According to a myth, Varuna and Surya fell in love with a nymph Uravashi at the same time. The nymph gave birth to a son who was named Agastya, and became famous as an ascetic. Varuna is omnipresent and is witness to every action. (Ramayana says that Agastya welcomed Ram at his hermitage at Mount Kunjar in Kerala). May we say that a different lettering of Mitra as Mithra causes a lots of confusion.

MARUTS

The Satpath Brahman refers to 49 Maruts. But Jaimani Brahman refers to only 40 Maruts, perhaps the rest nine are goddesses like Marichi.

The Maruts (Devas), sons of Kashyap and Prisni, are invoked with Indra and they come from solar space in the sky. Indra drinks soma in their company and they send rains and ripen fruits. They are pure, powerful and radiant. They wear ornaments and put lances on their shoulders. They are brave and roar like lions in battle. They are benevolent and scatter water. They lead horses, bring cloud and milk. They are knowledgeable, quick and vigorous on their ruddy mares. They are invoked for riches. Sometimes they decorate themselves as females, glide through air, yoke deer to chariot and moisten the earth. They have numerous achievements to their credit. Indra slayed Vrittra with the help of Maruts. They bore a well aloft sage Gautama and sprinkled water on him. They did not leave Indra, like others, in battle and pleased with them, Indra gave them 9 shares in his litany. They are vital breaths and have attained mid-heavens. Minor divinities like Vayu and females stationed in mid-air are Maruts.

Indra broke the caves to find his wealth stolen by Dasyus. Other cave breakers with him were Usha. Agni, Soma, Ashvins, Angiras and Saraswati. Of these Usha and Saraswati were females.

SOMA

Soma is an efficient and venerable deity. But Soma is referred to first and foremost as a plant, juice prepared from which was offered at sacrifice. It is a nector of gods which symbolizes immortality. Soma is described differently in different myths. He is a celestial bull, a bird, an embryo, a giant of the waters, a divine power, prince of piety, and an inspirer. He awards virtue and heroism, and is a link between heaven and mankind. Soma later personified Moon.

Soma was born from Samudra Manthan. As per a legend the 27 lunar stations are Soma's wives, who are daughters of Daksha Prajapti. (One of Daksha's daughters was married to Shiva and another to Kashyap). The moon waves because gods in 27 houses drink by turns during citation. Waning of Soma is attributed to a curse of Daksha that Soma will die of consumption because of his affair with Rohini. Later he revised the curse to periodical waning. Another legend says that Soma sprang from the eye of Rishi Atri.

Still in another legend Soma abducts Tara, wife of Brihaspati. He does not return her in spite of the Rishi's and Brahma's requests. A war ensued between Tara and gods on one side and Soma and demons on the other side. Finally Soma agreed to return her. But Brihaspati refused to accept her as she was in a family way, adding that after delivery he would accept her. That very moment a child was born. He was so beautiful that each of Soma and Brihaspati claimed it as his own. When Tara was pressed to reply whose child it was, she blushed and said it was Soma's. Soma jovially said 'that is well, you are Buddha (intelligent)'. (This Buddha is different from Buddha, propounder of Buddhism). Tribes claimed descent from Sun (Surya) and Moon (Chandra) and called themselves as Suryavanshis and Chandravanshis.

USHA

Maiden Usha serves as the time index. She comes before the sun rise in a 100 horse driven chariot and illumines the world. She motivates men still asleep to wake and move out to do their chores. After that the Sun follows her in a 7-horse driven chariot. In Rig-Veda she is prayed for destroying demons.

Ever smiling, with her powerful charms, Usha moves forward half-opening her veil. Thanks to her that birds can fly in the morning. She motivates them to fly.

Usha is the daughter of Heaven, sister of night, relative of Varuna and a friend of Ashvins. Sometime the Sun is spoken of as her husband and sometime as her son. Indra was sometime thought of as her creator but at another time he is hostile to her and destroys her chariot. When Indra's cows were stolen and he went out in search of them with the hound, Soma, Brihaspati and Angirases, Usha opened out the darkness on the pen of cows where Panis (tribals) had hidden them.

PUSHAN

A hymn in Rigveda invokes Pushan : "May, Pushan meet with a wise man who will guide us, and take care of our cows and horses. May he give us food." Pushan is the guide and patron of travellers. He makes smooth our path when we travel. (The authors came across a reference to a place named Pushan in AVESTA and another one in South Korea. It is difficult to explain any connection among the three.)

PRAJPATI

Father of Devas and Asuras, Prajapati is identical with Vishvakarma. But Visvakarma as an epithet was applied to Indra and Soma also. He made foundations and gave distinction to everything. Whereas the name Prajapati was applied to Savitar and Soma also, he is father and protector of those who beget progeny. Prajapati is not a god, he is a thought. (Taittariya Brahman II, 2,9,10 : Brahadaranyaka – Upanishad V.5.1)

SARANYU

An immortal daughter of god Tvastra, Saranyu fell in love with Vivasvat and had children from him. She wanted to get married to Vivasvat. When Vivasvat came to marry her, Tvastru in stead gave him in marriage another girl, named Suvarna. Saranyu felt sad and asked Suvarna to keep the matter secret, and to look after the children. She then left the place and took the form of a mare. Vivasvat on realizing that he was living with a female other than Saranyu, went out in search of her. He took the form of a horse and joined the mare (Saranyu). They begot children whom they named Ashvin.

BRIHASPATI

Brihaspati or Brahmanaspati was a priest. He was the master of magical powers, even involved in rituals. Brishpati's wife was Tara, who was abducted by Soma. Yet her chastity was not doubted and she is counted amongst the Panchakanyas – Five Virgins.

ASHVINS

During his metamorphosis the Sun begot from Saranyu two sons endowed with perpetual youth and beauty. He named them Ashvins. They had knowledge of medicine and became physicians of gods. Ashvins rode horse which is symbolic of force, enjoyment and health. They were swift, violent and irresistible. They created bliss. They were powers of truth and intelligent action. They gave men energy that impelled them beyond darkness to the other shore, beyond human mind to the supramental consciousness.

Ashvins won a competition and carried in their chariot their bride Surya, the daughter of Sun and brought riches from beyond the sky – from the innermost realms of our life complex – from the regions of Vijnan and Anandsmaya Kosha. They are also known as sun and moon and Prana-Upana (breath in breath out).

This myth associates Ashwins with Chyavan; an old man who had an extremely beautiful young wife named Sukanya. She attracted the Ashvins. With the help of medicines, they made Chyavan Rishi into a young man looking like themselves. But Sukanya was not misled and went with the right man, her husband Chyavan, now a young man. Such was the vitality of the drink. Chyavan Rishi himself evolved the medicinal drink – brand name Chyavanprash – that is quite popular. In jest it is said – but taken seriously be people – drink Chyavanprash and remain ever young.

VISHWAMITRA

Vishwamitra was an enlightened sage and seer of ancient India. He was a Kshatriya who by virtue of his austere practices and deeds attained the enviable status of Brahmarshi. He was opposed to the predatory role of religion. The story of Trishanku and the role of Vishwamitra in it is important and its outline is presented below:

One day the warrior King Vishwamitra went out hunting in the forest. While hotly pursuing a prey he got separated from his companions and lost his way. Searching for them, he reached the hermitage of Brahmarshi Vashistha. Soon, the companions also arrived there. It was afternoon and Vashishtha entertained his guests who were perplexed that a hermit could provide such a delectable food at no notice. The guest King enquired of Vashistha how he could manage to entertain such a large number of guests. The sage said it was all because of the cow. She provided him nectar like milk from which varied food could be prepared. Vishwamitra offered him any number of cows in exchange for it, he also offered immense wealth but nothing could tempt Vashistha. The king tried to take it forcibly but the army failed to take it away.

Vishwamitra then practiced penance to please Lord Shiva. The severity of the penance frightened Indra and to sidetrack him, he sent a nymph, Menaka. Vishwamitra fell a prey to Menaka's charm and had a union with her. This undid his penance. He realized his mistake and began the penance again to secure from Shiva a boon for a celestial cow. This time Indira sent another nymph, Rambha. Wiser by his previous experience, Vishwamitra did not succumb to her temptations and cursed her. The use of curse again caused a setback. He lost the virtue he had earned from the penance. Howeve the penance pleased Brahma who blessed the Rishi that he would attain the status of Brahmarshi, provided he was blessed by Vashistha. He had been a rival of Vashistha and felt so humiliated that he thought of ending his life. At this juncture Vashistha's wife, Arundhati intervened with her husband. The Brahmarshi blessed Vishwamitra who achieved his goal – he also became a Brahmarshi. This gave him knowledge about the creation of cosmos with seven rhythms and Gayatri Mantra, with the limitation that it should be recited only by high castes. (Shudras and women of all castes were excluded).

With Brahmarshi Vishwamitra is assosciated a story of Trishanku, a king who keenly desired to physically enter the heavens. He approached first Brahmarshi Vashistha who declined to help him in his mission. Dismayed, he approached Vishwamitra who listened to the king's story. He sent Trishanku physically on an arrow to heaven. But his old rival, Indra, the lord of the heaven sent Trishanku back to the earth. The Brahmarshi was determined and could not be taken lightly. This time he sent Trishanku not to return, and when Indra again tried to send him to earth, Vishwamitra placed him in the stellar system where he put stay and will rule for all time to come.

We heard a similar anecdote about Vikramaditya and Kalidas. The king was pleased with a barber and told him to ask for anything he wanted. The barber said, "If your Majesty is pleased, please make me a Brahmin". The king nodded. He called his ministers and told them to teach the Vedas to the barber in three days and make him a Brahmin. The ministers tried to do as they were asked for. But it was a stupendous task. They were discussing what to do when Kalidas, the great poet, passed that way. They placed the problem before him. He said, "Don't worry. Have the final ritual for the third day and call the king to witness it". The Brahmins did as advised and on the third day the king graced the occasion by his presence. The priests chanted the mantras. There was a lot of noise – A donkey was also braying. It could not be silenced though Kalidas rubbed its skin. The rubbing caused pain and hence, the cry. When the king came to know of it, he went out and asked Kalidas to postpone rubbing till the ceremony was over. Kalidas said, "It is difficult. What is that you are doing? You are trying to turn a barber into a Brahmin in three days. Surely a donkey can't be turned into a horse in a day – which is what I am doing". The king was amused and realized the reality hidden behind it.

APSARAS AND GANDHARVAS

The Apsaras and Gandharvas are well known characters to Hindu epics. Gandharvas were men-horses, and played heavenly music. They were licentious mates of the Apsaras, nymphs, who were first aquatic and then rustic, and in early Brahamanic period dwelt on fig trees and banana plants, as per the myths.

The Vedic Apsara Urvashi has an interesting story. One day while hunting, King Pururvas heard a female voice calling for help. He noticed that two Apsaras playing in a wood were being abducted by demons. Pururvas saved the women from the demons. He was charmed by them and sought one of them to be his wife. Urvashi agreed but on one condition that he will never show himself undressed to her. They lived long together and Urvashi thought she had a child.

The Gandharvas felt her absence and planned a stratagem. They stole lambs of whom Urvashi was very fond. When Urvashi mocked how the lambs were stolen in the presence of a man, Pururvas jumped out of bed and went out without wearing clothes. Urvashi saw him undressed and she disappeared. She ignored Pururvas's distress and did not come back. But she told him to come back on the last day of the year, when he could spend the night with her and also take away his child. Pururvas came on the appointed day. Urvashi told him that Gandharvas will grant him a boon if he told them that he wants to be one of them and he could then live with them for ever. Next morning he made the wish which was conditionally granted. Pururvas learnt lighting fire from them and lived with Urvashi ever after.

MANU

Indian civilization is the oldest surviving civilization of the world. The Indo-Gangetic plains in South Asia are the oldest and the most extensive plains. The other two ancient civilizations were Egyptian (Nile Valley) and Assyrian (Tigris-Euphrates Valley) but the two civilizations are extinct while the valleys and the rivers continue. Which makes the surviving Indian civilization unique. In one of his poems, Urdu poet Iqbal proudly said, "Sare Jahan Se Achcha Hindostan Hamara" (Our land, India, is the most magnificient among the lands in the world). The poet finds himself at loss to account for the survival of Indian civilization. Iqbal's poem continues, "How is it that while all other ancient civilizations disappeared from the face of the earth, the Indian civilization has survived and continues to thrive".

Several myths relate to Ganga. The river cascades from the high Himalayas and brings the purest water with medicinal value to the plains. She brings prosperity to the land and people address it as "Ganga Maiya

– Mother Ganga." Innumerable myths abound the land and its people. The scriptures, epics and even secular literature say hymns and verses in her praise.

The Satpath Brahman records the beginning of the new world with floods, followed by chaos that flushed away obscurities of the older order and people's movement from west to east and their active engagement in clearing the green wilderness of forests and swamps. With the flood hangs the myth of Manu's survival and Vishnu's avatar. Manu escaped the fury of the flood, as a quid fro quo for the good turn he did to a fish. The fish gave her benefactor prior information about the calamity that would visit the world soon. The information was an escape packet, telling Manu how and when to move out in a boat and with what accessories he ought to.

The flood dates 3102 BCE, the date when the Kaliyuga started. Manu who escaped the devastation became the progenitor of the mankind. Excavations have confirmed the independent status of Indian civilization. Some historians assign the date 3102 BCE to the Kaurava-Pandava battle at Kurukshetra. This date of Mahabharata is not acceptable to many.

About the date of flood, the Indian geologists and archaeologists do not see eye to eye. The geologists date inundation of lower Indus plains to 2000 BC whereas the archaeologists assign 800 BCE to the destruction it caused to Ganga. The Aihole Inscription substantiates the Mahabharat war. Puranas assign 400 BCE to both the floods and to the war. In their eastward movement people had to clear lands with the help of copper and iron-made shoves. They found metals and used them into making arms, swords, arrows, missiles, etc. The armament proved of great benefit compared to the horse driven chariots. Manu is best known for codifying social laws.

Manu's avatar and time are important. For most of the humanity, the moment the linear time stops it is death. "In a world where the only certainty is uncertainty", the great myths offer wisdom and comfort to prepare man for his journey into an unknown god's hands.

SURYA- I

Vishnu Purana (III.11) describes Surya as a dark red man with three eyes and four arms. He is seated on lotus and rays of glory spread from his body.

Surya married Sanjna daughter of Vishwakarma. After begetting three sons from him, she left them because she could no longer bear her husband's perpetually dazzling light. But he noticed her leaving and brought Sanjna back home. Vishwakarma took away one-eighth of Surya's splendours so that Surya become bearable to Sanjna. (He used the sledged energy for forging disk for Vishnu, trident for Shiva, lance for Kartikeya, and weapons for Kubera, the guardian of wealth.)

(Brahma Purana alludes to 12 names of Surya, each with an epiteth. These are : Indra, Dhata, Parjanya, Tvashra, Pushan, Aryman, Alms-giving, Vivasvan, Vishnu, Anshuman, Varuna, and Mitra).

YAMA

Yama is guardian of truth. Rigveda's funeral hymn mentions how Yama's messenger Sarma, a 4-eyed hound of heaven, with its two sons of black and white colour, rescued Indra's cows stolen by Vrittra and Panis. In Kathopanishad Yama is **the guardian of Dharma**. Yama is also known as the god of death. Nachiketa, a young boy, went to Yama's house and posed a question : What death is? Yama did not reply to the point, but Nachiketa was satisfied with his efforts.

RISHIS

Vedas refer to many myths relating to Rishis who have penetrating in-sight. They are commentators and not authors of hymns. Some myths are connected with the philosophy and spiritual experiences of seers of a single truth. The Brihatdevata of Sonak contains 40 legends about Rishis. The messages of these legends are mostly symbolic.

The songs of Rishis vary in mannerism, approach and value from topical to obscure. Their styles also differ. For instance, the style of Dirghatmas Antachya is deep and mystic; of Medhatithi Kanva, it is melodious and lucid, and of Vashishtha, it is harmonious.

In Aurobindo's opinion, Rishis are persons of divine experience. According to Dayananda the Vedas take us from simple truth to the depths of transcendental mystic realities.

Rishis have their genealogies, which is explained by the Theory of Pravar and the Theory of Gotra. There are many lady seers also. (e.g.: Lopamudra, Romesha, Vishvavara, Angirishi, Shasvati, Apala, Yantri, Shraddha, Kamayani, Vashukipatni, Ghosha, Surya, Indirani, Urvashi, Sarma, Juhu (Brahmavadini or Brahmajaya.)

ADITI

Amongst the Vedic deities there were a few prominent female deities who were worshipped. They were Aditi, Nritti and Usha. Aditi was daughter of Daksha Prajapati. She was the mother of Adityas, Mitra, Varuna, Sun and Moon, Day and Night. As the end name suggests, Aditi represented Regeneration and bestowed life. The Rig-Veda praised her:

Aditi is heaven, Aditi is mid-air
Aditi is mother, father and son,
Aditi is all gods, Aditi is all that
Has been and shall be born

People prayed Aditi for abundance. 'Bounless spirit', she protected people from enemies. The Brahmins identify her with Prithvi.

TVASTAR

He forged the thunderbolt for Indra and ambrosia cup for the Moon.

NRITTI

Nritti, opposed to Aditi, was malficence and represented death, ill luck and destruction. With Vritti and Danu, she was binder, chthonic and underworld goddess. She was one, and from one she was fragmented and in her death aspect, she was worshipped as a goddess. She was bloodthirsty but in a hymn she has been asked for giving protection. She was a Tantric and manifested herself in the form of decay, want, cowardice, anger, old age and death. She dwells in the southern area which was death's destination.

RATRI

The natural phenomenon of night (Ratri) also needed protection.

SURYA II

Surya was a pretty damsel. Her father decided to give her in marriage to the person who would win the race. The Ashvins won the race and took her as a bride in their chariot.

ARANYANI

Goddess of forests and mistress of animals, Aranyani was like a Yakshi.

SARMA

She was known for seeking out thieves and led Indra to Panis who had stolen his cows. It is also referred to Indra's bitch.

6

VISHNU AND ASSOCIATES

DASAVATAR

Vishnu, the God of preservation among the Trinity, has been very popular among people, and that is why he has always had good many devotees. Also, a large volume of devotional literature and music is devoted to him and his avatars. The Bhagvat Puran and Vishnu Purana are two of these voluminous works, and messages in these and other works on Vishnu speak high of Brahmins (not Brahman) which is jarring and detestable. Even so, there are instances to show that in ancient times there was not much rigidity. Shudra Upavaran's birth as Narada is an instance.

Vishnu was not much talked about in the Rig-Veda but he penetrates the Hindu mythology – in entire world! His figure in the gold and precious stone studded in the Vaikuntha (heaven) with consort Lakshmi (or Shri) and Ganga incessantly flowing from his hair and resting on the multi-hooded Sheshnag, simultaneously engaged in creating another universe is pleasing to the sight. This is not all, as the myth goes he takes avatars in animal, animal-human, human forms. He has already incarnated in nine forms and the tenth of Kalki is to occur. The first nine avatars are Matsya (fish), Kurma (tortoise), Varaha (boar), Nra-Simha (man-lion), Waman (dwarf), Parashuram, Ram, Krishna, and Buddha. Vishnu appears in his avatars with Lakshmi, and is portrayed with four arms with Shankha, Chakra, Gada and Padma (shell, discus, mace and lotus). The incarnations, in brief, are described below :

1. Matsya :

During an evolution, Vaisasvat Manu, one day, found a small fish in his hands, and he heard it tell, "allow me to live and I will protect you." Manu safely put it in a jar but it grew soon large and had to be released in a reservoir of water. The fish cautioned; Manu of an impending disaster (deluge) and advised him to load two species of each live animal and seeds of every plant and board a ship. Manu complied with the advice placed species of all existence when he saw everything submerging fast in water, leaving none except one horned fish (an avatar of Vishnu). He hooked and moved the boat to the horn of the fish and took it to a high mountain. Manu and all life was saved. Manu went to the plains and reoriented life in the new age.

2. Kurma (Tortoise) :

During the Samudra Manthan (Churning of the Sea – see next page, the Kurma held up Mount Meru and helped gods to reclaim 14 treasures from the sea, including Halahal (poison), Varuni (wine), Parijata, Chandrama, Lakshmi, Dhanvantari, Uchhaishrava, Kaustik, Airavat, Kalpataru, Sura, Kamadhenu.

3. Varaha :

The demons captured the earth that was submerged in the deluge. Dashing across the heaven, Vishnu in the avatar of wild boar (40 miles wide and 400 miles tall) dived to the sea bottom and snatching the earth from the demon who held it, brought it on its tusks to the surface of the water. Thus in Varahavatar Vishnu saved the earth.

4. Nrasimha :

In the form of man-lion Vishnu killed the Asura Hiranyakashipu who had terrorized the world.

5. Waman :

To cut the power of the conceited demon king Maha Bali, Vishnu took the avatar of Waman (dwarf), and killed him and restored peace for the rishis. Vishnu disguised to as a dwarf Brahman, whom Bali gave world as gift in land measuring three steps. The dwarf grew in size and covered earth in one step and sky in another step. No land was left to cover the third step. Bali gave his body to cover the third step. This, according to some, is celebrated as Onam in Kerala.

6. Parashuram :

Vishnu incarnated as Parashuram to destroy the Kshatriyas, since the Brahmins were not satisfied with their rule and governance. With his axe, Parashuram destroyed the Kshatriyas thrice (some say 21 times) from the face of the earth. He slew Kartavirya, the 1000 armed king.

7. Rama :

Vishnu in his avatar of Rama killed Ravana.

8. Krishna :

He took the avatar as a lover of Radha and gopis. He was charioteer to Partha (Arjuna) in the Kaurava-Pandava war at Kurukshetra. He recited the famous celestial song (Bhagvat Gita).

9. The Buddha :

In his ninth avatar, Vishnu taught mankind to liberate themselves from desire, Maya (illusion) and rebirth. The Jatakas recount Buddha's previous incarnations.

10. Kalki :

The Puranas forecast that Vishunu will incarnate as Kalki on a white horse with a flaming sword when man is totally degenerated and takes to plundering. Kalki will destroy the wicked and the world will then prosper.

The Bhagvat Purana (3.25) says that at the conjunation of two yugas the Lord will take birth as the Kalki as a son of Vishnu Yasha.

After the War at Kurukshetra, the Vedic system (9 yagya) gave way to worship of images at home as well as in temples where they were installed. The worship of Vishnu as Rama and Krishna, and of Shiva gained popularity among people. Their temples came up in different types of architecture. Even geography affected the architecture of temples and images. Rama and Krishna images were well presented, while Shiva appeared in ascetic form.

Note : Some devotees allude to Vishnu's 20 avatars. Bhagvat Ch. 3 mentions Sanat Kumar, Narada, Nar Narayana, Kapil, Dattatreya, Yajneshwar, Rishabh, Prithu, Dhanvantari, Ved Vyasa, Mohan, Haranyashrisha as other avatars.

SAMUDRA MANTHAN (CHURNING OF OCEAN)

In this cosmic event the Devas and Asuras churned the ocean and their combined efforts produced 14 precious things, one of which was Amrit (nectar), about which it was said that whosoever drank Amrit became immortal. The Devatas apprehended that if the Asuras who had captured the jar of nectar, possess and drink it they would become immortal and the Devatas would become weak for good.

The myth (in Mahabharat) begins with a visit by Durbasha, an intemperate sage, to Indra, the lord of gods. He was received with warmth but somehow the Rishi was not pleased and cursed Indra that he would lose sovereignty to the Asuras. This upset Indra, who to ward off the curse, met Vishnu. Vishnu advised him to patch up with the asuras and thus retain sovereignty, and in the meantime they should make efforts to churn the ocean and secure ambrosia which would make them indestructible. Indra and gods decided to act on Vishnu's advice.

But churning the ocean was not an easy job. The Devatas had to find a rope, a rod, and a support to churn the ocean, because it was a mass of potential energy. To make the plan workable, Vishnu stood metamorphosed as a tortoise in the center of the ocean, and on the tortoise's back rested Mt. Mandara, around which was coiled Ananta, the serpent. The Devatas pulled the tail of the snake, and approached the asuras to pull the rope (of serpent) from the front, which Brahma supported. It was agreed that the Devas and Asuras would share the finds from the churning. As they pulled, the ocean became milky and turned into butter. From the ocean emerged the 14 coveted jewels. Both gods and asuras clamoured to taste Amrit but none was willing to touch Kalakuta Halahal (poison).

Which called for immediate dissolution. Shiva, the god of destruction, came forward and drank it to retain the liquid in his throat. This changed the complexion of Shiva's throat to blue. (That is why Shiva is called Neela Kantha – blue throated). Next came Kamadhenu, the cow that could fulfill the possessor's desires, Uuchchaishrava (horse with erect ears), Kaushtubhamani (great gem), Kalpavriksha (wish fulfilling tree), Sri Lakshmi, Sura (Varuni), Dhanvantari, Airavat, Parijat, Chandrama, Rambha and Conch.

Rishi Vashistha took away the cow Kamadhenu, Indra took Airavat, the horse, Vishnu took Shri Lakshmi and Kaustubhamani, Asuras took Sura and staked their claim to ambrosia and snatched it from Dhanvantari's hands. The devas were frightened that if the asuras drank it Asuras would become amar (immortal) and sovereign for good and immune to death. Vishnu asked the Devas and Asuras to form two queues. When they had done so, Vishnu began to serve ambrosia. But in the melee Rahu took a sip. Vishnu cut off his head and then started serving it. First he served it to the Devas. Vishnu ensured that by the time he served the last Deva in the queue, the jar's content was consumed to the last drop, as the demons looked on. That is how the Devas became immortal.

Kurma has been translated as 'tortoise' 'turtle'. The difference between the two explained by Joanna William in "The Churning of the Ocean of Milk-Myth image and Ecology" (IIC quarterly : 40 years – a Look Back) is important to understand how the animal could have been used in churning. The turtle is acquatic, while the tortoise is a land animal. (Some turtles are terrestrial also.) The parable of churning has been used in theological, archacological and ecological studies. Hindu temples in Java and Bali Islands (Indonesia), Angkorbat (Cambodia) and even some Buddhist temples in South-East Asia also depict Samudra Manthan.

Joanna's stresses on the practical and developmental use of the creature – as a natural resource for human good in irrigation system for rice cultivation. An inference has been drawn that gods and demons used Vasuki to produce water Kurma an "animal strength, adaptability and ancestor cults." It was interesting to note that the myth is recited in weddings in South India. Perhaps there were frequent travels and communication between South India and Indonesia.

7

VISHNU ASSOCIATES

1. Lakshmi (Shri)

Lakshmi, the consort of Vishnu, is the embodiment of marital bliss and harmony. She is the goddess of prosperity, well-being and power. She possesses unique qualities of beauty, lustre, glory and majesty. For these qualities, she is the most popular goddess in India. She is worshipped on Deepawali in Kartik but irrespective of her being a Hindu goddess, the gaiety of the Deepawali celebration is observed by all communities. It is a secular occasion and every one participates in it. Deepawali (or Diwali) means rows of light (or earthen pots).

The Sri Sukta describes Lakshmi as Shri, and details her traits. On Deepawali day people pray her for bestowing prosperity on them. While the business men ask for good business (it is called businessman's function), farmers pray her for good crops.

Lakshmi is fond of gold ornaments, elephants and lotus. In pictures she is shown holding lotus in hands and flanked by elephants. Even so, Lakshmi is known for her frickle mindedness. May be her worshipper one day enjoys an enviable life but the next day he may be on the road. However, as Vishnu's consort, she is an ideal wife.

Lakshmi emerged from Samudra Manthan and was taken away by Vishnu. She is Vishnu's Shakti. She incarnates every time Vishnu takes avatar. She played a central role in creation and evolution of the universe. She takes over cosmic function whenever Vishnu is inactive. She helps Vishnu's worshippers to reach him. She is also shown as Rukmini's epiphany.

2. Dadhichi

Once Vrittrasura, a demon, observed extreme austerities. Pleased by this, Shiva blessed him with a boon of immortality. Assured of life, Vrittrasura decided to destroy Indrapuri (the city of Indra). When gods learnt of this, they went to Dadhichi, who was recipient of a similar boon from Shiva. If they could procure that weapon, they would match Vrittrasura. But the weapon could be made from Dadhichi's bone but how could they secure so long he was alive. When they approached Dadhichi, in an act of supreme sacrifice he renounced life, permitting them to manufacture the weapon from his bones. They made bows of many makes – Gandiva (Arjuna brand), Pinak (Shiva's type), Sarang (Krishna's style).

The weapon which the devas made eliminated Vrittasura. Could this be true? The fact is legends are exaggerated accounts of people's experiences. They could turn cronches into witches, snakes could turn into dragons (in Chinese legends), and fleet footed stead could go on flying.

The myth of Dadhichi's bones has many messages – Don't become over benevolent (like Shiva) to the people who are of violent nature and could unscrupulously exploit generosity; even discarded material like bones can prove of great use; collective thinking is of great advantage. (Should you think it is all fiction, laught at the story; there is nothing unethical in making goods from the dead. If shoes could be made from cattle remains, so could weapon be made from human bones, says one rationalist. Lastly, when a man faces a mighty enemy, scruples could be temporarily suspended).

3. Narada

Who do you think was the most enlightened Devata? You may unhesitatingly name Narada for the honour. A well informed Narada was as a hobby ever on move and kept all known to him informed of the latest events. He made his presentations delightful. Male, female, child - everyone liked him and awaited his arrival and obviously the captive audience was a good platform for propaganda, which could sometime intentionally become malicious – though Narada never had such a motive.

Narada's arrival was known by his chant 'Narayana, Narayana' and remembrance of god's name was to people's liking. Like it or not, Narada was at the door and welcome him to be spoken of as a good host. A good entertainer, Narada was heard with rapt attention. Some of the things he recited, people thought were gossip.

Narada was a well accomplished personage – handsome, connoisseur of music, and himself a good musician too; hearing him could be thought music was coming from some eminent Gandharva (who are great artistes.) He could be prompted to give a performance, and for this quality was known as Upavaran, a moody and conceited person. Once at a sacrifice, the congregation asked him to sing a song. He entertained the sages but with a worldly song, which offended the listeners and they cursed him to be born of a Shudra woman in the next birth. Narada received the punishment without a protest, and determined to improve his lot. Those were the days when by conscious efforts one could improve not only one's lot but caste also! Those were the Vedic days – not the Brahmanical period as of now. As it is the curse was effective and Narada was born son of a sweeper named Upavaran. Sweepers are a devoted lot to their work, honest and sincere. As a five year-old Upavaran once accompanied his mother to an assembly of sages. It was a rainy season and while his mother helped the sages with removal of remains, the boy heard them talking in praise of Ishvar. The stories purified Narada's 'Shudra' mind (as if anatomy could change) and he instantaneously became a devotee. When the sages departed, they imparted Gyan (knowledge) to Narada. But a tragedy struck him. His mother died of a snake bite. (Were she a devi, she would have been immortal). Much distressed, he went to a jungle and set down under a tree where he did severe penance. The Bhagwan appeared in his devotee's mind and told him that his mind was still impure and he would see him only in the next birth. The voice asked the boy to continue his *tapas* and blessed that he would be pure. Saying so, he disappeared. Narada was transformed into the spiritual body of eternal life, bliss and knowledge.

When the proper time came Narada's Shudra body left and he entered the bosom of Brahma. During the Pralaya, Narada lay on ocean and in the beginning of the Kalpa he emerged out of Brahma with nine other Prajapatis. Even today Narada is spoken of high as a person who would entertain, be a confidant, a good adviser and a good companion. He would tell the host about his previous host without any malice, very much unlike today's guest who would not be pleased to speak well of the host however lavishly and to the host's capacity, he was entertained.

Narada was fond of physically flying in air by the path of sky. (That was an advantage with Devatas.) Brahma once advised Narada to amplify the teachings of Bhagvat Dharma, so that people may be true devotees of Bhagwan. Narada communicated the message to Vyasa Badarayana who wrote the Bhagwat.

4. Bhrigu

Bhrigu is known for his Samhita relating to jyotisha (predictions). A legend about Bhrigu (descendants of Bhrigu) is that they are aerial gods of storms who bring heaven and earth into communication. According to Vishnu Purana Bhrigu was one of the first wise men. Bhrigu literally means one born of flames. One day Agni told on Bhrigu to a demon who was bethrotted to a to a very beautiful girl, Puloma. Bhrigu had fallen in love with her and abducted and hid her in a place. The demon brought Puloma from where she was hidden. Bhrigu cursed Agni for telling on him "Hence forth thou shalt eat remains of all things". Agni demanded of Bhrigu the reason for the curse as he had told the demon only truth (because one should never tell a lie). He added that if he

(Agni) liked he too could hurl curses, "but I respect Brahmins and control my anger. I am the mount of gods, who receive oblations because of me". Hearing this Bhrigu withdrew the curse and changed it, 'As the Sun purifies all Prakriti with his light and heat, so Agni shall purify everything which enters his flame."

Once Bhrigu, the legend is, went to Vishnu's abode. That time Vishnu was resting and Bhrigu had to wait for sometime. Bhrigu was so annoyed that he kicked Vishnu. The latter got up and took Bhrigu's feet in his hand and said' "I hope you are not hurt." This modesty of Vishnu has bēen versified by the Hindi saint poet Tulasidas: "Kaha Vishnu ko ghat gayo, jo Bhrigu Mari lat". What did Vishnu lose if Brigu kicked him?"

5. Prahlad

Brahma was pleased with the austere penance of demon Hiranyakashipu and blessed him possession of whatever he asked for – power, not to be killed by god or demon, man or beast, neither during day or at night, not on earth or in air, nor inside or outside a building. No one should be capable of killing him.

Hiranyakashipu brought the three lokas (worlds) under his control. He superseded Indra, Kubera and Yama and appropriated for himself the sacrifices made to gods. He became conceited of his power and declared that he alone was the God. He hated Vishnu and could not withstand Vishnu's praise. It so happened that his own son Prahlad turned to the devotion of Vishnu, much to his annoyance. The demon admonished the child and sent him to a teacher. But nothing would change Prahlad.

Hiranyakashipu was so much annoyed that he ordered Prahlad to be killed. All methods like drowning, piercing with weapons, seating on fire failed to harm the child. Prahlad pleaded with his father to rid himself of the demonic nature, and instead conquer his own five senses and mind, and devote himself to the great deity. Hiranyakashipu chided, "Where is your lord of the universe?" Prahlad answered, 'Everywhere". Scoffed the demon and hitting a pillar asked Prahlad, "Even in that pillar?" "Yes in all objects," Prahlad said. In annoyance the demon said, "then let him appear in any form he likes."

Suddenly the pillar cracked and from it emerged an unusual creature Nrasimha – man-lion, at the threshold of the building who picked up the all powerful Hiranyakhashipu and tore him apart. Nrasimha was neither god nore demon, nor human nor beast; the time was dusk that was neither day nor night, the man-lion killed him in lap, that is neither on earth nor in sky nor in air. This met all the conditions of the boon. The mysterious creature granted boon to the child that his father should attain a high state and be freed of his sins. This was Vishnu in the avatar of Nrasimha.

6. Mohini and Bhashmasura

Like Indra, who was the head of Devatas, Vrittra was the head of Asuras (demons) who revered him as Vrittrasura. Once he did severe penance which pleased Shiva who granted his prayer that neither god nor human being would have power to kill him, and secondly, the person on whose head Vrittra placed his hand would die. To find the effectiveness of the boon, Vrittra raised his hand and tried to place it on Shiva's head. Sensing danger, Shiva fled the spot, hotly pursued by the demon.

Vishnu was amused and also annoyed at Shiva's simplicity and at the demon's treachery - trying to bite a benevolent hand. He tactfully distracted the demon's attention by appearing in the form of an enchanting damsel in a dancing posture. Seeing a pretty damsel dancing, Vrittra forgot all about Shiva and approached the dancer with the request to dance with him as his partner. Mohini agreed but added that he had to appear in appropriate Mudras if he wished to dance with her. The demon asked for a demonstration of that Mudra. She performed it – placed one hand on her waist and the other on her head. 'So easy', the demon said.

And now, Vrittra came nearby and imitiated her. But the moment, he placed his hand on his waist and brought the other on his head, he was turned into ashes and perished. Bhashmasura's action was like self immolation.

Message : Beware, whom you are doing good. A 'bad man' can be tricky even with his benefactor.

5. Prithvi (Earth)

The earth is the mother, nurse, receptacle and nourisher of all things. Believe it that such a great being, was born, according to a myth, from the sole of Vishnu's foot, Vishnu Purana says.

King Prithu granted life to Earth which gave her the patronymic appellation Prithvi – daughter of Prithu; and it was during his reign that all cultivation, pasture, agriculture, high ways, villages, urban areas and civilization originated. Prithu made Swayam-bhuva Manu, from the calf that milked the Earth for the benefit of mankind. Thence came up corns, vegetables etc. for people's subsistence.

The story has a religious background. Prithu was son of Vena and Sunita (who was born daughter of Mrityu). On father's death, Prithu was inaugurated 'Monarch of the Ear' by the Rishis but he did not give them any presents in view of his father's wish at the time of his death. Vena at his tragic end had proclaimed that people should not worship Hari (Vishnu) and that a portion of the sacrifices should revert to the king. The Rishis-Munis were furious as they found Prithu adamant to act according to his father's wish and in anger they slew him.

Now, there was no king and in the absence of an authority, dishonest men started indulging in loot.. Robbers increased and "their clusters raised dust that rose like storms". The sages confabulated and found a 'Yukti'. They rubbed the thigh of the slain king who had left no son to succeed. From the thigh emerged a being – Nishad – wickedness. The sages then rubbed the right arm of the dead king from which emerged Prithu, and from the sky fell down Ajagava, Shiva's bow and arrows. Then Brahma and Angiras performed the consecration of Venu's son as Rajan. Prithu enquired of the sages about the king's duties. The sages said the king's conduct has to be virtuous.

Then came a time when Prithu's subjects experienced bad times. There was no produce from earth. The Praja (subjects) approached Prithu to mitigate their sufferings. Prithu marched with the Ajagava to assail the earth. The earth assumed the form of a cow and fled but she could find none to give her protection from the furious king. Then she addressed Prithu, "He was going to commit a sin by killing a female". Prithu replied, "the death of one malignant being is virtuous to secure the happiness of many", so the king has to act. The Earth remonstrated that if she was killed to promote the welfare of subjects whence will they derive their sustenance and support. Prithu replied, "If I destroy you, I will support my people by the efficacy of my devotion". Earth responded, "What matters is suitable means. I will impart you the means of success, if you like to use them. I will restore all products destroyed by me from my milk for the mankind's benefit. Please give me the calf to secrete milk. For this you level up all the land". Prithu got the land levelled and gave the calf. Swayambhuva Manu milked the earth for mankind's benefit.

Prithvi is associated with Purusha Sukta (in Rig-Veda). When Purusha performed sacrifice, she was fragmented by Vayu into Dyous (sky) and Prithvi (earth) from whom originated gods and goddesses. Hymns in Atharva Veda praise Prithvi and her consort Indra. Vishnu and Agni pervaded over her. She is protected by Parjanya, Prajapati and Vishwakarma and has been described as mother of plants, crops and creatures. She supports them without any discrimination. She as Mother and Nurse was called Bhu Devi.

6. Ram, Ravana and Valmiki

"Ramayana is not history or biography. It is a part of Hindu Mythology" – C. Rajagopalachari. The lettering "RAM" written on small trucks intrigued us during our first visit to USA in 1982. Had car manufacturers in America become Ram's devotees that they had named their sturdy product, after a Hindu-god? But it did not take us long to learn the reality that the vehicle revealed the sturdiness of a small animal in a difficult terrain.

Ram's story – the Ramayana, authored by legendary Valmiki runs into as many as 24000 shlokas. Devotion to truth, faithfulness to wife, and compassion for mankind in thought, speech and deed were the hallmarks of Ram's character that immortalized him as the most virtous human being. Tulasidas treated Ram as Vishnu's incarnation. Ram's reign was ideal. It was dominated by social harmony, order, longevity, and socio-economic and political virtues.

Say about five thousand years ago (a devotee carried the date as back as 84000 years), a king named Dasarath ruled over Koshala with capital at Ayodhya. He had from his three queens – Kaushalya, Kaikeyi and Sumitra – four sons- Ram, Bharat, Lakshmana and Shatrughna. When they grew up, guru Vishwamitra took Ram and Lakshaman for protection from Rakshasas who were harassing the Rishi – Munis.

The Demoness Taraka was their first target. Then came Khar-Dushan who were done away with. Then travelling through the forests in the east they reached Mithila where King Janak's daughter Sita's swayamvar was on. The condition for the marriage was: whosoever succeeded in breaking the bow of God Shiva would win Sita's hand. It was invicible and no one could break it. Ram succeeded in his effort and he won the hand of the beautiful princess. Ram's three other brothers were married to Sita's sisters and cousins.

As time passed, Dasarath decided to anoint his eldest son Ram as the prince-regent. But Kaikeyi wanted her son Bharat to be the next king. Incited by her maid, Manthara, she intrigued. Ram was exiled for 14 years and he proceeded with Sita and Lakshamana. Then Bharat who was away was brought to Ayodhya to ascend the throne. Dasarath missed Ram so much that he died. Bharat tried, but Ram could not be persuaded to return. So Bharat carried on the administration in Ram's name and his sandals as the symbol of authority.

Ram moved on from hermitage to hermitage. When he reached Nasik. He took ahode on the banks of Godavari, a beautiful natural spot. One day a demoness damsel Surpanakha imagined the princes were in love with her. But they churned out her advances, and when she could not be put off, Lakshman cut off her nose and ears. Thus humiliated, she turned to her mighty brother Ravana, King of Lanka to avenge the insult. (Ravana was son of Visravas and grandson of Malyavan.) With the help of Marich who took magical form of a golden deer he abducted Sita and took her to Lanka.

Ram and Lakshmana were out of their hut that time and on return they did not find Sita and the two brothers went out in search of her. Ram's sorrow knew no bounds. He met Sugreev, the monkey prince who had been wronged by his brother Bali. Sugreev promised to help find Sita. Meanwhile Ram killed Bali and placed Sugreeva on the throne. Sugreeva's commander Hanuman with monkeys went out in search, and he found her in Ashok Vatika in Lanka. Angry with the behaviour of the Rakshasas, Hanuman burnt Lanka when his tail was set on fire. After meeting Sita and assuring her of Ram's imminent invasion to retrieve her, Hanuman left. (Ram met sage Agastya at the Kanyar Hills in Kerala).

A great battle ensued. Ravana's brothers Vibhishana and Kumbhakaran tried to persuade him to return Sita but in vain. Vibhishana joined Ram's camp. In the battle Ravana with his army was annihilated. Vibhishana was anointed as the king of Lanka. Sita joined Ram after a fire test that she was pure. The two brothers and Sita with select friends returned to Ayodhya in Pushpak Viman, an aeroplane of Ravana. The day of return was celebrated as Deepavali Day. Ram was crowned as king and his glorious reign began.

Ram's happiness was however short lived. Because of aspersions by a washerman on Sita's character in relation to Ravana, Ram sent Sita to Valmiki's Ashram where she gave brith to two sons – Luv and Kush. Sita was persuaded to came back. But when she was again put to fire test to prove her innocence, she begged mother Prithvi to give her shelter. The Prithvi fragmented and she entered the earth.

Ram, after Sita's departure, lived alone and led a life full of sorrow. After a long just rule, for which he would ever be remembered, Ram entered the Sarayu river and "into the glory of Vishnu". He is regarded as an avatar of Vishnu who saved the cosmos from destruction by demons. After that Ram kept a gold image of Sita for rituals.

An authoress, Sylvan Devi has beautifully summarized Ram's character and rule : "The hero created by Valmiki still remains for contemporary India the most perfect model of humanity. Ram's devotion to duty, his fine delicate sensibility, his filial piety, his conjugal tenderness, the communion of his spirit with all nature are traits of eternal beauty, which time can neither destroy nor weaken". Ram was divinized during the Gupta period (4th to 6th Century BC), and many interpolations were made in the story, and temples of Ram came up.

Saint-poet Tulsidas raised human Ram to the pedestal of Lord of the Universe, and Sita to the status of a Devi. The Avadhoot Ramayan adds one more episode confrontation by a 1000 headed Ravana, another demon. Ram was unable to kill this demon. Sita then assumed the form of Kali and slew the formidable menace. Feminists criticize Ram for slaying a woman. They add that Rama might have been an ideal King but not an ideal husband. Social scientists consider the episodes connected with Ram as royal intrigues.

Ram's story has been popular not only in India, where one finds its interesting linguistic versions but also in South East Asia and other parts of the world. Ramayana is a folk literature. In south India Ravana's story takes a twist when Saraswati intervenes in bestowal of Shiva's blessing of invincibility to Kumbhakarna. His request for Nirodhatvam is turned to Nidravastham (from invincibility to sleeplessness).

Unlike other great characters who appear either as hero or leader, not both, Ram is both a leader and hero. With courage, honesty and integrity, he matches to the tasks and proves an ideal man and ruler. Unlike stories which have a moment of redemption, myths deal with trial and revelations. In a story hero saves woman from a dragon, fights for city escaping obliteration – he comes out of danger in the nick of time. Had Ram not succeeded in recovering Sita from Ravana, he "would have looked a clown." That is the difference between a hero and a mere leader.

One of Ram's act of heroism was the hot pursuit of the deer, Sita wanted. He suddenly came face to face of the deer transforming into demon Mareecha and faced the danger he was not prepared for. This was a quality of Ram's character. He kept cool which led to his triumph – a moment of delight and manifestation of hero's character.

Ram was both a hero and a leader, so were Buddha and Christ, Gandhi and Churchill. Buddha and Christ followed similar paths; Buddha set under a Bodh tree, Jesus after baptism went into a desert for 40 days and returned with a message. Buddha received enlightenment, taught ways of liberation (Nirvana) – there was no escape from sorrow, attempt release from desire and fear, and harmonize with life. The place to find peace is within oneself. Gandhi and Churchill also were both hero and leaders. Prometheus and Shivaji are other instances. Prometheus brought fire that helped development of civilization. Napolean is also both for French but the English consider him a leader, not hero. Aurangzeb is neither hero nor leader. Whether one is hero or leader, depends on the focus of the audience.

9. Sita

Ram and Sita are a supreme model couple. She is the role model of a wife, a paradigm of the Hindu legend. Sita's name first figures in the Rig Veda, as a goddess associated with the fertility of the earth. Literally, Sita means a furrow or line made by plough.

In a Kausitaki Sukta, Sita is the wife of Parijanya, the god of rain. She is petitioned for growth and prosperity. She was invoked with the prayer :

Auspicious sita, come thou near
We venerate and worship thee
That those mayst bless and prosper us
And bring us fruits abundantly.

In the Parasara Sukta, Sita, the wife of Indra, is offered cooked rice and barley in the sacrificial fire, and furrows are drawn in a sacrificial ritual.

In Harvansha, she is invoked.

O goddess you are the altar's center in the sacrifice,

The priests' fee

She is Sita to those who hold the plough, and earth to all living beings. Prior to the reign of Prithu, the earth was inhospitable, Prithu leveled the terrain and made it suitable for agriculture. He milked the earth like it were a cow.

The Ramayana portrays Ram as an ideal king, a model of social perfection, and Sita as an ideal devoted wife. Ram's devotees say that events connected with Ram and Sita should be understood as an expression of basic pattern in Indian religion. Sita's birth from the furrow is supernatural. She is Anonija i.e. not born of a womb. The legend is that Janak got her while engaged in some royal ritual of ploughing the fields. (Some westerners consider ploughing as symbolic of sexual intercourse.) There came out a baby from a furrow and she was named Sita. Ram has been criticized for sending her to exile in a state of pregnancy to the forest merely because a Dhobi had mentioned that she had been infidel to her husband. She gave birth to twins – Luv and Kush. When she came back to Ayodhya she merged in earth.

10. Krishna, Radha, Mahabharat, Bhagvat Gita

i) Krishna

Krishna is the most celebrated and popular hero of Indian mythology. The vast mass of legends and fables that has gathered around him invests his character with a degree of mysticism. His inspirational address to Arjuna in the Bhagvad Gita gives strength to the weak and solace to the suffering.

Krishna's mischievous traunts of a child, follies of a boy, the amours of youth and the wisdom of the adult, catholic outlook and philosophy of immortality of the soul and action (Karma) have an immediate, universal appeal. They are a source of wonder and delight. The best work on Krishnaleela is Surasagar, authored by Hindi poet Surdas.

Krishna came of the Yadava race of Mathura, on the bank of river Yamuna and ruled by his maternal uncle Kansa. (Kansa was his mother Devaki's cousin). Kansa was cruel to her when he learnt that he would be killed by a son of Devaki and her husband Vasudeva, and to avert the prophesy he imprisoned Devaki and Vasudeva and killed the children born to them. Krishna was born in prison, and according to legend the gates of the prison opened automatically to herald the coming of the saviour. They took the baby to their relative Nanda and Yashoda. Yashoda had given birth to a child at that very time. They exchanged the children and Vasudeva came back to the prison with the baby girl. Next morning

Kansa seized the girl and struck it against a stone but she escaped and flew in the sky. She announced that his assassinator was already born. Kansa indulged in bloodshed and violence. (About the girl the myth is that she flew to Vindhyachal. See Vindhyaeshwari Devi).

Child Krishna grew up in the company of his cousin Balaram and other cowherds – gopas and gopis – of whom Radha was the most prominent. A playful boy, Krishna indulged in all sorts of pranks. He played the flute melodiously which attracted the gopis as also the cows. The romance of Krishna and Radha has attained a religious mystique and is legendary.

Krishna grew up facing numerous adversaries whom he vanquished. He killed demoness Putana who was sent to feed her poisoned milk to baby Krishna. He frustrated her design. Next time he overpowered the mighty Nag in Yamuna when he went to fetch a ball thrown by a cowboy in the river. He slew Kansa and his relative Jarasandha and Sishupal, mighty warriors. He shifted his capital to Dwarka in Gujarat and carried off Rukmini, a princess and married her. To pacify his friends in the Brajabhoomi who complained of ignoring them, he sent his emissary Udhav whose high flown philosophy was beyond their grasp. But he realized the truth from gopis who were deep in love with Krishna and they saw him everywhere for that reason.

Krishna was related to Kauravas and Pandavas and when the war broke out between them he acted as the charioteer of Pandava prince Arjuna. When Arjuna showed diffidence to fight against his own kith and kin, Krishna inspired him to do his duty as a Kshatriya – to fight for a right cause. Arjuna then took up arms and Pandavas came out victorious. Mahabharat describes the 18 Days War.

One day Krishna was struck by a hunter's arrow that killed him instantaneously. Over the centuries Mathura – Brindavan have been centres of pilgrimage and magical tales woven around Krishna's exploits. He has been deified as Vishnu's 8th incarnation and is worshipped in all parts of India.

(ii) Radha

Radha's name is inextricably connected with that of Krishna who is irresistibly handsome and so attractive that Radha, though married (to one Ayana) is enamoured of Krishna. Unable to control her emotions, she breaks all the social norms and willfully pursues her love outside the realm of dharma. Their brief affair relates to their adolescent age, and ends when Krishna leaves Brija for Dwarka. Radha is love sick and overcome by emotions.

The tradition of Krishna's dalliance with Radha (and gopis) developed among the Vaishnavas to whom Krishna represents the God and Radha the devotee (soul) who gives up everything for her lord.

The myth begins with the spiriting away of new born Krishna by his father from Kansa's jail in Mathura and leaving him in the home of Nanda and Yashoda, a cowherd couple who raise the child. Krishna grows up with Balarama (also called Haladhar) and other gopas and gopis among whom Radha is the most prominent. Krishna shows his divine acts, like killing Putana, a demoness; controlling the Sheshanag in the Yamuna where perchance their ball had fallen and many other deeds of courage and adventure. The village women dote on Krishna, the child and their interest turns in to passion as they grow up. He retires to woods and plays flute, hearing which the gopis leave their domestic chores and dash to the bowers of Vrindavan to be with Krishna. Krishna's love is for all and not exclusive for Radha. Radha's love is the central theme of the poetry of Vidyapati, while Jaideva's approach is devotional. Both Radha and Krishna, it appears, are enchanted of each other and see each other everywhere. Brahma-vaivarta Purana assumes Radha as a goddess but except to devotees her description might appear unreasonable. Radha has been treated as the cosmic lady. Mirabai is the only person who can be compared with Radha. (Krishna was married to Rukmini and Satyabhama.)

Vidyapati shows Radha as one torn between seeking out Krishna and protecting his reputation, while Chandidas shows her as strong willed. Chaitannya's approach is devotional. Rup Goswami's drama portrays her as a lover, completely devoted. Kiritanias portray Radha as entangled in a web of emotional relationship that unfolds.

MAHABHARAT

Having the Mahabharata or/and replica of Taj mahal in a living house can be a curse for family.

A controversy raged for long: which precedes – Ramayana or Mahabharata? (event-wise and creation –wise) It is generally agreed that the events of Ramayana took place before those of the Mahabharata. But from closer scrutiny of their socio-political, historical backgrounds and linguistic analysis, the Mahabharata appears to have been authored before the Ramayana. Mahabharata is much bulkier in volume. Both are real and it is incorrect to say that the Ramayana is fictitious and Mahabharata an imaginary and speculative work.

The writing of the Mahabharata started in about 1000 BCE and was brought update in 500 CE. Its 18 books consist of as many as one hundred thousand verses. (Shanti and Anushasan Parvas and the Bhagvat Gita are major interpolations.) Many a folklore (for instance Shakuntala – Dushyant, Savitri-Satyavan, Raja Harishchandra, Nal-Damayanti, besides Rama's story) are also sandwitched in the voluminous epic. Vyasa is credited with its authorship. The myth is that he composed the entire work in three years. He dictated it to Ganesh who alone was competent and swift to follow and write down Vyasa's speech. Vaishampayan narrated it to Janmejaya after the Rajsuya Yajya. Our friend Patrick S. Bresnan is of the view that the Mahabharata was composed sometime between the fifth and fourth centuries BCE because this was the likely time when the Bhagvat-Gita was composed in response to certain spiritual movements, including early Buddhism.

Vyasa's legend is also interesting. Vyasa was a son of the renowned sage, Parasar, born in a not very happy situation. One day Parasar wanting to go across a river hired the services of a boat being ferried by a pretty fisher girl, Satyavati. Seeing her he was consumed with lust and she yielded to his persuasion, when he promised that she would retain her virginity. Magically, he conjured a fog and in that dense mist, they united. She conceived without losing her virginity and gave birth to a son – named Vyasa – an early child. In course of time Satyavati became the wife of Kuru King Santanu. Bound by the sage's bow, she could not produce a child – and in the meantime Santanu's son by another wife died leaving behind two wives but no progeny. Santanu was distressed. To console Santanu Satyavati summoned her son Vyasa to help the two wives with progeny. Vyasa reluctantly did so. But one woman seeing the ugly face of Vyasa turned her face away and closed her eyes. Seeing this he was angry and cursed her. So the son born of her, Dhritarashtra was blind. The other girl behaved normally and her son Pandu was normal.

Dhritarashtra born blind, could not succeed Santanu to the throne and Pandu became the emperor. Vyasa who was familiar with the family events was obviously the best choice to author the 18-day war, that became famous as Mahabharata. The epic tells a stirring story of conflicts and family rivalry between the 100 children of Dhiratarashtra known as Kauravas and five children of Pandu as Pandavas.

Pandu unexpectedly died young, leaving behind two widows, Kunti and Madri (and five sons - three – Yudhister, Bhim and Arjun from the former and two Nakul and Sahdev from the latter). Dhritarashtra seized the throne proposing to make it over to Yudhisthir when he came of age. Dhritarashtra's eldest son Duryodhana assisted his father to carry out the royalty's functions. Duryodhana was jealous of his cousins. Both thought they had the legitimate right to the throne and claimed Kuruland with capital at Hastinapur on the banks of the Ganga river. The Kaurava brothers were determined to get rid of their cousins and they invited the Pandavas to play a game. The Pandavas were put up in an ivory palace, which in fact was made of wax. In the night they put it on fire. The Pandavas somehow escaped and reached the land of Panchals ruled by Drupat. The Pandavas participated in a swayamvar of princess Drupadi.

Arjuna succeeded and Draupadi was married to him. With the intervention of Krishna and the Yadavas, the Pandavas and Kauravas reached a compromise to divide the kingdom. Kauravas got a major share and Pandavas a smaller one.

Pandavas made their capital at Indraprashtha, while the Kauravas continued to rule from Hastinapur in the name of Dhritarashtra. In a gambling contest Yudhisthir lost not only their property but also wife Draupadi who was brought to the court and Duhsashan tried to disrobe her. Though he failed, this was a humiliation and insult to the Pandavas who would never forgive the Kauravas.

To avoid further damage, Dhritarashtra asked his sons to return Draupadi to the Pandavas. Later the Kauravas manipulated to send the Pandavas to exile for 13 years. They passed the time in disguise doing odd jobs. When the period was over, the Pandavas asked their cousins to return their kingdom. But the Kauravas would not give even five villages, what to say of the kingdom. A war became inevitable to settle the matter and the two warring camps met at Kurukshetra.

The Pandavas were advised by Krishna who served also as Arjuna's charioteer in the battle. Arjuna showed reluctance to fight and kill his relatives and gurus, but Krishna's advice, as in the Bhagvat Gita, motivated them. The 18 day war destroyed the Kauravas and much of the Pandava army. The nation became weak. Yudhisthira as the ruler ruled the kingdom for many years.

The above narrative covers 16 books, of the total of 18 books. Books 17 and 18 are later additions. They show a more advanced ethics influenced by Ahimsa, Yudhisthira's abdication, and the journey of the five Pandavas and Draupadi to the Himalayas to find heaven. Divested of its didactic interpolations, Mahabharata is a story of vicissitudes, heroic deeds, treachery and loyalty. Some critics are of the view that Bhargavas, a Brahmamic clan, had a special hand in the elargement and transmission of the tale. The Mahabharat was for the first time recited at Takshashila.

BHAGVAT GITA

Among the scriptures of India, the one that commands people's utmost respect is the Bhagvat Gita. It has given solace to innumerable people and served as a beacon light to eminent Indians, such as Vivekananda, B.G. Tilak, M.K. Gandhi. It left impression on Emerson and Thoreau, the great scholars and philosophers of the West. It is worth while to know what they said.

"It was the first of books, it was as if an empire spoke to us, nothing small or unworthy but large, serene, consistent, the voice of an age-old intelligence which in another age and climate had pondered and thus disposed of the same questions which exercise us". - Emerson.

"The reader is nowhere raised into and sustained in a higher, purer or rarer region of thought than in the Bhagvat Gita. Besides, even our Shakespear seems sometime youthfully greater and practical merely." – Thoreau.

"Vivekananda asked monks to transform their energies for achieving spiritual liberation; B.G. Tilak found in its teachings devotion and compassion and performance of selfless duty. Its Central teaching is the attainment of liberation by performing duty to life".

The great scientist Robert Oppenheimer cited from Gita at the time of the first atomic explosion. "Arjun saw the whole universe enfolded with its countless billions of life forms, gathered together in the body of God of Gods and Krishna dazzled Arjuna's sight blazing in the measures, massive, sun-flame splendour of radiant form".

Gandhi called Gita his "eternal mother" – a love song to reality, a hymn in praise of everything excellent and beautiful and brave.

The Bhagvat Gita (the culmination of the Aupanishadic tradition) was written between 5th century BCE and 1st century CE. It elevated Vishnu, in his avatar of Krishna to the status of the ultimate God – the source of entire cosmos. The Gita's teachings are : selfless action, need to annihilate desire and ego, way to control mind and senses, and attain liberation from rebirths.

The Gita has a dramatic beginning : two armies assembled by the Kauravas and Pandavas draw the battle lines at Kurukshetra. Arjuna's chariot drawn by Krishna stands mid way and the battle is to start. Arjuna surveys the combatants and tells Krishna that he is not afraid of fighting nor of being killed but that there are among the opponents close relatives and friends with whom he does not feel like fighting. He would rather give up his claim to the kingdom than kill his relatives and friends. He admits he is confused and seeks Krishna's advice about his duty.

Krishna's response in 650 verses to questions posed by Arjuna is : the body may be killed in fight but the soul is eternal. Pleasure, pain and sensory experiences are transitory and must be put up with. Arjuna must do what his dharma demands of him. As a Kshatriya his dharma is to fight in a just war. If he does not fight he will be scorned at, but if he is killed, he will go to heaven. The spirit being eternal passes from one state to another. The whole thing sounds odd when it is kept in view that the response is in as many as 650 verses, that too in the battle field when the battle is likely to commence any moment. Moreover, the response is not to the point.

Some critics view the entire discourse imaginary and think that if there had to be dialogues to weave a philosophic subject or subjects, the responses from Krishna would have not been so lengthy, even if poetic license and additions of interpolations were conceded.

Much work has been done on Bhagvat Gita. Recent studies have laid stress on the social aspect of Gita. Satya P. Agarwal's interpretation of Gita makes out a case for revision of forms of worship (rituals?) and social customs. He is critical of rigorous and excessive measures relating to preservation of caste hierarchy and inhuman treatment of untouchables, mentioned in Gita and pleads for a solution for social and political impasse conflicting modern India. Does not at the end of the war, Arjuna behave very insensitively? When he tells Draupadi, "Only when I behead Ashvatthama, I will wipe tears from your eyes and then after burning the dead bodies of your five sons, you may take bath standing on the beheaded man's body." This transpired when Draupadi cried incessantly on hearing that Ashvatthama had beheaded her five sons. The killer was the son of guru Dronacharya.

Basham, the well known writer of "India That Was Wonder" makes a brief critical analysis of the contents of the Bhagvat Gita and says that the Gita is not in its original form and that many interpolations have been made "very intelligently" by Brahmin scholars. These are in three sub stratums viz. (i) In the explanation of nature of cosmos and Brahman, Krishna refers to himself as the highest god (chapters 2(38 to end), 3,5,6,8,13,14(7 to 25), 16,17,18(1 to 53) and in the process theistic verses have been interpolated in chapters 4,7,9,10,11,14 (1 to 6 and 26), 15,17(54 to end). (ii) Some passages adumbrating doctrines of Hinduism introduce the concept of three gunas – Sattva, Rajas, Tamas. Of these the soul wants to be detached so as to seek liberation and become Brahman (6.27). (iii) Chapter 13 enunciates Sankhya and links ego (Ahankar) and distinguishes the material world from soul, and adds emotions and sensations– (desire, aversion, pleasure, pain, thought, constancy (13.16). The union of Purusha and Prakriti (13.20) leads to realization of reality. Distinguishing the two helps in release from rebirth. At the back of all this is Brahman who subdues desires and causes loss of egoity. The man on death attains Nirvana (2.71-72). Man should do all activities as Nishkam Karma (without expecting results). It should be treated as sacrifice. Virtuous deeds, instead of sacrifice, are more effective. An individual should realize that the achievement of spiritual endeavour is higher than heaven where God dwells among gods. Here Krishna becomes incarnate of Vishnu, from whom emanates Brahmin, and Bhagvat Gita becomes God's work. Critics also say that contents of Chapter 5 (24 to 29) dealing with Nirvana are superfluous and are interpolations.

The doctrine of Karma prescribes that every one reaps the fruits of his Karma. It can be modified by man's faith in Krishna (God) and his grace. Krishna teaches Arjuna Nishkam Karma and devotion (Bhakti) in God. This is the most important doctrine of Gita. Whatever one does he should do it for the love and glory of God. Whoever has perfected Bhakti is relieved of the burden of his past karmas; even Shudras and women can relieve themselves of the burden of past karmas. Krishna does not reject the reality of other gods but they are all subsumed in him and emanate from him.

The Gita also propounds the Doctrine of incarnation. Krishna is born for the protection of good and destruction of evil; thereby he establishes righteousness. Krishna is both God and man.

Obviously, Bhagvat Gita supports tradition, including casteism (3.35 and 18.47). It says it is better to perform ones' duty, howsoever bad (or menial) than doing another's. It is better to die engaged in ones' duty, doing somebody else's duty is dangerous. The duty is dharma. Thus Gita defends not only Kshatriyas' duty but whole Brahmamic system.

Messages of Krishna and Christ in Gita and Bible, resemble. Krishna says "All those who love and trust me, even the lowest of them, prostitutes, beggars, slaves will attain the ultimate goal' (9.30-32). The Bible refers to cure of the ill, slaves, poor and prostitutes by Christ. Krishna and Christ sound alike. Even their appearances are similar. Krishna showed Arjuna his real form, which frightened the latter. Jesus Christ too showed his form to his apostles. ('John' in Bible).

One of the disciples, Judas (not Iscariot) asked Jesus "Lord, what can have happened, that you mean to disclose yourself to us alone and not to the world." Jesus replied, "Anyone who loves me will heed what I say, then my father will love him, and we will come to him and make our dwelling with him….and the word you hear is not mine; it is the word of the Father who sent me. Peace is my parting gift to you, my own peace, such as the world cannot give" (John 14).

"I am the real vine and my father is the Gardner. You are the branches. He who dwells in him, bears much fruit, for apart from me you can do nothing. If you dwell in me and my words dwell in you, ask what you will and you shall have it. This is my father's glory that you may bear fruit in plenty and so be my disciples" (John 15).

Jesus looked up to heaven and said, "Father, the hour has come to glorify the son. For the last made him sovereign over all mankind, to give eternal life to all whom thou hast given him. This is eternal life, to know thee who alone art truly God, and Jesus Christ whom thou hast sent. (John 17).

There is a myth that the mortal remains of Jesus lie buried and resting in Kashmir, a state of India. (Krishna breathed last in Gujarat).

VINDHYAVASINI DEVI

The identity of the Great Goddess is shrouded in mystery. To the Shaivites, she is Uma. - Parvati – incarnate of Mahadevi. To the Shakta pantheon she is Vindhyavasini Devi who dwells on the Mount Vindhya as the Adishakti (primeval power). She incarnated as the prime Vaishnavite deity to assist Vishnu in completing his mission of destruction of demons who were disturbing sages engaged in austere penance.

The Mahadevi manifests herself to devotees according to their conviction, faith and appeal in different forms. She is not bound to a place.

There is an interesting myth behind Vindhyavasini Devi. When Vishnu appeared in the avatar of Krishna in the house of the cowherd couple Vasudeva and Devaki, the Yogini Yoganidra Mahamaya too took birth for Vishnu's sake in the house of their relatives, Nanda and Yashoda. Vasudeva took the new born from the Karagar (Jail) of Mathura, where Krishna was born across the swollen Jamuna river in the pitch dark night. With the spell of Mahamaya the doors of the prison opened automatically and the Jamuna made passage for Vasudeva carrying the baby on head. He exchanged the male child Krishna with Yashodas' newly born daughter. Vasudeva returned with the female baby to the jail in Mathura. The baby boy was thus assured security from Kansa.

When Kansa came to know of the birth to his sister Devaki, he rushed to the jail, grabbed the baby and dashed her against a stone. The baby slipped from Kansa's hand and flew in the sky. Therefrom she broadcast the news terrifying Kansa that Kansa's slayer was born. Saying so the baby girl flew off to Vindhyachal. From the mount's name she came to be known as Vindhyasvasini, Vindhyeshwari, etc. She is associated in a big way with Tantra Vidya.

The Vindhya Mahatmya praises the deity. It includes instructions for tantrics – how to attain siddhis (i.e. supernatural powers) by constructing a yantra. The precept is that Mahalakshmi is the ultimate reality which exists in the form of a Yantra with its base on a triangle superimposed over Brahman a Bindu (point). At each corner Vindhyavasini transfers herself into three Mahdevis (viz. Mahasaraswati, Mahalakshmi and Mahakali known by their attributes and each manifesting herself). Mahasaraswati becomes Ashtabhog, Mahakali becomes Kalikhoh and Mahalakshmi as Vindhyavasini.

Still another group of devotees Vedicized Vindhyavasini. In the Devi Mahatmya, she is vegetarian, universalist and her identity is cosmopolitan. From imminence, she moves to transcendence in which state she is the ultimate reality – beyond human history. But in her manifest form, she transforms herself and moves within and throughout humanity.

Strangely, the devotees offer liqor and animal sacrifice at the Deity's shrine. Perhaps the tribals and other peripheral groups of people in the past indulged in sacrifice to curry Devi's favour. The Devi herself, as also her worship, were incorporated into the Brahmanical traditions.

SAVITRI

Mahabharata has several stories of didactic value. One interesting tale is that of Savitri, daughter of King Ashvapati of Ujjain. When she came of marriageable age, the parents tried to find a suitable match for her. But they did not succeed in their efforts and they gave Savitri freedom to choose her own husband. She visited many cities accompanied by maids. One day she met a handsome youth, son of a hermit, named Satyvan. She told her parents who felt embarrassed that a princess should marry a hermit's son. That time Narada came to their house and the king placed the matter before him. Narada tried to dissuade because the boy was destined to live only one year more, after that he would die. But Savitri was determined and finally they were married.

The couple lived happily. When the day of the prophecy arrived, she persuaded Satyavan to take him with her in the forest where he used to cut the wood. When he climbed the tree, he had a terrible pain and fell down at his wife's feet and told her that he was dying. Satyavan became unconscious. Savitri kept on sitting having her husband's head in her lap.

Yamraj's messages came to fetch Satyavan. But they returned seeing him like a burning flame. Then Yama himself arrived to take him. He told Savitri that he had to take Satyavan who was now his property. She said Satyavan is your property. So will he be, you may take him but not without me. Yama failed to convince that he could not carry a living person. Yama was pleased with her devotion and told her if she had any wish, except life of her husband, he would fulfill.

Savitri told him, "If you are pleased, then grant me a boon that my father who has no son, will have a son to hand down his name to posterity. "It will be so", said the Yama. But when Yama started going with Satyakama, he found she was following him like a shadow. Yama dissuaded her and offered one more boon. Now she asked that her in-laws should see grand children. Yama okayed. But how could Savitri have a child without husband? Realizing the truth, Yama released Satyavan

8

SHIVA AND ASSOCIATES

Shiva is both creator and destroyer. His consort Parvati (reincarnate of Sati) is a creative energy (shakti) as well as an aspect of Devi (Great Goddess).

Shiva's family tree

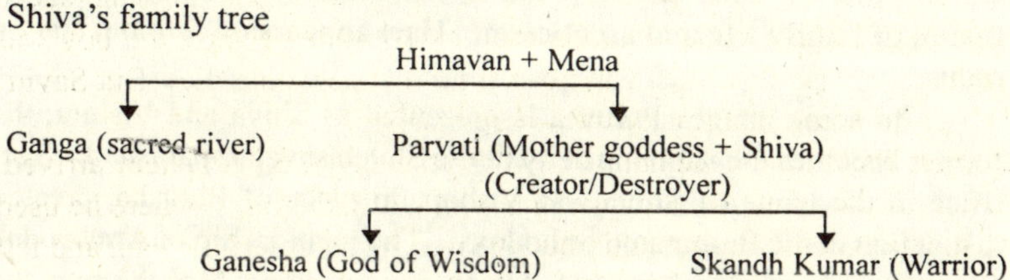

SHIVA

Shiva, one of the trinity, the lord of destruction of the universe, is benevolent to a fault. When pleased with a devotee, he bestows on him whatever asked for. This large heartedness has placed Shiva in odd situations. Overlooking these, he shows magnanimity and forgives the wrong doers. More devotees flock to worship him in his anthromorphic form of Shiva linga. The cult of Shiva has developed into a magnificent cosmic synthesis where life and death continually give birth to each other.

Shiva and his consort, Parvati, are two aspects of the ultimate reality. Shiva is Purusha and Parvati is Prakriti (Shakti). Without Purusha, Prakriti would be inert. On the other hand Shakti is necessary for creation and only with her Shiva can manifest his potential. He is the male principle and she is the female principle. Shiva in his dance posture is Nataraja. Parvati is an ideal danseuse of Lasya, while Shiva is in Tandava. Moulded in metal, the image of Nataraja in the Chidambaram Temple is a piece of art.

Shiva is popular with the media. He is portrayed as a handsome youth. His body besmeared with ashes, he is depicted with three eyes, the third one being in the middle of the forehead. He has four arms, two of which hold Damru and Trishul and the two are extended in Abhaya (fearless) and Varada (favour bestowing) mudras. Shiva has a crescent moon on forehead, with Ganga flowing from his matted hair and forehead. He is wrapped with Janeu (Yagyopaveeta) and garlands around his neck.

Shiva led a family life, with Parvati. His movement was a spectacle, when he left his abode in the Himalayas on Kailash. Himself on Nandi (bull), and in company of ghosts, goblins, imps, three legged Bhringi Rishi, sons – Ganesha on mouse and Skandha (Subramanyam) on peacock–the procession looked like a pageant.

Who is greater Shiva or Vishnu? This question would have been discussed among the devotees of the two deities. Asceticism and devotion each claimed to be more beneficient but they did not go together. Liberal devotees thought Bhagvan was one – Shiva and Vishnu were worshipped by them as one God, in the form of Hari Har Murti, a fusion of family life and asceticism. Hari appears on left and Har on right.

In some images Purusha is presented as Shiva and Vishnu, the former becomes the supreme deity in the Shvetashvetaropanishad. Sacrifice in the name of Shiva and Vishnu, in place of Purusha, created distinction in the Brahmanic orthodoxy. The relationship of Atman also changed. However, by itself Atman cannot attain Moksha and the Upanishad calls for the help of guru. But as yoga progressed, the importance of guru (Brahmin) decreased and it was thought that perfection in yoga may ensure attainment of Moksha. But yoga won't do for everyone. Total involvement in asceticism would bring disaster to the world. Therefore yoga and bhoga have to complement each other.

Every deity has three forms – Moorti, Yantra and Mantra. Yantra is drawn and installed. It changes and binds the deity to the yantra.

Another form shows Shiva as Ardhanareeshvar (half male, half female) which shows their bipolar nature in equal and complementary roles. Shiva's other popular forms are : Anugrahamurti, Dakshinamurti, Haryasva, Ugra, Lingodbhava, Tandavamurti and Bhikshatanamurti. Each of these has its own myth. The Shivalinga is venerated universally as Mangalmurti/Utsavamurti in the sanctum sanctorum. The androgenous image of shiva emphasizes that the two are necessary for each other.

The linga installed in the temple is *achal* (static) in land – in three parts – two of which, relating to Bramha and Vishnu, are embedded inside the pedestal. The third part, Shiva in cylindrical form is visible and worshipped. Shiva, in images, is shown Panchanan (five faced) pointing in four directions. Facing east, he is Tatpurusha, facing west he is Aghora, facing north he is Vamadeva and facing south he is Sadyojata.

There are innumerable myths about Shiva. Here are a few:

KIRTIMUKHA : Once a demon who had overthrown gods, confronted Shiva and had the audacity to ask him to hand over his wife goddess Parvati. Enraged, he opened his third eye which hit the earth and made a bolt. There appeared a demon larger than the one who had earlier confronted Shiva. The latter was frightened and threw himself at Shiva's mercy. Shiva gave him the protection. The larger demon told Shiva he was hungry "What do I eat?" Shiva replied, "Eat yourself". So he started eating himself. He began with his feet and ate the whole body except the face which looked glorious. Shiva named it "Kirtimukha" (face of glory) and blessed that he would be above the doors of Shivalayas and that devotees will worship Kritimukha before Shiva.

The message from the myth is that life itself is monstrous and should be recognized as such. There are pain and sorrow in life which have to be borne during life time. Without realization of this, man's entry in God's house is barred. This is relative to the past and present and will be so in future also. To help the world, know of this and tell others how to live in it – with joyful sorrows and sorrowful joys. That is what Kritimukha (face of glory) means. To know Shiva and Parvati, man has to bow to the master in reverence and then pass through.

The three devas (of Trinity) saw one day a burning pillar. Inquisitive about it, Brahma and Vishnu travelled with it for 1000 years. Tired of the ardous journey, they gave up the effort. But when they were getting off, they saw Shiva inside the pillar, proving that Shiva was the greatest deity. An extension of the legend makes Brahma tell a lie that he had reached the bottom of the pillar, but when he was getting off he saw Shiva inside the pillar. Thus Shiva was the proven greatest deity. Because of telling a lie, Brahma suffered. He lost his right to be worshipped.

Other important myths about Shiva are :

- Shiva cut off one head of Brahma who was in an amorous pose with his mind-born daughter Saraswati. (Don't let the mind be engaged with evil thoughts).
- Shiva destroyed Asuras – Tripura, Gajasura.
- Shiva gave Pashupatastra to Arjuna.
- He took the form of Ardhanareeshvar to dispel Bhringi's ignorance.
- Vanished Yama to save Markandeya.
- Minor deities associated with Shiva are : Nandi, son of Salankayan; Veerabhadra, personifying Shiva's anger, (Veerabhadra's counterpart Bhadrakali was created by Parvati).
- Shiva's abode was on Kailash Parvat, in the neighbourhood of Mansarovar Lake. The legend shows that both the Parvat and lake in Tibet were closely linked with India. As this is a book on Mythology, not politics, we leave it here.

SATI-PARVATI

Parvati, the consort of Shiva, personifies the Deity's shakti (power). She appeared in many forms e.g. as Uma, the gracious; Sati, the good wife; Bhairavi, the terrible; Gauri, the brilliant; Kali, the terrible black; Durga, the inaccessible. Shiva's followers are generally ascetic, poles apart in thought and living from the followers of Brahmanic order. A ghastly situation arose when Daksha Prajapati organized a Yajna to which he invited every god and goddess but not his daughter Sati and son-in-law Shiva, who were not from the Brahmanic order, though the highest in this order, the Brahma was the Purohit in their marriage. The father-in-law was annoyed that Shiva had showed indifference to social propriety, smoked hemp and wandered around funeral grounds in the company of ghosts and devils (even today orthodox parents disapprove of their daughter marrying outside the caste). Shiva kept cool but the daughter took it as an insult and went to the Yajna. She was not received properly and so finding her father rude, she threw herself in the fire.

Shiva, distraught at this consort's death, ordered Veerbhadra, his commander, to undo the yajna, which he did. Not only that in his fury he and his associates, according to one verson, wounded Daksha. That was excessive reaction and Shiva resuscitated him. The Rig Brahman does not mention 'Shiva-worship' because, being from a different (ascetic) order he was not entitled to participate in Pooja. There is an opinion that Shiva's worship began much later, in Mahabharta times. Perhaps Shaivites were not welcome to Vaishnavite rites.

Sobbing in grief, Shiva carried Sati's corpse on his shoulders and during his wanderings parts of her body fell apart at different places and all such places were declared sacred Piths for worship. Sati's death was sacralized. Shiva, perhaps, joined the Brahmanic order which ushered in reconciliation between the two cults. [Author has visited a few piths. At Datia (MP), he was told about Mrs. Indira Gandhi's visit to the Piths at Datia].

A legend is that Sati's yoni fell at a place in Assam. Shiva's linga was installed therein. It settled down as a symbol of regeneration. Soon Shivlinga worship began there. Shiva then repaired to his abode on Mt.Kailash and began an austere penance. This affected regeneration and its decline began. Gods were worried at this. They knew that only a son of Shiva would destroy demon Tarak (not to be donfused with Taraka, Ravana's sister. So they planned to distract Shiva's attention from penance to worldly life. Meantime Sati took birth as Parvati.

The gods conspired and persuaded Kamadeva, the God of Love, to distract Shiva, which he did. But in doing so, he was rendered to ashes. In the meantime Himavan's daughter Parvati did penance to secure Shiva as husband, the two were united. Kumar destroyed the demon.

108 Names of Durga (Devi)

1. Sati	2. Sadhvi	3. Bhavaprita
4. Bhavani	5. Bhavamochini	6. Arya
7. Durga	8. Jaya	9. Adya
10. Trinetra	11. Shooladharini	12. Pinakadharini
13. Chitra	14. Chandraghanta	15. Mahaatapaa
16. Manch	17. Buddhi	18. Ahankar
19. Chittarupa	20. Chitta	21. Chitih
22. Sarvamantramaya	23. Salta	24. Satyanandaswarupani
25. Ananta	26. Bhavani	27. Bharya
28. Bhavya	29. Atihavya	30. Sadagatih
31. Shambhavi	32. Devamata	33. Chinta
34. Ranapriya	35. Sarvavidya	36. Dakshapriya
37. Dakshayajna Vinashini	38. Aparva	39. Anekavarna
40. Patola	41. Patolavati	42. Pattambaraparidharnee
43. Kalamanjaira rangini	44. ameyanikrama	45. Krura
46. Sundari	47. surasundari	48. Vanadurga
49. Matangi	50. Matangamuni pugita	51. Brahmi
52. Maheshwari	53. Aindri	54. Kaumari
55. Vaishnavi	56. chamunda	57. Varahi
58. Lakshmi	59. Purushakratih	60. Vimala
61. Utakarshni	62. Jnanaa	63. Kriya
64. Nitya	65. Budhida	66. Bahula
67. Bahulaprema	68. Sarvevahana vahana	69. Nishumbashumbahrini
70. Mahisasuramardini	71. Madhukaitana hantini	72. chandemundevi nashini
73. Sarvasuravinashy	74. Sarvadanavaghatini	75. Sarvashastramayi
76. Satya	77. Sarvastradharini	78. Anekashastrahasta
79. Anekashtradharini	80. Kumari	81. Ekkanyaa
82. Kaishori	83. Yuvati	84. Yatih
85. Apraudha	86. Praudha	87. Vriddhamata
88. Balaprada	89. Mahodari	90. Muktakeshi
91. Ghorarupa	92. Mahabala	93. Agniwali
94. Raudramukhi	95. Kalevatrih	96. Tapasvini
97. Narayani	98. Bhadrakali	99. Vishnumaya
100. Jalodari	101. Shivadooti	102. Karaali
103. Anentaa	104. Parameshvari	105. Katyayani
106. Savitri	107. Pratyaksha	108. Brahmavadini

The episodes of Shiva do not find place in Vedic literature. Parvati's incarnation as Ambika (later Durga) finds mention in the Vajasaneyi Samhita. Uma is mentioned in Kenopanishad as an inquisitive person.

She elicits information from Shiva on Tantric and esoteric practices. Shiva and Parvati are expert dancers, Shiva as Tandava and Parvati as Lasya dancer. Kali was Parvati's alter ego and she fought on her behalf as and when she was called upon.

As Uma, Parvati practiced asceticism. As Parvati she is a beautiful girl, and under the name of Uma, she undertakes to destroy demons. A question is often asked: Was Shakti associated as Shiva's feminine aspect with Durga, Kali, Parvati?

Durga's 108 names are recited by her devotees. (Besides there are a few more names not listed here, viz, Annapoorna, Gayatri, Indrakshi, Kameshwari, Manmohini, Rajeshwari

GANGAAVATARAN

Gangavataran, a poetic work of Pandit Jagannath describes the descent of the mighty but graceful Ganga from Heaven to Himalayas to earth for the welfare of mankind. The Ganga, reverentially addressed as Gangaji, sustains millions of lives and out of a sense of gratitude people worship her as 'Mother Ganga'. She descends from Gangotri in the Himalayas and breaks into plains at Haridwar, that is the door of God. Flowing down a few hundreds of miles, she is joined at Prayag (Allahabad) by river Yamuna and the mystical underground Saraswati. Further down at Varanasi (Banaras), she makes a long sweep to north and flowing down a few hundred miles again meets the Bay of Bengal at Gangasagar.

Ganga is the quintessence of sacred waters. She flows in several mythic images of cosmos. With six other rivers, namely Yamuna and Saraswati (the confluence known as Triveni), Narmada, Sindhu, Kaveri and Godavari she enjoys great sanctity among the people of India. Pilgrims- mostly Hindus- from different parts of the country and abroad - flock to the sacred Tirtha. Her descent to the earth is celebrated each year on Ganga Dussehra, which is the tenth day of Jyestha of Hindu Calendar.

The Vedic myth is that the Demon Vrittasura had coiled around heaven and stopped the flow of the celestial water to earth, forcing Indra, the lord of the Devatas in Heaven, to combat. With the help of Vishnu, Indra overpowered the demon. For this reason the Vaishnavas call Ganga Vishnupadi. Released from the custody of the demon, Ganga descended to earth with great force, after Vishnu had taken three strides, pierced his toe and released the water for the nourishment of earth.

Ganga is known as the consort of both Vishnu and Shiva. The story of Ganga's release from Vishnu's toe has been narrated above, but the devotees of Shiva have their own version, according to which Ganga flows from Heaven through Dhruva upon the 'lotus petal continent'.. One of its branches, Alaknanda flows into Bharatavarsha. From heaven it falls to revive the 60,000 sons of King Sagar who had disturbed Kapila while he was absorbed in mediation, and the glance of the sage had turned them into ashes.

Sagar was upset and wished to revive the dead which was possible only through the Ganga's water. Sagar prayed her and pleased with Sagar, Ganga acceded to his request to descend to earth. But there was yet a problem, who would take her forceful water which could destroy the earth. The benevolent Shiva agreed to Sagar's prayers and promised to hold her in his hair. He took Ganga in his matted hair from where Bhagirath took her to the sea wherefrom she reached the underworld and revived king Sagar's 60,000 sons.

According to the Vedic hymns, the Ganga splits into seven streams and replenished the ocean that had been, according to another story (myth), swallowed by sage Agastya. Still another myth associates Ganga as the mother of Bhishma, as narrated in the Mahabharta. Mother Ganga had conceived him and when Bhishma died she rose in human form to greet her son.

Several myths relating to Ganga, Vishnu and Krishna find place in the Devi Mahatmya and Brahmavaivasvat Purana.

KALI

The sight of a naked woman is sufficient to disturb onlookes. Kali's image, as it is seen, besides being naked, is dark, ferocious, blood-sucking and destructive also and can upset anyone. That is why she is feared as the cause of instability and disorder in society. Her looks frighten more when she is seen wearing a necklace of skulls, a girdle of arms and corpses of infants. She has four arms which hold a bloodied cleaver, human head. Nevertheless to her devotees, she is the goddess divine, protecting mother, reassuring, deity who confers boon on them.

Kali is associated with Durga, Parvati and Shiva. She dwells in battlefields and cremation grounds. In the battlefield she carries a skull topped staff, howls ferociously, devours enemy's flesh and drinks his blood. In the cremation ground she sits on corpses, surrounded by jackals, serpents, ghosts (bhoots and prets). She has no vahan (vehicle) of her own, but rides on a preta. She is one of the Dasamahavidyas, an uncontrollable aspect of Devi.

The myth about her origin is that when demons Shund Munda attacked Durga, Kali sprang up from her brow. Howling and wading into the enemy camp, she decapacitated the two demons. Next time when Durga called her, she killed the demon Raktabeeja, every drop of whose blood produced a demon. She killed them all and finally sucked their blood - no blood, no new demon. Next Kali destroyed demon Daruka and his army.

Kali, which means a 'dark' woman, was sensitive and took it as an insult if someone called her 'Kali'. Once when Shiva called her Kali, she was piqued and only when he addressed her as Gauri, that is fair, she forgave him. In the mediaeval times when Hinduism embodied concepts of Maya, Prakriti and Shakti, and Devi became growth, decay, death and rebirth, the Kali aspect also changed. Through rituals of pacification, Kali placed Hindu Dharma into perspective.

Kali stands with her devotees if they are fighting against an injustice. The thugs were audacious and exploited her name. They took innocent lives for material benefit. They won the confidence of innocent travelers, killed them and all others who tried to obstruct them. They took away all their possessions. They popularized the myth that murders by Kali's devotees had her sanction. Land holders and merchants helped them in their nefarious activity. The British took a bold step to suppress thuggee. Sir William Sleeman especially selected for the purpose by Governor-General Sir William Bentink (1831-37), executed the operation ruthlessly and arrested as many as 30,000 thugs. They included both Hindus and Muslims. How could Muslims be devotees of Kali?

There are Kali's temples in all parts of India. But the one near Dakshineshwar, (near Kolkata) of which Ramakrishna Paramhansa was a Pujari is very well known.

Feminists in USA depict Kali as an embodiment of woman's power and saviour. One Marlyn Stone conducted a study "when god was a woman", "to know our past heritage as more than a broken and buried fragment of male culture". Rachall Fell MeDormet compared Kali with the goddess of love and war who are paradoxical and dangerous. In the recent past Rani Lakshmi Bai of Jhansi and Indira Gandhi were compared with Kali for their courage and ruthless fighting spirit.

Alien goddesses akin to Kali included Sumerian goddess Inanna, Babylonian Ishtar, Egyptian Isis, Anatolian Ceybala, pre-Hellenic Gorgon, Greek Hectate Demeter, Artemis, Rhea, Aphrodite, Athena, (Roman) Minerva, Syrian Anath, Aztech Coatlicve, Hebrew Lilith, and Shakinah Black Virgin, American-Indian the spider woman, and a heritage of hags, harpies and wicked step mothers. Another lady Barbar S. Walker described Finland's Kalma and Iceland's Calli based on Shakti Psyche, Anima, Gnostic Sophia and Catalistic Shekina variations of Kali.

Kali, the terrible Mother, combines in her person, duality of opposites – creation and destruction, birth and death, love and fear. In "Hindu Female Deities as a resource for the contemporary rediscovery of the Goddess", the authoress Rite M. Grass assigns her six characteristics viz. bisexuality, strength and capability, embodiment of polarities, and opposites of mother, universal range of activity and explicit sexuality. For American feminists sexuality is vital. Kali has three phases of moon waxing, full and waning.

The Harappans worshipped mother goddess. In the matriarchal society, Hindus worship Kali. "Aryan priests emphasized her dark sexual aspects and demonized her so as to dissuade people from worshipping her". Could it be so? Some people associate Kali with Kaliyuga. They recognize her spirituality and observe rituals in her worship. Stuart Ferra in 'Witch Goddess" discusses the weird "Goddess Recipes", one of which is "the blending of Kali incense, sandal wood chips, jasmine chips, rose petals and two days of one's own menstrual blood, burning during meditation at the onset of one's period and associates her with repressed female power and sexuality. But such a light hearted observation about their goddess hurts Hindu feelings. This is devoid of decency and insensitive to other's feelings. He needed not have talked of "Mother's menstrual blood drops".

In the traditional devotional India, speaking and writing about the Devi's sexuality and repressed sex is 'sin' and invites her wrath. Women in India have suffered from society's mores, attitudes, and evils like Sati, child marriage, child labour, widow's sufferings, bride burning.

Santoshi Maa has been called Kali's twentieth century version. Presently Santoshi Maa and Vaishno Devi are the most popular deities among their Hindu devotees. Hundreds of thousands of pilgrims go on arduous journey to Vaishno Devi near Jammu (J&K State).

LALITA

Lalita Tripurasundari, an important aspect of Devi, figures prominently in the eastern part of the country and two great works of poetry, namely *Lalit Sahasranam* and *Trisanti* praise her activities. Devotees to Lalita Devi are initiated through a mantra and she is honoured by Panchadashakshari, an esoteric rite,

The story of Lalita Devi is that she manifested herself in a disc in the sacrificial fire of a Yajna performed by Indra. Emerging from the fire, she married Kameshvar (Shiva). She killed Bhandasur and annihilated Sonitpur. Kameshvar built for Lalita Devi Sripur on Mount Meru where she resides. Her emblem Srichakra has a form and patterns of triangles and squares. She holds a bowl of sugarcane (which is a symbol of mind), Tanmatras (arrows), goad, noose, and a wire cup which symbolizes that she energizes and controls people's minds and sense organs. She frees devotees of attachments and helps them to control their temper.

Like other deities, Lalita Devi has three forms, viz. Moorti, Yantra and Mantra. The yantra is drawn and installed which changes and binds the deity to the yantra. (Devi Parvati's other forms are Annaporna, Bela, Bhadrakali, Chaumunda, Gayatri, Savitri, Indrakshi, Jagatadhatri, Kameshvari, Katyayani, Manamohini, Rajeshvari and Sridevi).

BHADRAKALI

Amrit recalls her annoyed grandmother yelling at the girls' for their pranks, and saying that they would be Bhadrakali. There was so much admonition of Bhadrakali that the gang of pranksters would disappear immediately. Not many temples in India are known to be housing Bhadrakali. However her name is familiar to people all over India. Kamarupa in Assam is known to have a temple. Far South Changannur, in Kerala, has a popular Bhadrakali temple. The myth is that Daruka, a fearful demon used to terrorize people. The Kali slayed the demon and freed people from his terror. This sounds like every other story. If there is a demon, there has to be a god who would bring relief by the ridding of the demon.

Bhadrakali has periods and the temple observes all sanitary formalities. A priest opens the sanctum sanctorum early morning and removes the previous day's decoration (Nirmalayam) with white petticoat (Udayada). These are handed over to the attendant. Generally a Varrier examines the dress for blood signs and a tantric confirms the menses.

It is surprising that the Udayada is sold to the members of the public at a fixed price. As Nirmalayam of the deity is something uncommon there is a competition to possess it. The buyer willingly pays a high price, several times of the fixed price. Even some dignitaries e.g. Sir CP Ramaswamy Aiyar and VV Giri, the late former President of India, were amongst the buyers.

When menses is declared, the sanctum is closed for three days. On the fourth day deity's image is taken on a female elephant in a procession to the Pampa river while many women hold lamps.

Mensturation of a deity is a miracle. It appears to be associated with Sati. When Shiva was carrying Sati's corpse with menses on his shoulder, her yoni (the female reproductive mandal) fell down on land which explains why the Devi gets the monthly period. Well myths could be bizarre.

GANESHA

Ganesha is the most popular god and is propitiated at the beginning of a function. He is prayed for removing obstacles. In Rig-Veda he is referred to as Ganapati, which figuratively means master with a clan or a group of singers and dancers. In icons he is depicted in various forms but in each one he is shown with an elephant head, a grotesque body, round belly and large ears.

Ganesha is known as Vighneshwar, the deity who undoes the affect of obstructions and hindrances when he is avoided. When pleased he brings joy and happiness. In some places Ganesha is worshipped as a god of fertility also.

The Puranas have many interesting stories about Ganesha. His birth is shrouded in mystery. A popular myth is that once Parvati made a child's image with the head of an elephant from unguents that were smeared on her body. After amusing herself with the toy, she threw it in the Ganga, which accepted it and claimed as her own child. Parvati also claimed it to be her child. Thus Ganesha is known to have two mothers – Parvati and Ganga. According to another story Parvati prepared a child's image from the scruff of her body and endowed it with life. She ordered the boy to guard the house and not to let anyone disturb her when she was resting. One day when Shiva came home, the boy prevented his entry into the house. Shiva was so much enraged that he beheaded the boy. At the loss of her son, Parvati became inconsolable. Shiva then grafted an elephant's head on his body and gave him life and appointed him as the head of the retinue (Gana). Thus he became Ganapati. He has two shaktis – Riddhi and Siddhi.

Lord Ganesha was known for his adventurous spirit and cleverness. Once in a fight with Parashuram he lost his tooth (tusk). He used it as a stylus to write the Mahabharata dictated by sage Vyasa. Another time his parents asked the children to go around the world and told that the winner of the race would be suitably awarded. While Subramaniam raced, Ganesha on his vehicle of mouse took three rounds of his parents and reported his return. How come, he had come so soon the parents quarried? Ganesha responded that going round the parents is as good as going round the world.

Ganesha had a weakness for *laddus (modaks)* i.e. sweets. His belly shows him as a glutton. The myth is that one day after gorging himself, he took a ride on his mouse. He was ambling in the moonlight alone when a snake barred his path. The rat was frightened and leaped to one side. Ganesha rebounded so violently that his belly was burst. To repair the damage caused by the snake, Ganesha rolled the snake round his damaged stomach. He heard moon jeering at his action. In a rage, Ganesha broke of his tusk and hit it hard at the moon.

SUBRAMANYAM

Subramanyam, the second son of Shiva and Parvati, younger brother of Ganesha fulfilled the purpose for which he was born. He effaced the tyranny of the Asuras led by Taraka, the demons who had made peoples' lives miserable. Subramaniam literally means one who tends to be an aspirant to spiritual growth. But he is a warlord first.

Subramaniam, born in a forest of arrow like grass, was brought up by six divine mothers of the constellation of Kartikeya (Pleiades) after whom he was called Kartikeya. Another myth is that when Shiva directed his third eye on a lake there instantly emerged six children who were suckled by the wives of six Rishis. One day while cuddling them, Parvati squeezed them so hard that they formed a single body. The six heads figure in most of Kartikeya's statutes. He is known by other names viz. Sadananda, Shanmukha, Sanatkumar, Swaminatha (father's preceptor), Brahma Shasta (the exposure of Brahma's ignorance of Vedas) and Gangeya (son of Ganga).

Sanat Kumar was a great warrior and was known for his youth and virility. Subramanyam had two consorts – Valli and Devesena, Valli was a farmer's daughter and Devasena of Indra. This shows the deity did not make any distinction between the humble folk and elite. His mount was peacock who belabours snake with its legs. The peocock represents creation in all its glory and Subramanyam's ride on peacock signifies that he is master of creation. The snake pervades everywhere. Some people associate him with the Naga cult and say he was a sylvan deity. Tree worship is also popular among his followers. Subramanyam is popular in southern India and his temples are on hill tops.

Kubera: Kubera is god of wealth. He is another of Shiva's son. He is fond of music of Gandharvas and Kinnaras.

MARKANDEYA

Every Hindu craves for a progeny, particularly a male because only a son can perform the last rites of his father. Having no progeny was therefore considered a curse. Even sages could not ignore this. Markandeya's case is a good illustration.

Markandeya was leading a good life with his family. But he was not blessed with a son and began observing austerities to beget a son. Lord Shiva was pleased with him and blessed Markandeya that he would beget a son but he would have a short life of 16 years.

Though the constraint of a short life of their son saddened Markandeya and his wife, they were happy for the present to have a child who will bring joy in their life. A child was born and he dazzled everyone. The parents took all possible care of the child. He grew up to be a devotee of Shiva.

The parents enjoyed the child's frolicks and were impressed by the child's sharp intellect. Time passed and the boy entered into the sixteenth year of his life. The parents remembered about the short span of their son's life and were sad.

Markandeya felt bad when he saw sadness on his parent's faces. He asked them why they looked so gloomy. When he made querries persistently, the parents told him the truth. Markandeya told them not to worry and he continued to worship Shiva.

Then the day arrived when Markandeya was completing his sixteenth year. And, as time clicked, Yama came to fetch Markandeya and told him of his mission. Markandeya was amidst Pooja and told the Yama to wait till the Pooja was over. The Yama was angry at this insolence and threw his noose in Markandeya's neck. That very moment Shiva emerged from the linga and the Yama fell back. Markandeya saw the sudden appearance of his Aradhya and forgot everything. Shiva was pleased with Markandeya and granted him immortality. His parents were very happy and their joy knew no bounds. – ***from Skanda Purana***.

AYYAPPAN

The shrine of Lord Ayyappan is situated at the top of the Sabarmalai Hill in Kerala and devotees in thousand converge there to have the Lord's darshan.

Ayya, part of the name, is a corrupt form of Arya. He is known as Hariharputra or Sashtha. The temple at Sabarmalai was built by Vishvakarma and Ayyappan's image was installed in it by Parashuram.

A pilgrimage to the shrine is organized each year. A large number of visitors pour in, after having led a life of austerity for 41 days.

The myth about the temple is that after Durga had slain demon Mahishasur, the demon's spouse Mahisha secured a boon from Brahma that she could not be killed by Vishnu or Shiva. Mahisa became very bold and planned to destroy the gods. She began tormenting the devotees. In retaliation gods planned to destroy Mahishi and created a child. King Rajashekhara of Panthalur, in Kerala, found the child. At the age of 12, Manimekhalam, the child killed the demons.

Manimekhalam after killing the demon, disappeared from the scene, leaving behind a message for his father that he should build a temple at the spot where an arrow thrown by him might land. The arrow thrown by the King struck at Sabaramalai and on that spot he built a temple. This is the Ayappan temple. It has the image of Ayappan with his elephant Yogi. (The Balaji temple at Tirupati in Andhra Pradesh commands reverance from pilgrims all over India).

A RENUNCIATE

Sage Saubhari practiced austere penance in his ashram at the bank of a river. He felt he had mastered over his senses and conquered his desires. One day while absorbed in meditation he opened his eyes, he saw a fish king surrounded by its large family. The sight of the big and small fish kindled in the sage a desire that he too should have a happy family of his own. So he left his ashram and went out in search of a female companion who would help raise a family – happy and large.

One day he went to King Mandhata and asked for the hand of one of his daughters. Mandhata knew that his seven daughters had been raised in luxury and none of the princess, if he agreed to sage's proposal, would be happy. So the king tried to put off the sage, saying that it was for a princess, as per family tradition, to select her life partner and it would not be correct to force a daughter to break a tradition. Then thinking the sage might have felt hurt, the king added that he would have no objection, if any of the princesses liked him and he would gladly marry off the princess with Saubhari. Not to hurt the king's feelings, Saubhari told him "Let the princesses have a look at me and decide". The king approved.

The sage by his yogic powers turned himself into a handsome youth. When the princesses saw him, each one expressed her desire to marry Saubhari. It was now Mandhata's turn to feel embarrassed and he said if they all liked him, he could take all of them. So the king gave all his daughters in marriage to Saubhari.

Saubhari took them all to a palace he constructed by his yogic power and placed the princesses one each in a beautiful mansion. They all lived happily and forgot even to call on parents. One day Mandhata came to meet his daughters and to see whether they were happy and, finding them all happy and enjoying life, the king told his son-in-law that he had misjudged him. Saying so, Mandhata left for his place.

As time passed, Saubhari raised a big family and was happy to see his children running about. But one day he woke up and thought, "I am a fool, I have wasted my penance for worldly things. As one desire is fulfilled, another awakens. Why should I have yearned for a life like the one I live. Pity, I allowed temptation to get over my intelligence and fell down from my spiritual path. It is true attachment destroys power of austerities. I shall now strive to free myself from all attachments. I shall mediate the Lord and recover my soul and attain immortality". Making the resolve Saubhari left his wives and all his possessions. Going back on the path of penance, he reached the panache from which no one returns.

[Prajapati used penance three times in different sequences. The key was da, da, da for self control, charity, compassion. Yet another story is about Chudala and Sikhadwaj. The lesson was by discrimination one knows what renunciation is. Renounce the ego, it gives the appearance of diversity. Peace follows renunciation].

Nrasimha-Man, Lion, the fourth Avatar of Vishnu

9

GREAT MOTHER

MOTHER GODDESS

Everything originated from mother goddess, that was the belief of humankind in ancient times. She genuinely loved people without any expectation of reciprocity. They worshipped her and gave her different names. Materials and remnants of human civilizations that thrived in India, Mesopotamia, Egypt, Mediterranean Sea Coasts, Central Asia and China prove peoples' love for Mother Earth. In India one's own mother and mother earth (synonym for goddess) were regarded more endearingly and were coveted more than heaven *(Janani Janmabhoomishch Swargadapi Gariyashi)*.

The Egyptian and Mesopotamian civilizations evolved a religious ideology. The Egyptians worshipped mother goddess in her martial forms as Ugarit, Ishtar, Anat and Hathor. The Greeks worshipped her as Aphrodite, Artemis, Athena and Hera, whom they considered embodiments of love, chastity, wisdom and modesty, respectively. The Romans adopted these goddesses as their own but changed their names to Venus, Diana, Minerva and Juno, respectively. Other goddesses were also elevated e.g. Persephone and Demeter. Demeter took the name Ceres.

Indians worshipped three great goddesses viz. Saraswati, Lakshmi and Parvati, consorts of Brahma, Vishnu and Shiva, respectively. The three goddesses became famous as deities of learning and knowledge, wealth and devotion, and courage respectively. Besides, elements of nature e.g. Usha (Dawn) were also worshipped.

For many centuries the mother goddesses were confined to their regions and did not influence others. In fact people of one region did not know much about goddesses of other regions. They had hierarchy but their influence was limited. In India the influence of the great goddesses welded their influence, and there were cravings among people for their kindness in very subtle ways. Seven decades ago we observed Saraswati Puja as students of primary class with *patti-puja* [i.e. writing board worship]. Saraswati Puja is still in vogue in parts of India. Lakshmi, the goddess of wealth and prosperity is worshipped on Deepawali, and Parvati has throughout been worshipped in different forms as Kali, Durga, Bhavani Rri (from ri-to attack), Devi (from div-sky), Maya is illusion, super natural mother, Danu-goddess of art, Shatrupa and Adiare Primary goddesses.

The concepts of Mother Earth (Prithvi/Dharati Mata) and Devi (as mother goddess) existed in Vedic times as has been inferred from the small figurines excavated in Indus Valley by Marshall and Cummingham in the first quarter of the 20th century. But their conclusion that the Indus Valley Civilization was a subsidiary of the Assyrian civilization has been discredited. Excavations elsewhere have led archaeologists and historians to assert that Indian civilization was extant in far larger areas then the Assyrian region. Some American institutions have made significant researches, especially in scriptural literature, and it is to the credit of the feminists that they dug up material on little known female deities like Saranyu and Sanjna. They found in Saranyu the toughness of an American female.

Some scholars believe that the original tribes of India were matriarchal and followed matrilineal and matrilocal customs. Women held positions of authority and families were traced through the maternal line. Husbands made their home near the home of wife's family. Later filial or parental imagery and sentiments were developed to unique levels in which human mother played eleborate roles that inspired elemental energy for the worship and propitiation of gods and goddesses. Mother earth has at times been envisioned as the sõurce of physical life and goddesses have been associated with water and brooks. Goddesses have been envisioned in terms of life giving and death-dealing aspects of nature as also protectors of culture because of her psychological and material realities. (Vyasa and Homer account for water nymphs. (Urvashi was one such nymph.)

The myths of Greek and Roman great goddesses establish hierarchy among them. In mid-19th century special attention was paid to social human evolution. A matriarchal phase gave rise to the idea of Mother Right, that is a matriarchal descent and matriarchy. A comparative study of fertility of earth with female fertility led to the revival of the idea of mother earth. A difference was noted. While human mother's emotions can be experienced, look genuine and the Mother earth's affection for her billions of children are figuratively genuine but these cannot be directly experienced. A case for a single mother was made out in 1849 by a German scholar, Edward Gerhard. Fourteen years later in 1863 John Jacob Bachofen, a Swiss jurist theorized that the society at its stage of inception had no concept of institution of marriage; promiscuity and institution of hitera prevailed. (This statement does not seem to be correct. We find ample references to prove that institution of marriage existed in India more than five thousand years ago. Similar is the case with Cretan, Greek and Egyptian societies.

Darwin's work *'On the Origin of Species'* (1859) support the story of human evolution. Female figures found in excavations also support the theory of human affection for Mother Earth in the Mediatarrerean, Middle East and India. Archaeologist Evans and poet-historian Frazer made significant contributions to the growth of the myth. Evans enriched Crete with stone, gold and ivory figures, and named the figurines as Mother Goddess, Mother Rhea etc. which captivated people's hearts. The scope of regional civilization was enlarged to universal civilization, creating a myth of 'shared human cultures' and a Utopian Future Beyond. This sounded like the old Hindu concepts of *'Vishwa Bandhutva'* (i.e. the entire wold is bound by one brotherhood), and *'Ekosat Viprah Vahudha Vadanti'* (i.e. Truth is one, sages call it by different names').

Reverting to excavations, the archaeologists considered the Minoan culture as the starting point and the earliest stage in the highway of western civilization. The Cretan story is fascinating. It related to King Minos, a son of god Zeus, and Europa, daughter of King of Phoenicia Zeus was unfaithful to his wife Hera (Roman Juna). Gods can afford to be unfaithful. Though mortals fall prey to temptation, they don't go scot-free and have to suffer for infidelity.

In infancy mother is the power of nature and father the power of society.

Manu who is much maligned for his utterances about women, speaks about her in reverential tones also. He says, "A father excels ten upadhyayas in glory but a mother excels a thousand fathers".

Among great scholars who contributed Suktas to the Rigveda, 7 women figured as seven mothers (Saptamatrikas) and 5 virgins (Panchkanyas), 5 Virgins: Ahilya, Draupadi, Tara, Kunti, Mandodari.

The 27 Brahmavadinis are: Ghosha, godha, Vishvavara, Asalopanishan, Nishat, Brahmajaya, Jastur, Svasa, Aditi, Indrani, Chandramata, Sharma, Romasa, Urvashi, Lopamudra, Nadyash, Yami, Nari, Shasvati, Shri Laxmi, Vat, Shraddha, Medha, Dakshina, Ratri, Surya, Savitri.

Mothers: Lakshmi, Dhriti, Medha, Vidya, Sarasvati, Maheshvari, Kaumari, Vaishnavi, Varati Indrani, Chamunda.

MAHADEVI

The 'Shakti' of Tantrism, popularly known as Devi manifests herself as the universe and denotes Brahman. The cult of Shakti (or Devi) centres around Parvati, Shiva's consort. She appeared in the world to help her devotees in various forms representing various aspects and as Rudrani, Sarvani, Mradini, Aparna, Uma, Girija, Haimvati, Gauri, Amba, Ambika, Dakshayani, against the Asuras.

The myth of Devi is that once Asuras created serious problems for the gods and goddess. In order to eliminate them, a Devi emanated from the bodies of Brahma, Vishnu, Shiva, Indra, Skandha and two other deities. She incarnated herself, assailed the Asuras and rescued her devotees.

The Devi is both beneficent and maleficent. In her beneficent form she is beautiful, wild and auspicious and was worshipped as Uma, Parvati, Annapurna etc. She has four arms and represents Brahma Vidya (spiritual wisdom). In her maleficent form she is terrible and dreadful. She wore tiger skin and was drenched in blood as Kali, Durga, Chandi or Chandika, Mahishasuramardini. She had several arms holding sword in one and other weapons in the rest of arms. She rides tiger, and in this form she is known as Mahadevi, great goddess.

According to the Shakta theology, Devi is immanent in the world. It is said that women partake her female nature and tames the domestic passions. Devotees believe that rubbing Devi's Bibhuti (hierophanies) on forhead and arms empowers them.

Devi's name figures amongst Sapta matrikas (seven Shaktis) that sprang up from the bodies of seven sages. The other shaktis were: Brahmani, Maheshwari, Kumari, Vaishnavi, Varahi, Nrisimhi and Aindri. Besides, Devi possesses her own shakti – chandika- who is violent and uncontrollable. Some antics find in her a strange mixture of Aryan and Dravidian attributes. Whenever a soman becomes violent, she is called Chandi.

Durga means a deity difficult to know and approach. But on supplication she is tender love personified. Tantrics describe ten aspects of shakti known as Dasamahanidyas. These are:

i) Kali- goddess of time who destroys everything.
ii) Tara- the power of hiranyagarbha or void from which the universe evolves.
iii) Sodhasi – purification of fullness.
iv) Bhuvaneshvari, representative of material forces
v) Bhairavi, desires that lead to destruction and death
vi) Dhumavati (or Jyestha).
vii) Bagala, showing her ugly side of love.
viii) Chinnamasta, naked deity holding her severed head in hand and drinking her own blood.
ix) Matangi, power of domination
x) Kamala, pure consciousness of self

Durga's important aspects are — Yoganidra (power to sleep); Mahishasuramardini- she ride a lion and destroyed Mashisasura; later the gods were overpowered by Shumbha-Nikumbha and the Suras again approached her for help. They composed music and poetry (viz. *Ya devi bhuteshu*). Responding to this, Kali emerged from Devi's forehead and she killed the demon Dhumralochana and Chanda Munda and for killing them she became famous as Chamunda. Raktabeeja gave her the fiercest battle. As she would behead the demon, more would come up from his head, and she found it difficult to drink all the blood that fell, rushing out of his body. After she killed him, a Narayanastuti was recited in praise of her qualities as Vindhyavasini Devi, Raktadanta, Shatakshi, Shakambhari, Durga, Bhima and Bramani. She has three Maya manifestations of Mahakali, Mahalakshmi and Mahasarasvati. Brahma told Devi that Vishnu would kill demon Madhu Kaitabha. Devi is the personification of Maya. Unless she is pleased, Lord will not destroy anyone.

Andhaka was another demon whom Devi killed at Vishnu's request. Some other Matrikas Halima, Maloma, Brihi, Arya, Palala, Vamitra, –non-Aryans and mistresses of seven deities–were accused of devouring children. Troublesome spirits were–Vinata, Putana, Aditi (or Rohini) Diti, Surabhi, Sarma, Kadru, Lohityani, Arya, Hariti, Jara and Jyestha. Of these Putana's name to associated with Krishna. Jyestha's husband Dussadh complained against harassment by his wife to Vishnu (Linga Purana).

Ref: Devi Bhagavat Purana, Devi Mahatinya (part of Markandeya Purana), Saundarya Lahiri, Lalit Sahasranama, (The confluence of Akar Gang, Ganga on earth, Ganga in Patala, Saranyu and Sanjna who explore the truth that humanity was born in a moment of alienation from the gods. This has been portrayed in a film mentioned by John Howleg in his work on Devi).

Supreme Greek Deity Zeus (Roman-Jupiter) with wife goddess Hera.

BOOK III

10

SELECTED WESTERN MYTHS

PYGMALLION

Pygmallion, young and handsome, was king of Cypress. He looked for a perfect bride and remained bachelor even though he had been of a marriageable age for some years. He reasoned that the marital relations of many men had turned sour. He had himself seen many of his subjects married to daughters of Propeteus, but soon after marriage, the girls deserted their husbands and lived with Cerestea who were evil men. To make offerings to God, they killed people. This practice was disliked by gods and in their hatred they had turned these wicked men into bullocks and then into statutes in stone.

Pygmallion had therefore decided to remain bachelor and in his spare time he used to carve out statues. He carved out a girl's statue which was so lovely and perfect that he fell in love with it. But it was stone and could not reciprocate his sentiments. When the day of Feast of Aphrodite approached and Cypriots came to pray, Pygamallion joined them. He prayed the goddess that she give life to the statue. When he returned home he found life in the statue and kissed its cold lips peremptorily. As he was exhausted he lay at its fee and fell asleep. At dawn he dreamt that as he was kissing her lips, they were warm and she looked into his eyes with warmth. She enfolded him in her arms and when he opened his eyes, he saw the beautiful girl stood before him and she started bending towards him.

Before he could raise his eyes, he saw goddess Aphrodite before him. She told Pygmallion, "You, of all men, deserve happiness, a happiness you have yourself fashioned. Here is the queen before you, you have been seeking so long. Love her and guard her from harm".

ECHO and NARCISSUS

Echo, a nymph, was fond of music. She remembered the last words she heard from any one and repeated them. But she was not liked by Hero and was not allowed to exhibit or develop her talents.

One day Echo met a youth named Narcissus. She tried to engage him in a small talk. But the young man being in hurry paid her no attention and curtly left the place. But she followed him. Narcissus kept on moving and reached a river. He washed his face in the clean and clear river water and saw a beautiful face. Fascinated by its charm he tried to kiss the face but as the water was disturbed he missed seeing the face. He was frustrated and killed himself with a knife, saying, "I can not live without you beloved!" There was an echo from the tree, "I cannot live without you beloved." He died.

The gods pitied Narcissus. After some time a plant appeared at the place where his blood had fallen. From the plant sprouted a pretty flower with white petals and a clear red center. It was named and to this day it bears the same name "Narcissus", and its rebounded sound is called Echo. The two are immortal.

MIDAS

This is a tale of a king named Midas, of Phrygia, who was very greedy. One day Selenas, a great wanderer, lost his way and reached the palace of Midas. He was tired and asked Midas if he would let him stay for a while in the palace. He was not only permitted but was well looked after. The wanderer was pleased and told the king if he had any wish he would materialize it. Midas could not make up his mind. He though it would be good to have lots of gold and told his guest, "Let it be like this. Whatever I touch may turn into gold." Silenus said, "It will be so", and left the place.

The words of Silenus came true. Now whatever Midas touched, turned into gold. The table and chair he sat on turned into gold. When he set on the table for lunch and a servant brought him grapes, as he touched them, they turned into gold balls. He could not eat them. When his children touched Midas, they also turned into gold. He was now in great distress and tears came out from his eyes, and even the tears turned into gold. Exasperated, he consulted an oracle.

The oracle advised Midas to "go and take bath in river Pactotus. This will lift your curse and learn the lesson from this", As advised, Midas took bath in the Pactotus. But he could not control his greed. When he was approached to be a judge in a duet concert between two gods – Apollo on lyre, and Mersyas on pipes, he consented. When Apollo played lure, its clear notes silenced the birds. When his rival raised mournful pipes, squirrels scurried into trees. Midas declared the piper as the winner in the contest.

Apollo was furious and told Midas that a man like him should have ears to match his judgment, and cursed him, "You need ears of an ass". Midas noticed he had funny ears. He cursed his ears and let them grow. He looked wild. To shave the hair, he called his barber. The barber was shocked to see the king having the ears of an ass. He was agitated but was afraid to tell any one about the king's ears. But he could not resist his temptation and went to the river bank and said, "King Midas has an ass's ears". As the wind blew the reeds whispered, "Who is that who has the ears of an ass?" back came the reply, "Midas, the King".

ADONIS

Adonis was a personification of masculine beauty. Both the goddesses, Aphrodite and Persephone desired him exclusively and approached Zeus. Zeus ordered that Adonis be available to the two for six months each.

A Roman Tale

CUPID AND PSYCHE

Psyche was a pretty girl. She was so pretty that whenever people saw her they forgot to pay their regards and compliments to her. Venus was jealous of the attention being given to Psyche. She told her son cupid to teach Psyche a lesson. When Psyche learned of this she was worried, and consulted on oracle who prophesied that Psyche's husband will be a serpent. This disturbed Psyche's father. The oracle advised him to dress up Psyche as a corpse and leave her on a mountain. The father did as he was advised and left her on a high hill.

As Psyche lay there, a wind blew and bore her to a lovely valley. She found herself near a palace and made her way to it. A voice then told her, "Enjoy yourself inside the palace." She started living a comfortable life in the palace. An invisible bridegroom spent enchanting time with her in the night. One day Psyche's sisters visited her and told her to cut off the serpent's head when he was asleep before he devoured her. That night Psyche looked up at the serpent. She was confused and the candle she was carrying fell down from her hand. The candle scalded the young man's shoulder. Embarrassed and fearful Psyche fled the palace.

The handsome man was none else but Cupid. He met Psyche's father, Jupiter. The god bound the two into a nuptial knot. Psyche became immortal.

Cupid had a parallel in India – Kamadev, the love god. Cupid's consort was Rati.

Zeus's Divine and Human Families

(The most powerful Greek god, Zeus was married to Hera and had many children from her. But he had lover goddesses and women also; some unions are mythological.)

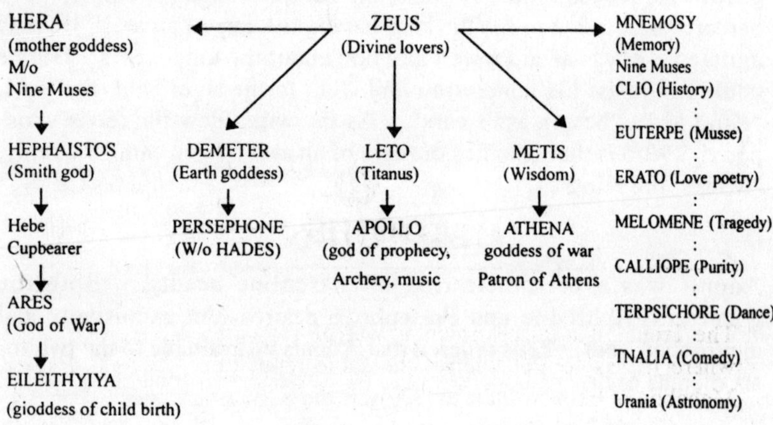

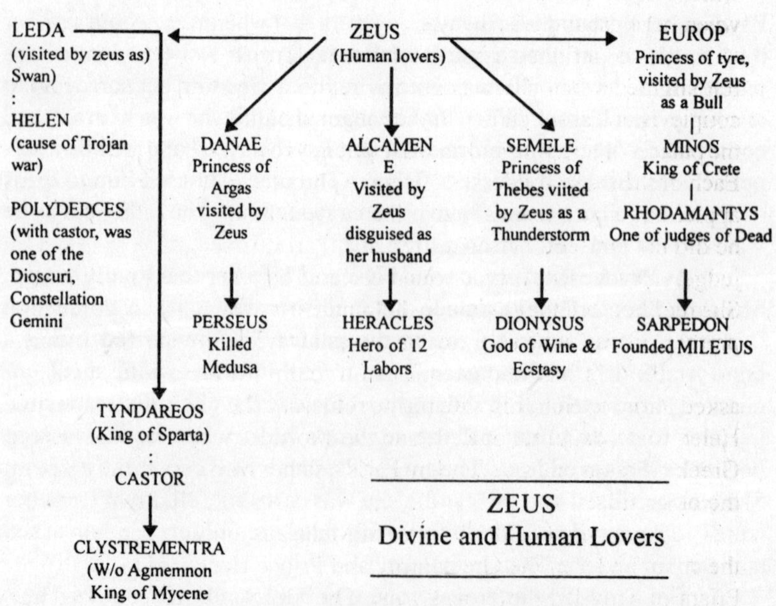

ZEUS
Divine and Human Lovers

11

THE TROJAN WAR

The Trojan War, also known as war of Troy after the name of the site where it was fought, enjoys the same reputation in Greek history as Mahabharat does in India's. Troy is the Kurukshetra of Greece. Both were fought over the honor of a lady. Helen is Draupadi of Troy War. (There is however some difference. A prince had tried to disrobe Draupadi, while Helen, queen of Sparta was abducted from her palace by a prince when her husband was away.)

It was a flimsy cause that led to the Trojan War. Eris, the goddess, felt slighted when she was not invited to a wedding by the Greek god couple Thetis and Peleus. In her anger she threw an apple in a room in the palace. The apple had an inscription, "To the most beautiful woman." Each of the three goddesses – Hera, Aphrodite and Athene – claimed the apple. A judge had to adjudge the contest, Zeus was approached. But he did not consent. As Zeus refused, Paris, prince of Troy, became the judge. He favored Aphrodite and declared her the most beautiful woman. She reciprocated the gesture by helping Paris abduct Helen, an extremely pretty princess, when her husband was away to another city.

Helen's husband Menalaus on return learned of the mishap and asked Paris to return his wife but he refused. The war became inevitable. Helen was a daughter of Zeus and the two sides were joined by rulers of Greek cities on one side, and by Paris's father with his friendly rulers on the other side.

Agmemnon, elder brother of Menalaus and ruler of Mycene was the commander of the Greek army and Prince Hector, elder son of King Priam of Troy led the Trojan army. The Greek supporters had many warriors, including Achilles, the hero of the conflict, Diomedes with soldiers of Argos and Tirnys, Ajax, captain of Locrians, Patroclus, a friend of Achilles, and Odysseus.

The noteworthy rulers to side Troy were the Amazon queen Penthasileia, Sarpandon and Glancus, leaders of Lycions, Rhesus of Thrace, Cyrnus son of Poseidon and Apollo. Cyrnus and Apollo fortified Troy.

The Greek army massed at the coast of Greece. One hundred ships were readied to carry the army to Troy. The entire Greek nobility joined to save the Greek honor and for a just cause. To the herald of fanfare, the soldiers boarded the ships. The white sails were unfurled and slowly the fleet moved out of the harbour and set off the Aegean Sea for Troy. At this poi it it was noticed that the great warrior Achilles had not joined the Greek army so the ships came back to Aulis. Soon Achilles was found and he joined the army which now sailed.

The Greek army passed through Hellespont. They were prevented from reaching the beach by the Trojan army. But Achilles made the course easy. Under his leadership, the Greek army drove away the Trojans. He defeated Cysnus son of Poseidon, who fled the battle ground on a white swan. The Trojans withdrew to the shelter of the city's walls. Both sides lost many of their men.

Even at this stage Menalaus wanted to spare human life. He sent an emissary to Priam suggesting to limit the war to a fight between Menalaus and Paris. If Paris won, Helen would be his and the Greek Army would return. If Paris died, his would be an honourable death. Paris accepted the challenge and the two fought long and hard battles at the city gates. At last Paris was wounded. But before Menalaus could strike the final blow, Trojan soldiers pulled Paris inside the gates and these were closed.

The Greeks held the siege for long, but the fortifications were hard to pierce. The Greek planned to starve Troy and devastated the surrounding areas and the Greek soldiers guarded the escape routes. Trojans evaded and collected food in the night. One day the Greeks accosted a Trojan party and found Priam's son Lycaon. Achilles spared his life but sold him as a slave. They raged Lyrnessus to the ground and as spoil found two beautiful girls, Cryseis and Briseis. Agmemnon took Cryseis and gave Briseis to Achilles. This was a sacrilege as the girls were from priestly class and a sickness spread. An oracle said the malady was occurring because of taking away a priestess by the Greek army and it would continue until the priestesses were returned. Agmemnon gave away Cryseis to the temple with gifts and sacrifices, and asked Achilles to give him Briseis, which he reluctantly did. He showed his resentment by refusing to join the battle. This proved disastrous and the Greek Army lost many of its brave fighters, including Achilles's friend Patroclus. Achilles was upset and joined the battle saying "By all the gods, tomorrow will be a day of rejoicing. In Patroclus's memory tomorrow Troy's hundred, nay thousand, men will die". Is it Arjna's voice?

The next day Achilles threw a spear and killed Hector. Tightening their defenses Troy's defenders closed six of the city's seven gates. Achilles who had captured Hector's body, tied the dead man's feet from the chariot and dragged him three times around the city's walls. In the night the dead body was thrown outside in the open to be consumed by vultures. Hector's father, King Priam invoked the help of Zeus, and asked for permission of Achilles to take Hector's body for burial. Achilles laid a condition that they could do so provided they gave equal gold in weight. The Trojans collected gold and to make up the deficiency in weight, Hector's sister Polyzena gave her necklace. Achilles sent a word to Priam that if he was given Polyzena, the battle would come to an end. Paris apprehended that he would lose Helen and resisted implementation of Achille's proposal though Priam agreed. And when Achilles come to settle terms, Paris let fly an arrow which pierced through the heel of Achilles and he died. That was Achilles's heel!

The Greeks fought a bitter battle. Then one morning the Troy Army found the enemy was gone. There was no trace of the Greeks except that there was a gigantic wooden horse with an inscription that read, "The horse is dedicated to goddess Athena for her help for the Army's safe return to their homeland." This proved Troy's victory over the Greeks. The Trojans brought the horse near the palace and all was quite when a secret door in the horses' body opened and from it emerged 50 Greek soldiers and also at the fall of night other Greek soldiers returned from a nearby island harbour. They killed the guards and opened the gates. The Trojans were not prepared for this surprise attack and lost the battle to the Greeks.

Helen returned to Menalaus. The two returned to Greece. The Trojans were killed in large numbers and their wives and children were taken as prisoners and sold as slaves. After the fall of Troy, the Greek army went back to their respective places. Odysseus, one of the great heroes, left for his place Ithaca. When the heroes returned, they found the noble families of the past had vanished and less worthy people were ruling in their place.

Odyssus Returns

When Maha Troy ended, Odyssus left for his place Ithaca. He faced several obstructions on the return journey and could not land at Thrace as intended. He proceeded and collected provisions from Libya. On way he berthed his boat in Sicily, the home of Cyclopes, a wild and unkempt people. They lived on human flesh. (Cyclopes had only one eye, in the middle of the forehead. Sicilian's leader Polyphemus was a son of Poseidon from a nymph and they manufactured thunderbolts for Zeus).

After berthing his boat, Odyssus realized that Polyphemus might create trouble for him. So in the night when Polyphemus was asleep, Odyssus blinded him with an iron rod and sailed to Ithaca. He sailed past Aeaea, which was ruled by sorceress Circe. He reached a place inhabited by two monsters – Scylla and Cherybids. He sailed back and with the help of King Alcinous reached Ithaca. There he learnt from goddess Athene about his wife Penelope and son Telemachus, and about the plots hetched against him. Everyone thought Odyssus was dead.

Nobles had been harassing Penalope for marriage. She had put them off saying she would marry the man who could shoot arrow from the bow of Odyssus. (Is it not similar to the episode of Rama breaking Shiva's bow in Mithila for Sita's hand?) When Odyssus reached the place, many men had turned up for the occasion and they tried to hold the bow but failed to shoot an arrow. In the end an old man emerged from the crowd, and with ease he drew an arrow and shot from the bow. The arrow flew straight through 12 axe rings.

The old man straightened and there stood Odyssus. With the help of his son, Odyssus killed those who had tormented Penelope. Some managed to escape. Odyssus had come home.

GODS, GODDESSES

Aphrodite

Hephaestus, son of Zeus and Hera he grew up to be a good sculptor and developed a deft hand at jewellery smithy, carpentry and intricate work. One day annoyed with him Zeus caught and threw him by hand on earth. But before he could hit the earth, he was caught by two nerids – Thetis and Eurenyme.

After many years one day Thetis attended a party arranged by Hera. Thetis was putting on a pendant. It was so pretty, it caught Hera's eye and she asked Thetis about the smith who had made it. When Hephaestus was brought to the palace by Thestis, Hera insisted that the artist should live in the palace. Since she insisted, he moved to her place. Zeus was also impressed and arranged his marriage with Aphrodite, known as goddess of love. It so happened that Aphrodite was caught in an affair with some one which soured the relations between the couple. (Aphrodite was like an Apsara.)

Apollo, Artemis

Apollo and Artemis were children of Zeus and Ledo. Apollo was a musician and played lyre par excellence. Artemis was protectoress of little children and goddess of chase. Hera did not like Zeus's relations with Ledo and when she (Ledo) was in a family way, Hera banished her. Not only that she sent out a serpent in pursuit of her. After nine months, she reached an island known as Delos where Apollo was born. After a few years, Apollo visited mother Ledo and the children. Zeus gave Apollo a chariot with white horses and golden bow and arrows, and to Artemis he gave a silver chariot, a pack of hounds, 20 wood-nymphs and 20 water-nymphs as companions.

At the command of Artemis, the hounds brought two deers which she harnessed to her chariot and drove away. She declined to marry

Alphins when the young man proposed her. Apollo instituted annual games at Delphi in an arena. He befriended a nymph. Dyrope, princess of Thessaly and the two got married. An interesting myth was associated with them. A white crew brought a message of Cornis's love to a man. He was cursed to be black. At Artemis's request Apollo threw an arrow which killed Cornis.

The child of Cornis and Apollo, named Ascelsius, learned surgery from Chiron, the centaur. Zeus killed the surgeon. At Ledo's request Apollo was saved from banishment to Tartarus.

Ares

Ares was the god of war. But he often lost war. Even so people sought support from Ares, secure in belief that he would not bother them about the justness of the cause of war. In the Trojan War, Ares fled to Olympus when Poseidon's two sons plotted to forcibly occupy the house of Zeus and to abduct Hera and Artemis but they failed in the end. Ares was taken as a prisoner and placed in a jar where he remained for a long time. One day while passing by, Hermes heard noise inside the jar. He opened the jar and set Ares free.

Athene Pallas

The city of Athens is named after Athena or Athene, the goddess of wisdom. She was daughter of Zeus and Titan goddess Metis. The courtship of Zeus and Metis had lasted long and their marriage was not liked by Hera. The oracle of Delphi had forecast that Metis would have two children, a girl followed by a boy, who will overthrow Zeus. Zeus decided not to take risk and swallowed Metis who was in the family way.

There is an interesting myth about the birth of Athena. Zeus suffered severe headache. At Zeus's command, Hephastus drew a wedge in Zeus's skull with a hammer to give the evil an escape route. But instead of evil there sprang up a pretty girl dressed in armour. Zeus knew that the girl was daughter of Metis and he named her Athene. She grew up to be a talented woman, well versed in arts and crafts. She possessed a judicial mind that settled people's disputes satisfactorily.

ATHENE

Athene could not stand up to the appreciation of creative work of another woman, Archene (meaning girl) by name who was expert in arts and crafts and lived in Lydia. She had designed a huge tapestry. People came to see it from distant places, they appreciated it. Athene also went to see it and was so upset that she tore it apart.

Archene felt very hurt and left the place. She wandered off in the woods and fainted. She was revived and was blessed that her works would be critically acclaimed. Archene turned into a spider and kept on weaving.

Athene's name and fame spread widely and brought her many suitors. When a man named Tiresia intruded on her privacy in bath, she cursed him to become blind. But when Tiresia beseeched her, she forgave him and gifted him with inward sight. He became the greatest prophet of his time.

Athene was known by a second name, Pallas about which there is a story. Athene had in Tritonis a friend named Pallas. By an accident Athene's spear pierced the heart of Pallas and she died. In remorse Athene added Pallas to her name and she was called Athene Pallas. Athene thereafter left Libya and settled in Greece.

According to another myth, Athene in Cretan and Mycenean civilizations meant mother earth. Athenians dedicated the temple of Parthenon on Acropolis to Athene. She was revered as the predecessor of Athens's first King Erichthonious. She helped Jason and Diomedes. Sophocles wrote about her. Athene possessed intellectual qualities and was a friend of Odysseus.

Ballerphone

The young prince of Corinth, Ballerphone lived for a while in the court of Argos King Proteus. Queen Antles fell in love with Ballerphone but he kept himself aloof and avoided her. Annoyed at this, she made a false complaint against Ballerphone of making advances towards her. Proteus was angry to know of the youngman's behaviour and sent Ballerphone with a letter to his father-in-law. In the letter he wrote what his queen had told and asked him to punish Ballerphone.

Ballerphone went to Iobates to meet the king's father-in-law. He was told that a monster known as Chimera was troubling people and that a brave man like him could kill it. Ballerphone agreed and took the challenge.

The monster was terrible. He spat poison from its fangs and could not be killed by arrows. Ballerphone met soothsayers and sought their advice. They told him that he could kill the monster if he was mounting Pegasus, a winged stallion while fighting the monster. Pegasus was an offspring of Poseidon and Medusa. Athene gave him for help a golden bridle that would control the wild stallion. Ballerphone managed to catch hold of Pegasus and mounted her. As Pegasus flew, Ballerphone saw the monster on a plateau and attacked it. When the monster opened its mouth, he thrust his spear in Chimera's mouth who instantaneously died.

Ballerphone returned to Iobates. The king was pleased and gave him his second daughter in marriage. He became conceited and went to Olympus to the annoyance of Zeus. When he was flying, Zeus released a gadfly which stung the stallion beneath the tail. As Ballerphone swerved to one side to control Pegasus, he fell down on earth and died. Zeus chuckled, "All those who seek to rival gods are punished."

Dionyssus

The name 'Dionyssus' should sound familiar to students of Indian history. Dionyssus visited India as per the Greek myths. Dionyssus was born son of Zeus and Semele, daughter of king of Thebes. Apprehending trouble from Hera, Dionyssus was taken to mount Nysa where he planted vines and lived long many years in the company of nymphs. But Hera searched him out and 'twisted' his brain. He left the company of caring nymphs and joined Amazons, wild and untamed women, who were dressed in animal skin and were armed with swords and serpents. In their company he roamed about and went to Egypt. Therefrom he travelled to India.

The myth is that Dionyssus had horns and fought many battles in India till the whole land was subdued. His story is that of madness, plunder and pillage. He took many elephants from India to Egypt. When he went to Greece, Rhea took pity on Dionyssus and defying Hera, she drove away madness from the youngman. But he could not give up his past careless life. He visited Thebes, north of Athens. There people refused to take to wild dancing and music from dusk to dawn as was Dionyssu's wont. From Thebes he sailed for Aegean Islands in a ship bound for Naxos. The crew bound him to the mast. But as he turned into a lion, the crew ran away. Dionyssus went to the underworld and got his mother released. He married the daughter of King Naxos and thereafter lived a happy life.

(Dionyssus has been compared by scholars with Shiva, the Hindu god of destruction, because of his ascetic life and liking for intoxication and dance. But Shiva's mysticism is absent in the Greek deity.)

Golden Fleece of Colchi

Theophanic, daughter of King Bisalles of Thrace, was very pretty. Whenever she swam in the sea, many suitors came to seek her hand. One day Poseidon also came but did not want to be seen. So he changed Theophanic into an ewe who got mixed up in a grazing flock. Now none could recognize her, except Zeus. Zeus ordered that the lamb with the golden fleece be brought to Greece. It was brought and placed in the plain of Argos, near Mycene. It was a prized possession and became a matter of contention. The oracle of Delphi decreed that that son of King Pelop who had the lamb would succed him. On the king's death, both his sons Atrenz and Thystor claimed throne and kingdom. The lamb was in possession of Atrenz.

It so happened that Atrens's wife was in love with Thystes and to help him she managed to place that lamb in her lover's flock. But when people came to know of this, with their support Atrenz drove away the imposter and became the king.

On the order of Zeus the lamb was taken to a place, near Thebes, whose king Athmos had two sons Phrixus and Halle from one wife and two other sons from Ino, the second wife. Ino was jealous of her stepsons and wanted to get rid of them. She got an opportunity as there was famine in the area and she told the king that Zeus had sent a message, viz. sacrifice Phrixus and Halle to ward off the famine. The city council favoured the sacrifice. So the two were taken for sacrifice. But on the way the children heard the voice of Hermes, "Children fly on lamb's back." The two children scrambled on the lamb's back who disappeared in the sky. When they neared a land, Halle let go off the fleece and he tumbled down near the sea of Propontis that separated Europe from Asia.

The ram flew with Phrixis and landed at Colchi. On the orders of Zeus the ram was sacrificed. The golden fleece from the lamb was hung on the branch of a tree near King Acetes's palace to be guarded by a dragon.

The second part of the story of golden fleece is connected with Jason, son of King Aeson of Thessaly. Aeson's kingdom was usurped by his step brother Pelias. Jason acting on the advice of Centaur Chiron set out and reached river Anairus where he helped an old woman to cross the river. On reaching the opposite bank the old woman who had turned into a young woman disclosed to him that she was Hera.

Jason pleaded with uncle Pelias to return the kingdom. Palias said he would if Jason brought the golden fleece from Colchi. Jason then travelled with thirty Greek heroes in an Argoship to bring the fleece.

The Argonaunts reached Hellespont where the king of Troy tried to bar their entry. But the crew soon crossed, except Hercules whose oar was broken and he had to fetch a new oar. The crew passed through a straight between two huge floating rocks, and after passing through the Phrigia and Amazon areas they reached the mouth of river Phosis and Colchi ruled by a wizard Acetes. The wizard said Jason would have the fleece provided he and his companions caught the fire breathing bulls, harnessed them to a plough and sowed the field with the dragon's teeth. Jason agreed to the terms. This was the wizard's ruse. He wanted to kill Jason.

Jason had an attractive personality and the wizard king's daughter Medea fell in love with him. She helped him in the venture. She gave him an ointment to escape search. Now Jason, Medea and a lyre player Orpheus rode three horses and reached the sacred grove wherefrom the fleece could be seen. It was guarded by a dragon monster. As Orpheus played lyre, the guard was lulled into sleep. Jason climbed the tree and took the fleece. The three left by Argos, reached the open sea and escaped. Jason reached Corinth where he married a princess. Medea was upset and left for Athens. Pelios returned the kingdom to Jason. But one day as bows fell from Argos on him he died.

Hades and Hermes

Hades is the name of a place, and also of a god. The place Hades was the destination of all dead – good or bad. Hades was reached by dark and gloomy passages. Hades, the man, was the ruler of the place. He ruled over all matters relating to man's fate. (Hades's equivalent in Hindu mythology is Yama and of Hermes it is Yamadoot.)

In Greece when a dead body was taken for burial, an abol (a small coin) was placed in its mouth before the actual burial. His shade was taken by Hermes, a messenger of Hades. It had to move beneath the earth and cross river Styx (Vaitarni, Hindu equivalent) bordering Tartarus and its four tributaries. Ferryman Charon had to be paid toll tax. Hermes left his charges on the bank which was guarded by a three headed dog Cerebrus. Thereafter he had to cross the meadows of Erebus and the pool of Lethe. On drinking its water the dead forgot their past. And, there stood Hades's palace where gods and invitees only could reach. Here the shades heard judgements on their past life delivered by three judges – Minos, Rhodamantos and Aceus. After hearing judgement, the shades were taken on one of the paths leading to Asphodel, Elysian Fields (which was a luxury palace) ruled by Rhodamantos and Tartarus with a bronze gate similar to hell's.

Hades had three Furies namely Tisiphone, Alecto and Mega. They had bodies of dogs, bats with wings, and snakes for hair. They kept a watch and no one could escape them. To the guilty they sent hounds, and winged red robed monsters with pointed teeth.

Hermes was the son of Zeus and Maia. As a child he was mischievous. Once he penned Apollo's white cows. During search Apollo found Hermes playing lyre and he was so pleased that he took him to Zeus who made him messenger of gods. Hades appointed Hermes to conduct the dying to the underground kingdom. Hermes invented Astronomy, Alphabets, medical scale, making fire. He was god of herds, business and thieves.

Hercules

The character of Hercules, a Greek god, has a universal appeal. His courage earned him recognition. We recall that in India even seven decades ago 'Hercules cycle' was considered the best two-wheel vehicle. That was for its quality make. The name Hercules was a symbol of sturdiness.

Hercules was son of Zeus and Alcemene, a mortal woman. Hera did not like him and resisted his presence. But her plan to destroy the child did not succeed and Hercules grew up to be a healthy and strong person. He took training in arms and wrestling from Autodyrus and in shooting arrows from Eurytes. He was an excellent lute player. His charming personality attracted young women. But he cared more for leading a virtuous life than for an easy going one.

Once while walking on Mount Catheron, he met two women named Pleasure and Virtue. He opted for Virtue though her company involved trial, struggle and sorrow. With virtue on his side, Hercules looked for a worthy cause to fight for. The first virtuous cause he took up was to relieve Thebes of a heavy debt. Its King Creon felt grateful to Heracules for this and gave him his daughter Megara in marriage. They had five children and lived a happy life for many years. But Hera had an evil eye on him and turned him mad. In a rage Hercules killed his family. When his madness passed, Hercules was remorseful and on the advice of the Oracle of Delphi, he atoned the tragedy. He went to King Eurytheus of Tiryus for a cure on Delphi's advice.

Eurytheus sent Heracleus to Corinth to kill a lion, who was laying the land waste and to flay the animal. Hercules set out with his sword, spear and club and a rope. On reaching the place he learnt that the lion's lair was in a crave. Hercules crouched near the cave's entrance. When the night fell and after hunt the lion came to the cave, Hercules hit it with his club. The lion sped inside the cave but as it did so it was trapped in the net and with his hands Hercules killed it. He took out a claw of the lion and with it removed the animal's skin and returned to Tirnys.

The king next sent him to kill Hydra, a snake like nine – headed monster. Hercules dressed himself in the skin of a Nimean lion and drove to the site, where Hydra was, in a chariot with Isolaus, as his charioteer. When Hercules reached the place, he sent an arrow in the direction of Hydra. As the monster came out Hercules met it with his sword and cut off its head. But as the monster flew in the air it had a new head. Hercules struck the monster time and again but every time new head kept on coming. Meanwhile Hydra coiled itself about the legs of Heracules. Not to be left behind, at that very time, Hera also sent out a giant size creature whose claws closed on Heracules's ankles. Hercules crushed them with his feet. At this moment Iolaus, the charioteering girl, came out to Hercules's help. She sheared stumps so that new heads would not come out. Gradually, Hydra weakened and with a sweep of the sword Hercules killed it. (Hydra is like Raktabeej of Hindu mythology.)

The king's two other jobs viz. to capture the hind of Cerneia, and kill a boar were also completed. Clearing the Augustean stables was a great imaginative job which he next performed. These stables had not been cleaned for long and pestilence was spreading in the area. Hercules built a dam across a nearby river. The water came rushing and swept off the filth. Hercules thereafter drove away stymphalion birds from a lake.

Hercules's other courageous jobs were : killing a half man and half bull in Marathon, killing King Diomedes of Tirida who used to feed his wild horses with the flesh of guests, bringing back the golden girdle from Hippolite the Amazon queen (near the Black Sea). He killed the Geryon in the Spanish Peninsula. Hercules crossed the narrow straight that separated it from Africa and set up two pillars, one in Spain and the other in Africa, to commemorate his crossing of the straight. The pillars are known as the Pillars of Hercules. Hercules next killed a two headed dog, Ortheus.

After completing ten assigned jobs, Hercules sailed for Greece. Even there he was asked to do two extremely difficult jobs : to bring an apple from the tree of Herseperides on Mount Atlas, and to bear the brunt of heavens. He went to the underworld where no man dared to go.

On completion of so many good deeds, Hercules was free from the quilt of destroying his family.

The pillars at Gibraltar named after Hercules, cleaning of the Augustean Stables and bearing the brunt of heavens are some of his great jobs for which Hercules's name will be remembered for ever.

Orpheus

Orpheus, a prince of Thrace, was a talented person. Besides being a supreme lyre player, he was a poet and singer. He got inspiration from Nine Muses. Once he met a Dryad named Eurydice in the forest and brought her home to be his wife. One day she was roaming throught the forest when Aristaeur, the god of hunter made an amorous approach to her. She resisted and escaped. But she was bitten by a scorpion and died.

Orpheus was inconsolable and decided to bring Eurydice back from the underworld. He journeyed to Oronum and therefrom through a narrow passage reached Styx, which was the only barrier to Hades. Orpheus played lyre to Charon, the ferryman, who was so pleased that he let Orpheus go across the river. Even dog Cerebrus did not prevent him. Orpheus was brought to Persephone, queen of the underworld. He played to Persephone which overwhelmed her. She agreed to let Orpheus take Eurydice to earth but on one condition that he would never look back for her. He agreed to this and left with Euridyce. But on reaching the end of the passage, he looked back and as he did so, Eurydice was gone for ever to the shadowy world.

(A similar story pertains to another famous lute player, Aries. However, Aries did not suffer loss. When he was returning home with awards after winning a competition, he was caught by a bandit. Fortunately, a dolphin saved his life.)

Paris

Abduction of queen Helen by Paris proved to be the cause of the War of Troy and ruin of prime youth Prince Paris. Paris was once a guest at a wedding party in Greece when an apple with an inscription "To the most beautiful woman" was found lying on the ground. Paris was asked to adjudge who was the most beautiful woman fit for award. He gave the verdict in favour of Aphrodite, ignoring the claims of Hera and Athena, who were aggrieved.

After sometime Paris fell in love with Helen and with the help of Aphrodite, he took her to Troy. Helen's husband King Menalaus asked Paris to return her but as he would not a war ensued. This war lasted for ten years.(see the Trojan War).

Persephone

One day when Persephone was collecting flowers in the fields, she was seen by Hades, who was going in a chariot. Charmed by her beauty, he abducted her. He took her to his palace in the underworld. Persephone was daughter of Demeter, sister of Zeus. Demeter searched for her in the fields but failed to find her. The fields became barren. Zeus was concerned and at his request Hades released Persephone but on the condition that for six months she would remain on earth and for six months in the underworld.

Perseus

The Greeks believed in astrology, and oracles enjoyed a status. Time could intervene and events passed by but often the prophecy would turn out to be correct. One such prophecy relates to Perseus, son of Denae, daughter of King Acricious of Argolis on the coast of Greece.

Acricious was happy when his queen gave birth to a beautiful girl. He named her Danae. But he felt distressed when it was prophesied that Danae's progeny would kill Acricious. So he placed Danae in an exclusive quarter where no one could enter. This he thought would prevent a birth and there would be no question of killing him. But one day an unusually strong beam of moon light entered Danae's place. This was Zeus. The guards did not notice the beam.

Denae bore Zeus a son whom she named Perseus. When the king came to know of the child, he was furious and on his order, Danae and Perseus were enclosed in a chaste which was set adrift in the sea. The chaste was noticed by one Dicty and he took it to his palace. Dicty was a brother of king of Siraphoes. The king fell in love with Danae and wanted to marry her. He sent away Perseus to kill monster Medusa who lived in the land of wolves and bring his head. Perseus accepted the challenge and proceeded to complete the job.

Before Perseus proceeded, he was given a helmet by Hades, wings to feet by Hermes, and a shield by Athena with the advice to look Medusa through the shield. When Perseus reachcd Medusa's place inside a ring of stones, he turned his back to stones and saw in the mirror Medusa's head and wide jaw agape. Perseus did not move and the monster could not see Perseus. The latter struck it with a sickle. Medusa was dead. Perseus placed its head in a sack, put on the sandals, and flew on the waves and reached a rock. Therefrom he proceeded to Siraphoes. His mother had married the king. (Perseus saved Andrameda from a monster on the rock, and married her). But the prophecy had to come true. When Perseus went to participate in a competition of discus throw a disc thrown by him hit Acricious, who died.

Poseidon

King Poseidon built a palace on Ebiola coast. He liked Thetis and wanted to marry her. But when he learnt that a son born to Thetis would be more famous than his father, he changed his mind. Instead he married Amphitrita from whom he begot three sons. But he was unfaithful to his wife and wanted to marry Athena, another daughter of Zeus. But Athena did not like Poseidon and they came to a clash. Zeus intervened and they parted company.

Helios

Helios was the charioteer of Sun. With a helmet on his head, he used to drive the chariot of gold driven by four fiery horses with golden manes each day from east to west across the sky, spreading light and warmth to the world. At night fall he used to return home in the east after encircling the earth. As morning drew near, he would set off on his journey. To look at him one had to shade his eyes, otherwise the shaft of Sun's light would blind any one looking at it.

Helios had a son from a neird named Clime, one of the 50 daughters of Sun God. Brought up in Egypt, Phaeton, the son could see Helios from a distance. Phaeton's friends did not know that Sun was his father and they won't believe when he told them about the relationship. So one day with the reluctant permission from father, Phaeton drove the chariot on the daily path. The horses were well behaved and drove in a disciplined way. But when he came to Egypt, and ensured that his friends saw him, he cracked the horses downward. But the Sun light became so bright that the fertile land of Egypt turned into desert. Seeing danger to the world, Zeus threw a thunderbolt which killed Phaeton and his body fell down on earth at Erydanus. This brought tear to the eyes of nymphs who turned into poplar trees and the tears turned into drops of amber. There they stand swaying in the wind and cooling the earth with their leaves.

The chariot was dishevelled. Helios set out to find it and he found it in Ethiopia. As the horses stumped in confusion, he threw his cloak on their eyes so as to calm them. He led them quietly back to their stable in the west. Darkness covered the path for the rest of the day.

Two Pairs of Twins

This myth relates to a pair of twins – Castor and Polydeuces–sons from the same mother but different fathers. (Castor was a charioteer and Polydeuces a boxer. They played in Olympics.) Together they were known as Dioscuri. Castor was son of a Spartan king and Polyduces of Zeus. The other pair was Lyceas and Idas. They were cousins. Lyceas's father was a human, Idas was son of deity Poseidon. The two were good fighters.

The four (two twins) were good friends but they quarelled over a woman. Lyceas and Idas were to marry two sisters. Ignoring friendship, Castor and Polydeuces eloped with the girls to Sparta. This caused bitterness among them. Then Idas fell in love with pricness Marpossa, daughter of Ares. Ares's condition for daughter Marposa's marriage was that her suitor should be a better charioteer than him (Ares) and if the suitor lost in a race he would be put to death. She detested the condition. So one day she went with Idas to Messne. It so happened that Apollo also got interested in Marposa. But Zeus intervened and Marposa remained with Idas.

After some time the four friends forgot the past and met in Sparta where they made a daring plot to steal grazing herds from the plains of Arcadia. They carried out the plot but failed to divide the loot. One early morning Castor and Polydeuces took away the cattle. Lyceas and Idas searched for the cattle and found them. There ensued a quarrel between them. Idas pierced his spear into Castor who died. Polydeuces killed Lyceas. Idas too died. Only Polydeuces survived. He buried Castor. Zeus came and took him to Olympus. He shared his time between the two places. He lived at Olympus for six months and passed next six months with Castor in the underworld.

Thesius

Thesius, king of Athens, was a man of great courage. He was born to Ethra, daughter of king of Trazen, and Algens, king of Athens. Algens left Ethra at Traozen, placing a pair of sandals and a sword under a rock near the city gate, and told her in the presence of six men that she will give birth to a son who will meet him at Athens with the sandals and sword as symbols of recognition.

In course of time a son was born to Ethra. She named him Thesius. When he grew up an adolescent he left for Athens with the symbols. On way he killed a giant named Simi who had terrorized people at Megara and would not let any one proceed without paying tribute. He also killed an Arcadian and a bandit near Demeter's shrine.

As Thesius neared Athens, he met Medea and her son Medus. Medea offered him a drink mixed with poison. At that time Algens also happened to be there and he recognized his son from the symbols. He gave the bowl a blow and threw the drink away. Medus was exposed and he fled to Colchi. Next he faced Minotaur a creature, in the labrynth of Knossos. He was born of a session of Persiphenea and a white bull and lived on human flesh. Each year seven boys and seven girls were sent to appease his hunger. Thesius offered himself as one of the seven boys and travelled with them on a boat to Crete. His courage won people's heart, including the heart of Adriane, the daughter of the king. Minotaur came forward when he saw the youth. But Thesius caught Minotaur's horn in a wrestler's grip. The horn cracked up and Thesius pierced a piece in the monster's head. It died. By chance King Algens also died and Thesius became king. He married Hippolyte, queen of Amazons. He fled when a rebellion occurred and was killed. From his giant remains and sword and sandle, it was inferred that the bones were of Thesius. They were brought to Athens and buried there. (With this is connected a story of sculptor Dedalus and his nephew Icarus. Dedalus was turned out of Athens. He went to Thebes and built many buildings, including labrynth of Knossos. The two died when they tried to fly with wings.)

Oedipus

Athens and Thebes were two prominent cities of ancient Greece. Athens owed its name to Athene. Thebes was founded by Cadmus, son of King Agnor of Tyre. Cadmus had a beautiful daughter, Europa. One day Zeus came to her in the form of a beautiful bull. It was so beautiful that Europa impulsively petted it and rode over it. The moment she rode, Zeus (the bull) eloped with her to Crete. She was frightened. But the moment bull tuned into Zeus, Europa forgot all her suffering.

King Agenor sent out a search party to find Europa, and on the advice of the oracle of Delphi, Cadmus took with him a cow to found a city at the place wherever it sat down. During their wanderings, the cow set down at a place. There Cadmus built a fort and a city which came to be known as Thebes. The fort turned into a cause of tragedy when Agenor was thrown out of Thebes by his grandson. In repentance Cadmus and his wife turned into snakes and the myth is that every child in Cadmus family will have on his/her body the mark of a serpent.

Much to the annoyance of people of Athens, Thebes grew as a rival city. Thebes did not form a confederation with other cities, whereas

Palatea joined Athens. During the Pelonnesion War, the Athenian army was defeated, and Thebes lost to Sparta. After Cadmus, the greatest family of Athens was of Laias, the usurper king. Laias was warned that he would be killed by his son. When the king got a son, he left the child at Mt. Citheron to die. But the shepherds who found the child took him to Corinth, where the king brought up the child as his own son and named him Oedipus. When he was grown up; he went to Oracle Delphi who predicted that he would kill his father and marry his mother.

Upset by this prediction, Oedipus left the place and went to live at Thebes. One day he met a charioteer who was rude to him. Oedipus who could not tolerate rudeness killed that man. The charioteer was Laias. Neither Laias knew that Oedipus was his son nor did the people of Thebes know this fact. Oedipus could not have thought that the charioteer was his father.

The people of Thebes made Oedipus their king. Oedipus took the queen as his wife. (The practice might have been for victor to take the wife of the vanquished as his wife). Soon thereafter the country suffered a severe famine. The Oracle of Delpi said the famine would be over when the man, who was the cause of famine, left Thebes. As Oedipus came to know of it, he left Thebes, the city of seven gates. The army of Polymices and Andrastus was divided into seven parts, one division each at a gate to fight the enemy.

The term 'Oedipus Complex' has come in vogue, after Oedipus who unknowingly had killed his father and married a woman not knowing that she was his mother. Freud has popularized the term in his Psychoanalysis.

Achilles

A proverbial hero of Greek mythology, Achilles fought many a battle and was known as a great hero. He was especially taken to the War of Troy where he showed his bravery by winning several battles.

Immediately after his birth, Achilles was taken to the river Styx to make him immortal. His mother held him by the heels and dipped him in Styx water. She was given to understand that one dip in Styx water made man immortal. Thus entire body of Achilles had become immortal except the heels. So when an enemy arrow pierced his heel, he died.

Hercules bearing the brunt of heavens

BOOK IV

12

HINDU

Hindu civilization is the ancient-most living civilization, and Hindu is the most liberal and tolerant and to some extent most rational religion. However, undeniably it is very conservative in certain respects. Hindus proudly call their religion – Dharma, 'a way of life'. It has survived several marauding onslaughts over millennia and continues evolving even today. The Hindu cultural pathway has been treaded by conservatives, middle pathwallahs and invaders, while Hindu philosophy encompassed varied deep and wide thought currents.

There are about one billion Hindus who constitute more than 15% of the world's population. Majority of them (about 85%) inhabit India and a few million are scattered over different lands. Traditionally they are peaceful and live in harmony with people professing different religions. India is not only multi religious but also multi linguist and claims to be a multi cultural entity. Hindus are proud of their accommodative spirit, though their attitude towards one of their own parts – Shudras – besmears their fair name.

Hindu civilization originated some five millennia ago in the Sindhu, Saraswati, Jamuna and Ganga valleys. These valleys were inhabited by Dravidians, Aryans and Austroloid-Mongoloids. The Dravidians – dark skinned and urban–professed an iconic religion and worshipped the Mother Goddess and a male deity resembling Shiva. The Aryans – cattle herders – followed an aniconic religion and prayed supernatural deities, initially only five (Indra, Varuna-Mitra, Nasatyas, Surya and Agni) but later the number swelled to 33. The Austroloid-Mongoloids' faith centered in Demonology. They practiced magical rites and witchcraft, and believed in spirits, imps, spells and incantations.

The assimilation of the communities led to an occupation – based Varna – Vyavastha, originating from the myth of division of Purusha into four parts, function-wise equal were termed Brahmin, Kshatriya, Vaishya and Shudra. They enjoyed flexibility of interchange of castes according to attitude and professional competence. With passage of time the castes developed rigidity and inter dining and marital relations among castes stopped. A complex developed and castes became hierarchical. Concepts of restrictions and impurity cropped up. The first three castes – Dwijas – evolved an Upanayan ceremony which gave them a superior status over Shudras. However they dreaded the magical effects of crafts and tabooed food. The Brahmins being intellectually advanced claimed godhood on earth and developed philosophical concepts of Atma-Paramatma, a universal immortal soul that showed predilection about a Trinity – Brahma, Vishnu, Shiva – each devoted to his function of creation, protection and destruction, respectively. Divisons of occupation became natural. With this (divison of society on caste basis), there developed the concept of natural elements (namely, earth, water, fire, sky and air). The changes from Vedic to Brahmanic to Hindu shaped their faith into Dharma which gradually spread all over the subcontinent, known as India after the mighty river Indus 'Hindu' evolved from 'Sindu(s)'.

The Hindu prayer showed cooperative spirit. It said,

Sah Nau Bhavatu
Sah Nau Bhunaktu
Sah Viryam Karvavahe
Tejasvinamavadhiyamastu
Ma vidhisamahe.
Om Shantih, Shantih, Shantih

(May we get together, dine together
may we act together, may our deeds be glorious
may it be without hassels, and may peace prevail.)

With society's fragmentation into castes, their unity started disappearing. The equality of status was cast aside. The modes of worship, on coming into contact with Persians, Greeks, Central Asian tribes, Romans and others, also changed. Persians worshipped fire. Hindu worshipped gods, including Agni (fire). Both Persians and Hindus believed in the existence of demons, devils and daityas. But beyond this they differed. From the Greeks they learnt image worship. Besides Hinduism, Buddhism also spread over Central, Eastern, Far Eastern and South Asian regions.

Politically also Brahmins expanded and gained political importance. As a creed, Hinduism had stood for overall development of personality. A Hindu was expected to know about literature, music, art. Without accompanishments in these "man was like a cattle without horns and tail". Dharma played supreme role in man's deeds and life. Dharma was considered as confirmation of cosmic law - Rita. Actions are Dharmic only when man's internal thought process and external actions are congruent. Dharma is explained as *Dharanatdharmah*. Castes should do their prescribed functions and uphold their responsibility. A caste member should remember to do balanced acts, ensure his spiritual welfare and avoid disintegration in mundane pursuits.

Hindus have a common history, literature and civilization. Each phase of its development gave impetus to creation of new myths, which is why, Hinduism is not a dogmatic creed, or an academic abstraction or a celebration of ceremonies. It is a spiritual thought with a specific attitude of self, mixed with intellectual outlook, aesthetics and moral values. The stress is on spiritual experience of the soul. Spiritualists lay stress on intutional experience.

Hinduism believes that different people possess different spiritual thoughts, logic and traditions and aim at realization of God in different ways. In the past contacts amongst Hindu, Islam and Christian religions brought in reforms and there developed many sects of Hinduism. However, each sect seeks happiness of all, as in

सर्वे भवन्तु सुखिनः
सर्वे सन्तु निरामयः.
सर्वे भद्राणि पश्यन्तु।

Hindu epics donot relate to conflicts of creeds nor is it a proselytizing creed. Hinduism absorbed ideas and symbols of various people. Not only that it absorbed mystic animals of many races and tribes. For instance, peacock, swan, bull, mouse were absorbed as companions of deities. Thus polytheism was organized in a monistic way, though tolerant of others. Whereas the image worship of deities was absorbed from Dravidians, Ahimsa and vegetarianism from Jain and Buddha religions – as a mark of regard for life of all beings - cults needing higher ideals were also assimilated with their rites and social institutions. Thus it is interesting to note that stories of developments through deities were admitted through assimilation of cultures. Buddha was incorproated as an avatar of Vishnu. Centuries afterwards social reformers like Kabir, Chaitanya, Nanak introduced liberal thoughts. Later contacts with Christianity ushered in movements like Arya Samaj, Brahma Smaj. Even so Vedantism continued through them. Hinduism recognizes God as Supreme, all kinowing, great lover and as the Trinity of Brahma, Vishnu and Shiva. Some seers thought the Sansar (world) is Maya (illusion).

Hindu polytheism was organized in a monistic way. It was tolerant of other views. Deities tell the story of developments and assimilation of cultures. Conflicts between Shiva and Daksha, and Krishna and Indra have become myths. Kali is another instance. Said to be associated with Kiratas, she was gradually identified with the Supreme godhood, inspite of her interests in wine, flesh and animal sacrifice.

Hinduism believes in realization of God in different ways as well through the help of diverse scriptures. The Upanishads were interpreted through Brahmasutras, and Yoga Vashistha guided religious life, while Vedanta remained at the core. Every religion stresses on experience and describes God in its own way. Seers sat silent and provided no answer as to who God was. Absolute silence was their reply. Absolute is silent, inexplicable, Neti-Neti according to Yagyavalkya. Hindus recognize God as Bhagwan, though sages call Him by different names. (Ekoham Viprah Vahudha Vadanti). There are many sects of Hindus who have differences of views. But these sects are like cultural units. Heterogenous Hindu elements have welded together; they live separately and there is no attempt to eliminate disagreeable creeds to bring uniformity.

Hinduism does not believe that some people are chosen by God; it lays stress on conduct and not on creed. Religion expects righteous living but it has no fixed form of worship. Hinduism binds together its multitudinal sects, mostly theists, and is opposed to fanaticism and violence. In the past many people persecuted in their own lands escaped to India where they found security and protection. Religions are not incompatible; they are complimentary, the goal of man's life is liberation. For Hindu God is both imminent and transcendant. Westerners make fun of Hindus for treating gods in royal manner. H.M. Eliot criticized Hinduism of being full of untruthfulness, and devoid of courage and fighting qualities, which has been proved wrong. For some people the symbols of Hindu religion are Dhruti (i.e. Dhairya), Kshama, Dama (control over senses), not to steal, Shauch (keeping body clean) Vivek, Gyan (knowledge), truthfulness, learning and to keep anger under control.

Manu, the first human creation, presents his philosophic account of creation of the universe and Beings. He consolidated for the first time Hindu socio-religious ideas and presented those in a codified form, known as Manusmriti, but in full its name was Manav Dharma Shastra. It is also a Hindu code of ethics based on ancient usages, customs, and conventions which guided peoples' socio-cultural life. The code was held in reverence and, it became mythic. Laws of Manu prescribed duties and discipline for the people. The creator is a divine power and everything in it is perfectly ordered. A king is a divine authority. Castes are ordained by God. Each caste has been assigned its duties and failure to conform to order would invite socio-religious punishment. But Manu has been criticized for giving too much to the 'Upper Castes', especially the Brahmins, which led to many social and political evils and proved detrimental to the progress of society. Manu has enjoyed the status of a mythological progenitor of mankind. Brahma created Manu and Shatarupa and several myths are associated with their names. The present day Hindu society is based on Manu's ideas, though many changes were made from time to time which no doubt had temporary affect. Then the changes were cancelled and later disappeared altogether. Hindu life is ordained by Manu's code.

According to Manusmriti, the life of Hindu is divided into stages – birth, marriage (house holders' life), renunciation, death, each of these is accompanied with rituals. Birth is introduction of a new identity to the society. It also gives a new binding relationship to the parents and the family. Upanayan (thread ceremony) makes the individual realize that he is crossing the threshold of childhood. Marriage rites inform the two persons that they are now beyond sentimental affairs. The ritual has a temporary purpose and loses its force but the marriage is an identity of permanent relationship, it is a spiritual exercise, witnessed by families and others and sanctified by the Agni (fire). The feeling of unity of the couple is cemented by Agni. Marriage is an ordeal requiring ego – sacrifice – an action by one of them is action done by the two together. The society is supposed to help them realize the implications of marriage, which are more than sensors or biological. Marriage is a commitment. The story of Savitri and Satyavan may look like a myth but its value for social relationship has no parellel. Myths do help us in looking at our imperfections, most of which accrue through sufferings. 'Marriage' illustrates how a myth can also help us in looking at our inner problems. Inner mysteries can harmonize life with reality. Should such code and practices, which have served useful purpose be allowed in religion – whichever religion it be?

While Hindus, we said in the beginning, constitute 85% of the Indian population, and the remaining 15% are Jains, Sikhs and Buddhists professing indigenous religions, and non-indigenous people who follow Islam, Christianity, Parsi, Judaism. All these people have over centuries lived together peacefully but there have been at times clashes among them. Political motivations have also been at the back of these clashes. Clerics and religious leaders have much to explain. Yet Hindus have shown commendable tolerance for each other and for others also. The accommodative spirit of Hindus covers their differences.

The constitution of India bestows on people equal rights to live together peacefully – and not for indulgence in conversions in the name of freedom of conscience or for improving economic conditions. The practices of conversion are unfair and not motivated by benevolence and generosity to poor. Bringing in politics in religious matters is unjustifiable.

To crub the evils that had intruded in Hindu society, and also to ameliorate the economic conditions of people, a number of amendments have been made in the Constitution. About the end of 20th century, a new class of OBC (Other Backward Castes) was added. This has not made much difference. The Hindu caste system needs sweeping changes, preferably total elimination. Is that possible?

A disappointing occurance relates to Hindu emigrants to USA, UK, Canada, Australia, etc. These immigrants are planting the caste system. They have Samaj on caste-basis, like Brahman Samaj, Kshatriya Samaj, Agarwal Samaj, Kayastha Samaj and other casteist Samajas. This is an unhealthy sign and should be stopped.

JAIN

Namo Arihantanam, Namo Siddhanam
Namo urajjhayanam, Namo Loye Savvasahunam
Esopanch Namukkaro, Savva Pavappanaasano
Mangalanam Cha Savvesim, Padhamam Havai Mangalam

According to Jain philosophy there is neither beginning nor end of the world, which is made up of conscious and unconscious Tattvas (substances). Soul is conscious; space, time, pudgal, dharma and adharma are unconscious. Each one of these follows its Dharma. *Vattu Subavo Dharmah*. The Tattvas are entangled in material world like a seam of gold in soil. Soul is purified through practice of Ahimsa, Sadachar and austerity. Sadachar (i.e. right conduct) includes Satya, Asteya, Jitendraditya and Aparigraha and helps in overcoming obstacles, sensuousness and Rag-Dwesha. Jainism does not believe in a creator god or Niyati but venerates 24 Trithankaras.

Who is a Jain? A Jain is that person who breaks the land of spiritual ignorance and attains liberation with the help of teachings of Tirthankaras (ford-makers). These guide him to cross over the Sansar. A Jain takes to Ahimsa like a fish takes to water. The concept of Ahimsa was propounded by Rishabhnath (Adinath). The last two in the series of Trithankars were Parasanath and Vardhman Mahavir. Mahavir preached liberation from Karmic bondage, the cycle of life.

The cardinal principles of Mahavira's life were besides Ahimsa, Aparigraha, Anekantavada (the doctrine of Manifold aspects or non-absolutism), and Atmaupamya (oneness of reality). Ahimsa underscrores Anekantavada which is relative to multiple viewpoints, non-absolution, comprehension, and acceptance of that which is beyond normal expression.

The Jain Epistemology is characterized by Syadavada, the theory that asserts different possibilities to affirm validaty of a statement about an object under one of several conditions, that is "can be" and Nayavada (doctrine of standpoints) meaning several modes of expression or points of view. To elaborate the idea : A man perceives a situation from his own angle : he perceives only one aspect not the totality. This understanding is relative and not total. His viewpoint may suffer from constraints of ego, while the situation needs to be perceived from various perspectives. His knowledge is a mixture of truth and ignorance. Even if all the perspectives were correct, they might represent an incomplete view of reality. Denial of truth, or seeing truth as total exclusive truth gives rise to dogmas. However, omniscience brings forth in him an understanding of the whole. This is Anekantavad. An allegory of gold ornaments will explain the point, gold ornaments may be of various shapes but they are gold – this is Vastu Dharma. This is like the story of elephant and blind men. Each blind man perceived the animal from his sensory contact with the animal's particular part of the body and each man's perception differed from that of other's. This is understanding of the reality. Anekantavad lays bare various possibilities of the recognition of reality in its manifold aspects.

Ekantavad takes note of variety, entirety and independent existence of matter. It stands for understanding viewpoints of others, thereafter it synthesizes these and realizes the reality of Tattvas. It is the synthesis of knowledge and Karma. It lays stress on discipline and self control. (Umaswati's *Tattvartha Sutras*) :

Nayavada and Saptangivada (doctrine of 7 - fold judgement) are corollaries of Anekantavad. Ekantavad emphazies the reality of the worlds, it believes in Atma and matter but it does so without the involvement.

A Jain's life is based on three jewels (tri-ratna) – right faith, right knowledge and right conduct. He observes five vows viz non-injury to life, speaking truth, not stealing, abstraining from sexual intercourse and sensuality, non-attachment to worldly possessions. Such a conduct prepares him for spiritual liberation. A Jain leads an ascetic life.

The Jain community consists of monks, nuns and lay people. The monks and nuns meditate, study scriptures and confine their daily life to be on rounds for alms and teaching lay people (called Shravanakas i.e. listeners) and Upasakas (i.e. practitioners). They observe a special 8-10 day festival – Paryushana – during the rains when they fast. On the last day of the festival the image of a Jina is carried in a procession.

Jains are divided into two sects : Digambaras (sky-clothed) and Shvetambaras (white clothed). Once there was a famine when people migrated to south. The migrants were called Digambaras. They believe that the oral teachings of Mahavir are lost. The Svetambaras on the other hand believe that their eleven (11) Agamas are based on Mahavira's teachings. They also consider the possibility of spiritual liberation of women. A group among Svetambaras, known as Sthanakavasis perform rites in halls and don't use images. Jain monks and nuns cover their mouths to minimize harm to living things. Jains believe that every living thing has life (or soul) which is embedded between one and five senses.

Jains don't believe in casteism and say that caste should be determined by actions. –

कबूना बंगाणे होइ कामुणा होई खत्तियो
वैसो क्रम्मुणा होइ सूद्धो हवें कम्मुणा। (उत्तराध्ययन)

A number of legends are prevalent about Tirthankaras. About Rishab Nath it is said that he was introduced to worldly life by a courtesan. After leading a full life he realized the futility of luxury. Feeling for the suffering of people, he gave up worldly life. Archaelogists found a mutilated freeze in Mathura on a Tilla which depicts the event on pillars that were presented by one Bal Hastini and a Bauddha. This was done at the request of Lokantaka gods, as per the Jatakas. Many temples, including those at Mount Abu and Kumbhalgarh depict the themes of Jain hagiology. In USA, the Jains of the Bay Area near Sanfransisco have built a beautiful temple at Milpitas in which images of Tirthankaras are displayed. We do not mean to raise a controversy but respectfully submit to our Jain friends that presentation of Mallinath's image in male form is not indisputable. While most Digambaras and Shvetambaras hold Mallinath in high esteem as a female, only a few think of Mallinath as male. We are inclined to consider Mallinath as a female on the basis of information collected from various sources, including *Trisastishalaka purushacharitra*. We also present some extracts about her life from our publication "Eminent Indian Women" (1976).

"One of the greatest women who led a pious life and influenced the people is Mallinath, the nineteenth Arhat in the long succession of 24 Tirthankaras of the Jain hagiology. Mallinath is rather an unusual name for a woman, it sounds like a man's. But for the saint who was spiritual minded and made no distinction between man and woman, the name was of no consequence. Many flocked to her in search of peace and solace and perhaps it was her disciples who, finding in their guru understanding and catholicity of outlook, gave Malli, which was her original name, the name 'Mallinath'.

Malli was the daughter of King Kumbha, of Mithila, and Padmavati. She grew up to be exceedingly beautiful, and her name travelled far and wide and attracted princes of Anga, Kashi, Koshala, Kunala, Karn and Panchal. They all sought her hand. But finding none equal to her daughter, Kumbha refused to give Malli to any one of them. Enraged at this the six attacked Mithila and laid a siege. Although Kumbha fought valiantly but it was an unequal match. Seeing her father on the verge of defeat, Malli requested him to invite the princes to meet her in her apartment. The king acted likewise.

Earlier, having sensed, the catastrophe, Malli had got installed a beautiful statue of herself on a gorgeous jewelled platform in an interior room of the palace. The room had six doors with double doors and lattices in the front wall of the statue's private room and six little private rooms in the front of the doors, and one door in the wall behind the statue. Daily she threw a ball of food into the statue's palate and covered it with the golden lotus.

When the six princes came and saw the statue of Malli through the lattices in the doors; they were taken aback by the charming figure. But they were soon disillusioned when the real Malli, more beautiful, entered by the door at the back of the statue and took off the lotus covering the statue's palate. The odour of the putrid food hurt their nostrils and the princes turned away.

Giving the analogy of the statue, Malli told them that beneath the external charm of the body lies a filthy matter of transitory nature. Malli made the princes realize that the way to genuine happiness lay not in enjoyment but in meditation and practice of austerity. The princess herself gave up the royal comforts and became an ascetic. Her austere living attracted the princes and ordinary men and women who bowed to her and became her followers. By her excellent character, she was acknowledged as a Tirthankar".

In a sermon, Mallinath advised a congregation : "The boundless ocean of a worldly existence grows of itself very much from love, et cetera, like the ocean from the day of full moon. The dirt of love and hate is destroyed at once for men who plunge into water of tranquility which produces great joy. Men who have adopted tranquility destroy Karma in half a moment which they would not destroy by severe penance in crores of births. When the destruction of the darkness of love et cetera has been by the rays of tranquility, Yogis see the true nature of the supreme soul in themselves". Malli died at a ripe age after a fast at Mount Sammatta. She preceded Mahavir who lived from 599-527 BCE.

Jains have a number of beautiful temples, some at natural spots on hills, where they go on pilgrimage. Of these one is at Shravan Belgola in Karnataka, with a tall granite statue of Bahubali.

In Ancient times a young Jain had to take a vow, 'I will desist from knowingly or intentionally destroying any soul with two or more senses so long I live, I will neither kill nor cause others to kill. By mind, speech and action, I will desist from all such activities. From this had followed other vows such as abstinence from falsehood, theift, carnality and possessiveness. On the positive side, he practiced truthfulness, Brahmacharya, honesty, detachment from external world and then attained equanimity.

The tradition that offers sacred knowledge is Sampradaya. The Jains have great traditions and in that sense some people use the term Jain Sampradaya. The Jain teachings are collectively called Agamas.

The Jains were the earliest dissenters from the mainstream of Hinduism. The Vedic culture had taken sharp turn towards Brahmanism, including casteism with which the Shramana culture clashed. This was at the time of Mahavira and Buddha. There were five great Shramanas namely Ghoshalak, Purna Kashyap, Ajit Keshkambali, Padukatyayan, Sanjay Belbathputra. The Jain philosophy drew inspiration mainly from the Shankhya philosophy of Hinduism.

Ghoshalak propounded Nityavada (pre-determinism). He said : What is destined to happen will happen. In the same strain it is said, Kapil, Buddha and other great saints were eminent physicians who specialized in the cure of disease of transmigratory existence. Jainism believed in soul and rebirth. Later Charvak protested against Brahmanism. He went to the other extreme. He believed in enjoying life, ignoring conduct.

Rishbhadeva, Chausa, Bihar
7th Century A.D.

BUDDHISM

Buddha's life epitomized spiritual detachment, lofty idealism and love for humanity. Buddhism is the cream of Buddha's thoughts. He has served as compassion personified for two and a half millennia. People flocked to him with their stories of suffering and sorrow, which he removed with his soothing words and guided them to the path of right conduct. Buddha kept his cool even when someone was rude and posed insolent questions to him. Once a man started abusing him. Buddha kept quiet. The man finally asked Buddha why he did not reply. Buddha questioned him. If a man declines to accept a gift from someone, to whom the gift would return. The man replied, "To the person who made the gift". Buddha said, "Now what if I don't accept your gift of abuses? Won't they return to you. So, whenever a wicked man abuses a virtuous man, it is like looking up and spitting up at heaven. Who gets spoiled? Not the heavens, the spit would fall back on the spitter". Buddha sometime explained his thoughts in parables. In respect of humaneness Buddha and Jesus Christ were alike. Their paths were alike. Their disciples were alike in character and played similar roles in carrying their master's message. To Ananda Buddha was hero. Both the great men left behind old ideas, went out in quest of new ideas, and led people to a new way of life. With Buddha (566 BCE – 486 BCE) began a new religion and theology. Five hundred years later Christ's message would be carried forward and propagated by his apostles.

There are innumerable legends and Jatakas about Buddha, including his former births. "After his visit to the heaven of Tushitas (blessed ones), he finally incarnated" as Siddhartha in the womb of 44 - year old Mayawati, queen of the Shakya King Shuddhodhana of Kapilvastu. One night she dreamt that a white elephant entered her belly. A group of Brahmanas interpreted the dream that the queen would give birth to one who would be either an emperor or Buddha, an elightened one. Mayawati gave birth to the Bodhisattva in a garden in Lumbini to which she had retired for delivery. She was under a tree and held its branch at the time of delivery. On that very day were born Yashodhara (Gotama's would be wife), his squire Chandaka, horse Kantaka, favorite disciple Ananda, and the Bodhi tree beneath which Siddhartha experienced enlightmenet. Asita, a man from the Himalayas predicted for him a high place in religion.

When Siddhartha was only five days old, Mayawati died and he was brought up by his step mother Mahaprajapati. When he was 12, a council of Brahmanas predicted that he would devote himself to asceticism. Worried by this Shuddhodhana arranged to ward off asceticism and kept the prince away from the sight of old age, sick people and dead bodies. Despite precautions, he saw an old man, a sick man and a corpse being carried. He enquired the cause of the condition of the body and decided to renounce the world. Father tried to divert his attention but neither he nor the birth of a son, Rahul could change his mind. Siddartha one night left the palace. He went into solitude, practiced austere exercises and wandered. Nothing happened. Finally he stopped at Uruvilva on the bank of a river and practiced penance with five disciples for six years. Austerities reduced his body to almost a skeleton. He realized that excessive exercises destroyed a man's strength and that he had to go beyond asceticism as he had gone beyond worldly life. So when a village girl took pity on his condition and offered him a bowl of rice, he accepted it and bathed in the river. Annoyed at this, the five disciples left him.

Siddhartha also left for Bodh Gaya and sat down under a Bodhi tree, the tree of wisdom uttering the words, "Here on the seat may my body dry up if I rise until I have attained the knowledge which can be attained during several Kalpas. Indra and Mara (Cupid) placed several obstructions and tried to tempt him but nothing could deflect him from his goal. He did not fear death. He remained steadfast on his decision. He had conquered desire and fear.

First he learnt about the exact conditions of living beings. They die and transmigrate. As he meditated on human suffering, he was enlightened about the causes of suffering and the means of destruction. At day light he attained perfect Bodhi (enlightenment) and attained Buddhaood. He had become Buddha. For several days he remained in meditation. Then he decided to spread the message of Nirvana, rather than taking his own Nirvana.

Siddhartha Gotama (he was of the Gotama tribe), the Buddha first went to Varanasi and Saranath and preached to the five disciples who had left him. In his address he set in motion the wheel of law. He said : Keep off extremes – keep off life of total pleasure, keep of self mortification – both are vain and ignoble. Take the Middle Path which consists of right views, aspirations, speech, conduct, living, efforts, recollection, meditation and salvation and leads to knowledge, enlightenment and Nirvana. Here is the truth about pain (suffering) - the origin of pain is the thirst for pleasure, for existence, for change. Here is the truth of suppression of pain, the extinction of that thirst through the annihilation of that desire. Giving alms, knowledge and virtue are good things. To do a little good is better than to accomplish difficult works. The perfect man is nothing if he does not diffuse benefits to creatures and consoles the lonely. This is the doctrine of mercy. The way of salvation is open to all. Destroy your passions and and know that a man can escape his passions by taking refuge in hermitage. "The only remedy for evil is healthy reality." People responded: Buddham-Sharanam Gachchhami Samgham Sharanam Gachchami Dhammam Sharanam Gachchhami. (I take shelter in Buddha, Sangha and Dharma).

With this began Buddha's wandering that lasted 44 years. Many legends of Buddha's life appear in legends and art. Two of these are : Siddhartha's cousin Devadutta, who was jealous of him, made an elephant drunk to kill Buddha. In stead the angry elephant killed a girl. Chided by Buddha the elephant knelt before him. The Buddha's whole family (father, mother, wife and son) was converted to Buddhism.

At the age of 80 Buddha died at Kushinagar near the bank of river Hiranyavati. At that time the trees were covered with flowers and the Gandharvas played heavenly music. His last words to his disciples were, "Decay is inherent in all things. Everything created must perish. A man must separate himself from everything he has loved. You need no longer have a master. When I am gone the Doctrine will be your master. Work out your own salvation." Buddha entered the Nirvana. His body was placed on a pyre which lighted itself. The relics of the Blessed one have been preserved in the Stupas which were raised soon after his Nirvana.

The Jatakas, folklore and fables give stories about Buddha's past life. They also contain his metaphysical dogma and popular beliefs. Buddha stressed to mankind the need of compassion and knowledge. It is strange that later day disciples associated Shakti (powers, like the one associated with Vishnu and Shiva) with Buddha. Tara, the Shakti of Avalokiteshvara is his most revered Shakti. Tara was born from his tears. Like Shiva's Shaktis, Tara can be both gentle and threatening.

Buddhism, after Buddha's death got divided into two sects – Mahayana and Hinayan. Mahayana (Great Vehicle) created the notion of transcendental persons Bodhisattvas. It was popular in Western India which had experienced besides Hindu, Persian and Greek influences. In the artistic representation of Buddhist themes Hindu Vaishnaism, Greece – Syrian gnosis, and Persian fire played important part. Hindu art symbolized Buddha either by a solar wheel and showed him with hand mudras. Greek art gave Buddha a plastic form and represented him like Apollo. (Later he evolved in the Japanese form). He appeared as Human (Manushi) Buddha - Dipankar, (the most ancient and precursor of Buddha), Sakya sages namely Vipasayin, Sikhin, Vishwabhu, Krakuchchanda followed by Kanakamuni, Kashyap and Maitreya and Dhyani Buddhas.

Mahayana Buddhism is popular in Tibet and Far East. It had 5 Dhyani or Meditating of Buddhas namely (i) Vairochana (white complexion with dragon as his stead) of solar race, popular with Japanese Shingon Sect, (ii) Ratna Sambhava (yellow, wears a jewel, rides a lion and reigns over south), (iii) Amitabh – infinite light, red, holds lotus, escorted by a peacock, reigns over west, presides over paradise, (iv) Amoghasiddhi (green, carries a vajra, vehicle lion, in north region) and (v) Dhyani Bodhisattvas. One, Samantabhadra (green, vehicle elephant, developed in Nepal), has a bearing of good action and symbolizes happiness, two, Vajrapani (Vajra in hand, appears as a Zeus, Eros, Hercules, Pan or Dionysus originally a yaksha, he became a Bodhisattva), three, Ratnapani (jewel in hand), four, Avilokiteshwar – completely enlightened Buddha, also known as Padmapani (Pink lotus in hand), wanders for charity, takes cooling drink to those in hell, converts the ogres of Sri Lanka, preaches law to beings incarnated as insects. He prefers world of suffering to the peace of Nirvana. China has endowed him with the feminine aspect of Queen Kwannon. With a child in arm, the queen resembles Virgin Mary and Jesus. India imagined Avilokiteshwar as a cosmic being with innumerable forms.

There are other Bodhisattvas: (i) Manjushri, venerated in China, (knowm as Panchashirsha, meaning mountain of five peaks or Jhava, patron of grammer and wisdom, portrayed as yellow, seated on blue lion, (ii) Maitreya – sits in heaven (Tushit) and he is Buddha of future. (iii) Kshitijgarbha in central Asia. The Buddhas had shakti – Prajna and Karuna; Tara Vidya or Matrika Devi. Buddhism affected by Tantra had Tara, Kurukul, Chhanda, Marichi, Saraswati, Prajna and Hariti.

Buddha had once declared that escape from sorrow is Nirvana, which is a psychological state of mind; a seeker is released from desire and fear and life becomes harmonious and finds peace. Bodhisattva compassionately participates in other's sorrows. Buddhism travelled and was popular abroad Emperor Ashok's conversion to Buddhism boosted Buddhism and the message of Buddha got wide spread in India and abroad.

Mahayan Buddhism has a large following in China, Taiwan, Tibet, Japan, and Indonesian Archipelago. (The message of Hinduism which had preceded survives in Java.) Sri Lanka, Burma, Thailand and Cambodia. The mythology of the Hinayan sect travelled to South East Asia. Buddhism reached Combodia in 11th Century and Angkor Vata is a living testimony of Avilokiteshwara's serene and compassionate posture with the Vat's far side towers.

China's spiritual history has three main traditions – Confucianism, Daoism (Taoism) and Buddhism. Confucianism and Daoism reach back to 6th Century. Confucius emphasized traditional views – appropriate behavior, modesty, restraint and respect of rituals. Daoism stressed the importance of naturalness and spontaneous living with Das (or way) i.e. the principle of reality. Buddhism reached China after the first century.

The Chinese believed that every person had two souls, besides the soul of dead man who after funeral rituals becomes ancestor and his possessions are remitted to the spirit. (Hired clergy also transfers merit.) They are honored by incense. Dead outside the family may appear as ghosts. According to Daoism, gods, man and Mo are deified forms of individuals. Man is god of literature and patron of civil servants and Mo is the god of martial arts, revered by people. Spirits of rivers and mountains are also worshipped.

The traditions of Confucianism, Daoism and Buddhism comingled and fused with Chinese folk beliefs and practices. Chinese officials criticize people for giving money for religious purposes but showing reluctance to pay taxes to the State.

During the first imperial period (221 BCE) kings performed sacrifices on Mount Tai (Taishan) which bends four other mountains possessing spiritual power. These are connected with certainty and change. Strangely the Chinese also emphasize the past played by the flux of existence and the need to predict it through divination or interpret it through customs and practices like Yin and Yang and five elements. The Chinese revere their monasteries on mountains.

(Yin and Yang represented two opposing but complimentary natural principles. Yin refers to the sunny side of a hill, bright, hard and masculine. Yin is perpetual interaction, dark, soft, feminine. Each of the five elements viz earth, wood, fire, metal and water was associated with a number of correspondences e.g. colours, directions which were connected with Tai and other mountains. A complex interlocking system makes 60 years of Chinese calendrical circle. In a smaller circle of 12 years, each is designated by an animal (e.g. snake, monkey, tiger).

Confucianism has influenced people of Korea and Japan. Confucian thoughts are centered on five classics viz. Vijing, Shijing, Shujing, Li ji, Chin Qin. Confucian resistance to change is poor. Mencius and Yunji elaborated Confucianism. Mencius said seeds of goodness are present in every one but these have to be developed. Yunji said initially people were not good and their immoral behaviour had to be resisted. Confucius once said, unless you know about life, how can you know about death.

(Indian traders and Mahayan monks (of whom Kumarjaiva was the most important) reached China in 2nd CCE).

An interesting incident relates to a Buddhist monk Muhar, who was adviser and confidant to the king of South Korea, Yi Song gye in 1392. The king asked Muhar to choose a site for a new capital. He selected the site where soul now sits. He had decided to select another site, which he was leaving when a farmer berating his ox said, "You are as stupid as Muhak and always going the wrong way." (Muhak means without learning). The perceptive monk enjoyed the pun and recommended the site suggested by the farmers. South Korea also has a large following of Buddhists.

Sri Lanka, Tibet and Burma also have large population of Buddhists. Shinto is popular in Japan. Shinto, which means 'way of the gods', began as a cult of 'Kami' which believed in innumerable deities that inhabited the trees, mountains, rocks, springs and other natural phenomena. The cult fused with the elements of the three 'isms' from the sixth century.

Ninety five percent of Japanese fallow Shintoism. But only 20% of them believe in the existence of Kami, supernatural power. Spirits of great people can become kami or these can be worshipped at home. Shinto consists of two traditions – popular and political. The tradition is for rulers. Shinto has no human founder or divine creator. It has no core text (like Bible) nor a codified system of ethics, though it has deities, rites, shrines and priests. Birth, marriage, funeral are followed on Buddhist lines. People participate in native rites also. The Japanese conduct crufication rites to perpetuate Kami.

The Kami cult originated because of the Chinese threat to Japanese to prove that Japan's emperor had directly descended from Amaterasn, and female Sun Kami from the Kami creator of the entire universe. (Since then the cult is known as Kami.) Buddhism won court patronage and merged with element of Shinto. Rapport between the two religions emerged at metaphysical level. The Kamis were identified as sinful spirits that needed salvation.The Sun Kami was identified with Vairochana. Buddhist temples were in compounds of Shinto shrines and Shinto rites were supervised by Buddhist priests. Later the role of Kami was reversed. Since the Buddhas as Kamis were in foreign dress, new dimensions were added. Shintoism imbibed concept of creation, judgement, heaven, loyalty and filial piety.

The Japanese don't suffer from any inferiority complex about their culture. An American narrated his experience as a member of a Japanese team of scholars visiting Japan. A respected American scholar after visiting a few shrines told a Japanese monk scholar that the sites conducted into a Japanese shrine did not reflect any theology or ideology. Why it was so? The monk replied, "We dance". That was too short, rather curt a reply. But the monk meant no curtness for the guest. He meant that in stead of observing any ideology or theology, the Japanese danced and enjoyed, which was the purpose of religion for the Japanese.

Falcon and Dove

Compassion for creatures is the principal virtue of Buddhists. Of this the story of Falcon and Dove is a telling one. The king of the Sibis was known for his generosity. To test this, once Indra assumed the form of a falcon and pursued a dove. The harried dove took shelter in the king's bosom. The king assured the dove not to fear anyone and added that he protected anyone who sought his protection, even at the cost of his kingdom and his life itself.

The falcon protested, "The dove is my food. You have no right to deprive me of my prey. I am very hungry. Think of me how if I die of hunger. If you protect the bird, give me an equal weight of your body's flesh". The king called for scales and cut off flesh from his thigh and placed it on the scale. The dove was heavier. The king continued to cut off flesh from his body but in vain. In the end he decided to give himself. The gods appeared and expressed their joy. A shower of *amrit* drenched Sibi's body. He was completely healed. Flowers fell from the heaven, Gandharvas and Apsaras danced and sang. Indra announced that the king would next be born in the form of Buddha.

Buddha passes away to Nirvana on couch prepared by disciple Ananda.

JUDAISM

Judaism, the religion of Jews, is one of the oldest religions of the world. Jews claim that they are the children of God, and follow spiritual traditions laid down in the Old Testament, the Holy Bible. Their symbol is 7 - point candelbra. (Prophet Moses authored Torah, first five chapters of Bible. Torah is a book of law which unites people to a covenant with God).

Jews trace their origin from Abraham, their patriarch who migrated from the city of Ur in Mestopotamia to find a new land. A monotheist, he rejected idols and founded a new faith. Hebrew pattern of life is based on pastoral economy. He made a covenant with God who promised them land and Abraham and his progeny would be circumcised. (That is how circumcision came to be a custom. But the promise of the land would elude them for long. Thus arose the concept of the promised land.

The Jews are monotheists. They worship the God as world's creator and follow the code of conduct prescribed in the commandments. They believe that a Messiah from the House of King David will descend and as per Pentateuch (Torah), human beings in partnership with God would complete creation. Jews believe in the immortality of the soul, Day of Judgement, and resurrection.

Jews have their own social practices which they follow right from birth to death. The new born starts with circumcision on the eighth day of his birth. (This is known as Mohel/bat Mitzvah). However, a first born can secure redemption). Next, a Herbrew marriage is a contract which is ready after the ring ceremony. On the occasion a glass is broken which tells the couple that life is full of joys and sorrows and is a reminder of the destruction of Jeruslem. Another event is Passover when Chedar meal is served. Passover is a recall for the Jews from their exodus from Egypt. Jews attach importance to death and abstain from Chedar during mourning rites to perpetuate the belief that death is a part of life. During Schlosim – a 40 day mourning period – mourners abstain from entertainment and fertility. They commemorate holocaust (also called Yom Ha Soa) by holding special services. They chant prayers on Friday and eat Kosher. They have passed their traditions from generation to generation.

The Jews are the most persecuted people. Many denigrating stories show them miser and wicked.

Sherlock is a typical instance. Since they had to make their living amongst different people of other persuations, they had to resort to practices like lending on interest and recovery of the loan without scruples which earned them hatred and bad name. They are also hated by Christians because of betrayal of Christ by a jew for 30 coins. This brought notoriety on the entire Jew community. After wandering for centuries their dream was realized when the new state of Israel was formed.

What suffering the jews underwent is shown in their history. A group of them found shelter in India. On persecution, they left their land and in 175 BCE reached Alibagh on the western coast of India near Bombay. Their descendants call themselves Ben Israelis (Ben means children – they were children of Aaron, brother of Abraham.) There at Ablibagh, they founded a community which they calim remained genetically pure. Another branch of Jews settled at Cochin in Kerala. Cochin has a small but beautiful synagogue. Generally a synagogue has a rabi but Alibagh has no rabi.

The Jews have had a turbulent history. We go back to 2000 years of Christ. In 1700 BCE Israel followed Josef into Egypt ruled by Hyksos kings. They led a peaceful life but on the overthrow of the king, they came under bondage of the new rulers and struggled to maintain their faith. About 250 years later, their leader Moses took them (Israel's children) out of slavery. After exodus from Egypt for four decades, they wandered in the desert and finally reached Cannan. But while reading a farewell address, Moses died. Then under Joshua's leadership they came to Israel, their promised land. They joined Judges, another leader into a confederation. Judges Deborah, Eli and Prophet Samual overcame enemies. But forgetting that they had followed so long a democratic pattern of polity, they looked for a king and appointed Saul (1021-1000 BCE) as the king of Israel. But when Saul quarreled with Samuel, he was replaced by David, who proved a good ruler. He united the tribes, conquered Jebu, authored Psalms. But as he indulged in adultery, he was replaced by his son Soloman who built a national shrine, known after him as Solmon's temple. His merchant fleet achieved successes that induced Queen Sheba to visit him. He died in 922 BCE. Soloman's son Rehoboam who ascended the throne faced a rebellion led by Jeroboam. He united 10 of the 12 tribes and formed a new kingdom consisting of Judah and Benjamin and the city of Jeruslam. In 878 BCE king Omri brought stability to the kingdom and established his capital at Samaria. His son Ahoh married Jezebel a princess of Tyre. As the rulers exploited the poor, Elijeh was annoyed. (We have cited these names as they figure frequently in literature and media).

Israel had three other prophets – Amoh (783-741 BCE), Hosea (774-743 BCE) and Isaiah (742-701 BCE). In 721 BCE Israeli kingdom came to an end after the invasion by Assyrian King Sargon II and deportation of 27000 Israelis from Israel. In 597 BCE the Babylonian King Nebuchandnezzer overran Judah and took many leaders to Babylon. Ten years later in 587 BCE people rebelled against the king of Judah. He was taken prisoner and blinded, and the Temple and Jerusslem were destroyed. In 538 BCE King Cyrus of Persia conquered Babylon and allowed Jews to return to Jeruslem. Led by Ezra, the Scribe and Nehemia, they returned and started rebuilding the temple at Jeruslem. Ezra established the Torah as the constitution of Jewish life. Time and again the temple at Jeruslam was demolished and built.

Then Alexander the Great conquered Palestine and its possession was later controlled by Alexander's successor in Egypt and Seleucus in Syria. Seleucus gained control over Judea. In 167 CE a priest of Hasmonean family rebelled and in 164 BCE liberated the land, despite opposition of the Pharisees. In 63 BCE Pompey intervened and brought Jeruslem under Roman control. He appointed Herod Antipater a pupet as the governor of Jeruslem from 37 to 4 BCE). He enlarged the Temple. After his death the kingdom was divided among his three sons. The city of Jeruslem has changed many hands. The temple was demolished and rebuilt and demolished by kings. That is what makes Jews wail at its wall.

The Jews were severely oppressed by the Romans and they hoped for the coming of a Messiah to lead them to victory over the enemy. In 66 CE the Zealots rose. But in 70th Romans retook Jeruslem and destroyed the temple. They also conquered Masaa, the last Jewish resistance and the Jewish independence came to an end. However, Judaism survived and developed on the Palestine coast. In 68 Zakkai besieged Jeruslem and founded a center which became the new Pharisaic center of Jewish learning. Galilee has continued to be the center of Jewish scholarship.

The Testament refers to several Jewish groups that had erupted. Some of these were :

Pharisees : A dominant people's representative group that arose as a sect after 70 BCE against the Hasmanean family. They created Talmud-oral law-opposed to Torah.

Sadduces : Wealthy aristocrats and priests who backed the Romans in return for their support to the temple cult. They disappeared in 70 BCE when the temple was destroyed by the Romans.

Essenes : A religious following based at Qamaran in the Dead Sea. They led a communal life based on asceticism.

Zealots : Jewish political activists who fought militarily and politically to liberate Judea from Rome.

Kabbalah (tradition) : A branch of Judaism concerned with secret mystic truths developed during Middle Ages.

Scriptures : The Jewish scriptures had become disorganized and these were reorganized by a scriptural authority in three sections : The Torah (Law), the Neviim (Prophets), and the Ketuvin (Writings). These became the Jewish Bible and guided Jewish conduct in future. At the end of the first century the texts were reviewed by an Assembly of Rabbis at Yavneh. While they expressed no doubt about Moses as the author of Torah and its being God's revelation, they made a distinction between the earlier prophets (Joshua, Judges, Samuel and kings) and later prophets (Isiah, Jeremiah and Ezekiel) they included other prophets in the Book of Twelve (namely Hoses, Joel, Amos, Obadiah, Jonab, Micah, Nahum, Habakkuk, Zephamiah, Haggai, Zechariah and Malachi). The Ketuvins include Psalms, Proverbs, Job, Song of Songs, Ruth, Lamentations, Ecclesiastes, Esther, Damiel, Ezra, Nehemiah and Chronicle.

The Torah remained the foundation of Jewish law. Rabbi Jonah, the prince, collected various interpretations into the Misnah in 200 CE. Since then the Babylonian academies of Sura and Pumbeditha prevailed over the Palestinian academies. Later the Jews prospered under the Persian Sesanian rulers. Around 500, a Babylonian rabi named Rav Ashi set a Gemera text, called Talmud, but it failed to get prominence.

The Jews experienced their golden age in Spain after the 8th century when Muslim armies, much to Jewish relief defeated the Christian Gotha who had oppressed the Jewish communities. The Shephardi jews flourished in Spain and Portugal. Among the outstanding Shephardis could be named Samuel Nagid, Vazir and General of Grenada (1022-1070), who authored books 'Royal Crown' and "Fountain of Life", Moses ibn Ezra, (1060-1139), and Yahuda el Levi (1075-1141), a poet influenced by el-Gazali.

The Jewish and Islamic cultures existed harmoniously for sometime but by the time of Moses Mammonoides (1135-1204), Muslim attitude hardened and they became intolerant towards Jews. When Christians took Grenada they expelled many Jews who fled to Netherlands, Turkey and Palestine. With this the golden age of Jews was over and to their misfortune the Synagogue of Taledo was converted into the church of Santa Mariade Blanca. By the Middle Ages, the Jewish Diaspora had become divided into Shephardis (living in Spain, Portugal and Meditarenean world) and Ashkenazin Jews (in Germany, and Central Europe). The Shephardis wrote in Arabic and Ladina while Ashkenazins wrote in Hebrew and spoke Yiddish. They form 70% of the world's Jews. They suffered from feudal system and at the hands of Christian guilds and were forced into money lending and peddling and had to live in ghettos. During crusades they were persecuted and many of them were killed. A false charge of 'ritual murder' about Passover bread was levied against them.

Far sometime they received good treatment in Poland but later they wer expelled from Germany. In 18th Century Elazer founded Hesiadic movement. The Catholics challenged Jews. Martin Luthar King was anti semitic. The Jews found solace in mysticism and hoped King David's descendants would come and create a better world for them.

The Age of Enlightement proved beneficial to Jews in 17th and 18th centuries. Full citizenship came by bits and many had first to convert to Christianity. Some of them did great work. Heinrich Heine (1767-1896) was a great lyric poet. Moses Mandelssohn was a great thinker. Judaism saw a reformation movement in 19th century and by the middle of the century it was well established in UK and USA. (Jews form now a sizeable population in USA.) The story of Judaism continues. Zionism rose after attacks by Christians in Europe. They turned to ancient learning when they said Jeruslem would be rebuilt to Zion and they would return to Israel. But the Dreyfuse affair in France shattered their hope of participation in European life. An Austrian journalist, Theodor Herzxl (1860-1904) founded a movement but it was opposed and Jews suffered. Even so the movement continued. On November 2, 1917 Chaim Weisman (1874-1952), a British scientist and Jewish leader, issued the Balfour Declaration expressing British government's support to the establishment of a national home for Jews in Palestine. In 1919 President Wilson confirmed US's support. Jews migrated in large number in 1939 to Palestine. After World War II, Holocaust ended much of opposition to a Jewish homeland. On November 29, 1949 UN voted to partition Palestine into Arab and Jewish States. (Israel was established on May 14, 1948). The conflict between Israel and Palestine continues and peace has eluded the two people.

CHRISTIANITY

Christianity declares belief in Jesus as Christ, that is divine manifestation of God, come in flesh to destroy incarnate error. Adherents of the belief are Christians.

Jesus' life is full of dramatic events and mysteries. Numerous myths are associated with events from his birth in a manger to death by crucifixion.

Jesus Christ was born a Jew, a descendant, in the family tree of Prophet Abraham – 42nd in generation – 14 from Abraham to David, 14 from David until deportation to Babylon, and 14 from deportation until Jesus became the Messiah. Jesus left behind the old in quest of a new idea.

Emperor Augustus had ordered general registration throughout the Roman empire. In compliance, Josef of Nazareth went with his betroth Mary via Galilee and Judea to Bethelhem. On way he learnt that Mary was pregnant. This upset Josef and he thought of setting aside the marriage quietly to save her reputation. But then an angel appeared to Josef in dream who said, "Don't be afraid of taking home Mary with you as your wife. She has conceived the child by the Holy Spirit and will bear a son and you shall give him the name Jesus (meaning Saviour) for he will save people from their sins.

When Josef and Mary reached Bethehem, they could not find any lodging and the pair stayed in a manger where Mary gave birth to a son. They named him Jesus. An angel of the Lord sang in praise of the God, "Glory to God in the highest heaven, and on earth his peace for men on whom his favour rests". The prayer was heard by some shepherds in the field who came over to see the new born. The child was taken to the temple where visiting Magis made predictions about the child. Apprehending trouble to the child from Herod, the Magis advised David and Mary to leave the place and move to Egypt. The two did as they were advised.

Herod was told that a child who was recently born would bring disaster on him, and to safeguard himself from it, he ordered "kill all children below two." But Herod's design had already been overridden.

Then, an angel appeared before Josef and bid him to leave with family back to Nazareth.

Jesus grew up at Nazareth. He led a conventional life and learned Jewish scriptures. As per their tradition the family went every year for Passover to Jerusalem and returned after the event to Nazareth. Then when he was of the age of 12 and was visiting Jeruslem, Jesus got separated from the family. He passed the time with teachers and familiarized with the place. Josef, after leaving the family at Nazsareth, came to Jeruslem and took back Jesus. Time passed by when Jesus learned of John the Baptist, son of Zacharias. John had received a world of God and was preaching baptism as repentance and forgiveness for sins. He baptized people in the river Jordan, inconsiderate of their pursuits and the baptaized included Pharisees and Seducees. John told them that a son of God was coming and that he would baptize them with Holy Spirit and fire. Sometime later when Jesus approached, John baptized him also.

When Jesus came out of water a voice from heaven said, "This is my son". And when Jesus prayed, the heaven opened and the Holy Spirit descended upon Jesus. The Holy Spirit took Jesus away in the wilderness where the devil tried to tempt him. Jesus fasted for 40 days and was famished. But he failed to deviate Jesus from his path. Then angels appeared and waited on Jesus. He left for Nazareth where he learnt of John's arrest. He left Nazareth for Capernaum and proclaimed "Repent for the Kingdom of Heaven is upon you".

Jesus began baptizing people. He went round Galilee and taught the lay in synagogues. He spread the gospel, his own companion when Jesus baptized were called apostles. When he was 30 his ministry grew. His Charisma cured the ill and infirm and those who were possessed by devils or were suffering from paralysis. He fed the people and performed acts beyond human capacity. Crowds flocked and aura and glamour were thrust on him. Jesus had his share of myths.

Day after day more and more people came to hear him. One day too many people came up. So he went up the hill where from he addressed; the message would become popular as the Sermon on the Mount :

How blest are those who hunger and thrist to see right prevail.
How blest are those who show mercy, mercy shall be shown to them.
How blest are those whose hearts are pure, they shall see God.
How blessed are peace-makers God shall call his sons.
How blessed are those who have suffered persecution for the cause of right.
The kingdom of heaven is theirs.

And the prayer :

Oh father in heaven, They name be hollowed
They Kingdom come, thy will be done
On earth as in heaven, give us today our daily bread.

Forgive us the wrong we have done,
As we have forgiven those who have wronged us.
And don't bring us to the test, But save us from the evil one.

Jesus thought of compassion and not of temple or animal sacrifices.

He said, "There is something greater than the temple". The scripture says, "It is kindness I want, not animal sacrifices". He was away from politics and said, "Don't suppose that I have come to abolish the law and the prophets; I did not come to abolish but to complete. If someone sue you, come to terms with him while you are on way to court; otherwise he may hand you over to the judge, and the judge to the constable, and you will be put in jail. "An eye for an eye and a tooth for a tooth", they say. But I tell you "Don't set yourself against the man who wrongs you. If someone slaps you on the right cheek, turn and offer him your left. If you forgive others the wrongs they have done, your father will also forgive you. No servant can be slave to masters. You cannot serve God and money. Treat others as you would like to be treated. A good tree yields good fruit, and a poor tree a poor. A poor tree cannot bear a good fruit.

Jesus performed many miracles. He touched a man and his leprosy was gone. Issiah seeing many cured said, "He took our illness and lifted our diseases from us." A girl declared dead, got up and walked when Jesus touched her. Two blind men got their eyesight when Jesus touched their eyes. He said, "It happened that way because of their faith". Another man who was dumb got his speech. The sight of the man moved him to pity, they were like sheep without a shepherd, harassed and helpless. The ill were many, so he gave authority to cast out unclean spirits and to cure every kind of ailment to his disciples viz Simon (named Peter), Simon's brother Andrew, James and John (sons of Zebeda), Philip and Bartholomew, Thomas and Mathew (tax gatherers), James (son of Alephens), Libbaes, Simon (Zealot), Judas (son of Simon) Iscariot. Jesus gave them instructions and left the place to teach and preach in the neighboring towns. His action fulfilled the prophecies that Jesus was the son of God who had been expected and was now come. He talked to people in parables which struck them as full of wisdom.

An interesting episode tells about Jesus's feeding crowds without food. One evening his disciples had just five loaves and two fish. Jesus asked to bring whatever food they had. He broke the breads into pieces and asked the disciples to feed people. Five thousand persons ate the food and yet 12 basket full bread pieces were left. Another day boat was not available, Jesus walked on the water and reached the other bank.

Jesus chided Pharisees, and lawyers questioned Jesus why his disciples had broken traditions? When will the Kingdom of God come? He replied, "the kingdom is among you, and that others and not he had broken any law."

One day he with Peter, James and John (James' brother) went up a mountain where in their presence he was transfigured. His face shone like the Sun as he was talking to Moses and Eliah. They were wonder struck (This resembles like Arjuna saw Krishna transfigured.) Jesus's asked them not to tell anyone that he was the Messiah nor about the vision they saw until the Son of Man (as he called himself) had been raised from the dead. When some one questioned him about miracles, he said it was all a matter of faith. Some one told his mother that Jessus was possessed of devil. She with her other sons came to meet him. (This reminds of Buddha's family come to meet him).

At Getsmane he took with him Peter, James and John, asking others to wait. He told the three disciples that his heart was full with grief. Then he prayed, "My father if it is possible, let this cup pass me by. Yet not as I will, but as thou wilt." When he came the disciples were sleeping, Thrice he asked them not to sleep but every time they slept. He told them, "The hour has come. The Son of Man is betrayed to sinful men. Up, let us go, the traitor is upon us".

Judas Iscarios betrayed him for 30 silver coins giving the opponents sign, "The one I kiss is your man, seize him". He had come with a crowd sent by the High Priest Caiaphas. They seized Jesus. One of his disciples struck Caiaphas 'servant with sword and cut off his car. But Jesus told him to put up his sword. "All who take the sword die by sword", he said. Then he touched the ear and the man was healed.

Jesus was put under arrest and led off to the High Priest. Peter followed him, others fled. Lawyers and elders who had assembled at the High Priest's place tried to find some excuse to give jesus a death sentence but they could find none. Finally two men alleged that Jesus had said, 'I can pull down the temple of God in three days and rebuild in three days." Jesus kept silent. The Priest said, "I charge you to tell us; Are you the Messiah, the son of god? " Jesus replied, "The words are yours. You will see the Son of Man coming on the clouds of heaven." The High Priest exclaimed "Blasphemy, He is guilty. He should die." They spat at his face, beat him and made fun of him. When morning came, they put him in chains and took him to the Pilate, the Roman Governor who had power to release one man at Passover.

The crowd insisted that the governor release another man named Jesus Bandar Abbas. It was the Jesus who was released. Sentence of Jesus son of David remained unchanged. (Judas felt remorse at what he had done. He went to the Priests to return the money. When they refused to take it, Judas threw it in the temple. From this money the priests purchased a potters' plot.) The crowd ridiculed Jesus. The soldiers of the Pilate stripped Jesus and dressed him in scarlet mantle, placed a crown of thorns on his head and hit him with a cane, "Hail King of the Jews." They then dressed him in his clothes and led him to be crucified.

On way they took one Simon and pressed him into carrying the cross. At Galgotha (literally it means place of kill), they gave him wine which he did not drink. At 3 it became dark. Jesus cried "Eli Eli lebasaliachthani" My god, My god, why hast thou forsaken me?" Jesus gave a loud cry and breathed his last. There then occurred an earthquake. At 9 they crucified him." With him were crucified two bandits, one on his right and the other on left".

A few women watched all this from a distance. Among them were Mary of Magdala, the mother of James and Josef, and mother of sons of Zebeda. When evening fell, Josef of Armathea, a member of the council and also a disciple of Jesus took the body with Pilate's permission, wrapped it in a clean cloth sheet and laid it in his own unused tomb and rolled a large stone against the entrance. Mary of Magdala and the other Mary were there, sitting opposite the grave. Saturday morning the priest placed a guard lest some deception about resurrection was played. On Sunday morning Mary of Magdala went to the grave. At that time an angel of the Lord appeared. There was earthquake and guards shook with fear.

The angel told the ladies, "Christ is not there. He was raised from the dead and is going on before you to Galilee. There you will see him. The ladies ran to tell the disciples. Suddenly Jesus was there in the path. He told them to tell the disciples to go to Galilee where they will see him. "The guards went to the Chief Priest and reported what had happened. He bribed and asked them to tell, 'His disciples came by night and stole the body, while we were asleep." They took the money and did as they were told. The 11 disciples made their way to Galilee where they saw Jesus who told them, "Full authority in heaven and on earth has been committed to me. Go forth and make all nations my disciples. Baptize men in the name of Father and Son and Holy Spirit and teach them to observe all I commended you."

The versions of Mark and John have minor variations from Mathews. John's version says, "I am the bread of life. Whosoever comes to me shall never be hungry and whoever believes in me shall never be thirsty. Whosoever eats the bread shall never die. The bread I give is my own flesh. I give it for the life of the world. My flesh is real food, my blood is my real drink. Whosoever eats my flesh and drinks my blood dwells continually in me, so I dwell in him. The spirit alone gives life. The flesh is of no avail. The words I have spoken to you are both spirit and life". Saul, initially anit-Christ, became devout Christian. With Barnabas he went to Cypress. The churches were built up throughout Judea, Galilee and Samaria. Peter proved a strong supporter he spread Christianity outwards. Mathias was elected 12th apostle in place of Judas. The word 'Christian' was first used in Antioch. Stephen was selected to consider on religious matters. There were some who played foul – Ananias and his wife Sapphire sold a property but did not give sale money to church, as promised.

Jesus was accused of flouting socio-religious conventions, conflicting with authorities, associating with corroborators, zealots, prostitutes. But this was a false accusation because Jesus was not associated with any of these activities or characters. He was not connected with any political revolution. The fact was that religious and political leaders felt their positions were threatened by Christ's humanitarian acts and so they conspired against him. Mathew and Luke cite many instances of the preaching's of non-violent resistance of Christ. Christ was questioned by priests and Ponteus Pilate. The priests told him that he held contempt for Jews and condemned him of blasphemy and crucifixion, the crueljn death the Roman Justice provided. It is said about the Roman governor that he was reluctant to and could not on facts charge Jesus of a civil offence and condemn him for blasphemy to appease Jewish leaders who demanded death penalty. The gospels say Jesus made no effort to save himself.

The life sketch of Jesus Christ figures in accounts of disciples. John says, "In the beginning was the word, the word was with the God and the word was God. The above account has been excerpted from the Holy Bible. In the modern age the Biblical accounts, life Noah's ARK, woman's creation from man's rib as described in the old Testament, and 'resurrection of Christ's as given in the New Testament lack validity and are regarded by all as myths, except the faithful. For some time Christianity was thought of as a sect of Judaism.

Luke's description that three ladies went to the tomb but found it empty and saw two men in brilliant clothes who explained to them the significance of death of Jesus. When the ladies told this to male disciples, they reacted that the ladies were talking nonsense. The versions of Mathew and Mark differ from his. Their version is that only one young man in white met an angel who asked them to tell the disciple, "He is not here, for he has risen." The church was built on resurrection, which has been celebrated for centuries. It is asserted that he ascended to the heaven. A ten times stronger band played in Jeruslem but without a clear vision of their future nor that Jesus would be the cause of separation of Christianity from Judaism." The separation was caused by the Holy Spirit at the feast of Pentecost in an upper room where the assembled saw tongues of fire on each other and spoke in tongues which filled them with joy. The Christian church with Paul, a Pharisee and Roman citizen, of quick temper and a central figure, detached itself from Judaism as he had gained faith in Jesus Christ, which revolutionized the course of Christianity. Paul was convinced that the Christian gospel was meant by God for all humanity which brought him in conflict with those Christians who insisted on maintaining purity of Judaism and its law, and insisted that Paul be first circumcised before he could join the Christian sect of Judaism.

Paul had thought of the death of Jesus on cross, and of its significance, as also of the significance of his memorial (of Jesus' body and blood) as representing sharing in wine and bread in the Eucharist. He undertook four journeys on Christian Mission during which he established Christian Churches in Asia Minor. Many became Paul's enemies, particularly in Jerusalem and Corinth. Through his epistles Paul had prepared some standard literature on Christ's life required to inform people, Mathew, Luke, Mark and John used gospels for preparing people for Christianity. The Pastoral Epistles 1 and 2 Timothy and Titus present their own problems. Jesus did not come the second time, as was expected. He was once called the Lamb of God, in which form he revealed himself to John. (Jesus was the sacrificial lamb killed by Jews at Passover.) After this came up compilation of other texts – sermons. Along with letters, threat of Gnostics (who relied on secret knowledge for salvation), challenge to heretics, the material led to the compilation of New Testament.

Now Gospel prepares man for his journey. John the Baptist had announced : the Messiah, that is Jesus has come to usher a new heaven on earth. Man should prepare for the journey with Christ to the Kingdom of God and an eternal life. You need a map, mirror, trash bag for the way, besides the creed of the church, hymns and theoligician's teachings.

Jesus Christ is criticized unfairly on many counts. One of these is that his followers came from the lowest classes of society and that it was a movement of the poor and homeless against the rich and propertied. For instance, Celsus said, the first Christians were 'slaves' women and children', the society's weak and illiterate. This is unfair because those referred to as poor, like Philoman, Barnabas and Timothy were not poor. Apphia (Philoman's wife) and Joanna (Steward Chuza's wife) who helped the early Christians were adults of means. John asked for help of Jerusalem's poor. It is irrefutable that those who took to Christianity came from various strata of society from cross sections and social levels. Of course slaves too joined. These social levels mixed in congregations, yet it is a pity that Christians later supported slavery.

During the Middle Ages the restoration of Christ to immortality was equated with tree of immortal life and the fruit of the tree was the crucified saviour who offered his flesh and blood to the mankind meat and drink. In this perspective mythology of Christ and Christianity is the poetic expression of 'transcendental seeing'.

The Christian tradition has four features viz. initiation, worship, ministry and good work. (Teaching scriptures is also a feature). The worship comprises of four parts – adoration, confession, thanks giving and intercession. Scriptures tell about preparation for baptism, repentance, forgiving and forgetting. Baptism is initiation (rite) into community, through which one comes out clear of morality, washing away his sins. Repentance is change of heart. Initiation is rebirth. Repentance brings joy and more joy comes when one forgives and forgets others. Do unto others what God has done to you. If a man does not repent, bitterness enters into heart. 'Forget and forgive' leads to peace and joy. John brought the good news that God, after estrangement, had come back to us and asked us to start life again. We will discharge garbage of the past and the road will lead to rebirth. The central act of Christian worship is Eucharist i.e. Holy communion or Mass.

The Christian trinity has three elements – God, people, matter. God, the Father, is the supreme self, primal matter is mother and infinitismal sons are matter. In the biological sense, He is neither father nor mother. He is neither born nor will he die. The son's capacity extends to know, to do and to enjoy, and in these respects, Father is infinite. The soul's limited dimensions, however, incapacitate him (the self) from acquiring true knowledge. The result is sinful behaviour, and man is part of sin, whereas god is infinite, perfect and free from sin. He is incarnated but does not assume body form.

Christianity in India is ages old – it is associated with St. Thomas and Assyrian Christians. The tomb of St. Thomas in Chennai (Madras, in South India) reminds of the Saint's arrival and reception in India. The Assyrian Christians, like the Jews, were a persecuted people and they found shelter in South India where their church flourished and South India has a sizeable Christian population. For two millennia they have been living peacefully (except for cruelty to locals for forcible conversion by Vasco da Gama's successors in Western Coast). However Christian missionaries unfortunately are vitiating the peaceful communal atmosphere by indulging in conversion. Christians have occupied the highest offices of the land, including Chief Ministers, Ministers in the Central and State Governments, Judges of the Supreme and High Courts. School and hospitals run by missionaries do yeomen work which speaks well about Christianity – not forcible conversion). They (aliens) can also help India by keeping off indulgence in the politics of States of Nagaland and Mizoram in the eastern part of India.

Jesus had ushered in a new religion, a new way of life and a new age. He was acknowledged as Christ, and was called Jesus Christ, that is a divine manifestation – Son of God. Some Jews thought the idea of Jesus Christ was an extension of Judaism, and Christianity an off shoot of the old religion-Judaism. But Christianity separated from Judaism and became a religion on its own when the apostles differentiated between the two, specially because of crucifixion of Jesus. The death of Jesus Christ was neither a penalty nor a ransom. Devout Christians treat the separation of the two from the time Jesus went into silence before the case was heard and he was crucified, and before Adam and Eve committed a sin in the Garden of Eden motivated by the devil and later atoned for it. It is said that God offered his son Jesus to the devil for redemption. Pope Gregory said that crucifixion was a bait to the devil. Analyst Abeland thought that crucifixion evoked compassion for the suffering and shifted man's mind from blind commitment to the good of the world. This turned man's compassion for the injured Christ who became Christ the Saviour.

In our view the importance of Christ lay in historical perspective and we need revert to the Holy Bible. The Pentateuch's Yahveh is a fearsome spirit, flaming up often in jealous wrath and commenting the slaughter of man, woman, child and beast whenever his wrath is aroused. The conception of the Holy one who loves mercy rather than sacrifice, who abominates burnt offerings, who reveals himself to those who yearn to him asserts itself in the writings of Isiah and Hosea. In the revolution of Jesus we have the conception of God as perfect love. The name 'Yahveh' is the common link.

It is difficult to reconcile superstitious practices involving spells and magic with Christianity. Hunting women for witches was savagery. Conversions too is a malpractice that does not go well with religion. Hindu converts to Christianity and Islam frequently turn to Hindu gods in cases of trouble, sickness, dread of death, of ghost. The intolerance of monotheism has caused a lot of bloodshed. One of the earliest instances is that of the tribes of Israel that burst into the land of Cannan. The worshippers of one Jealous god are egged on to aggressive wars against people of alien cults, and with divine sanctions inflict cruelties on the conquered. That spirit of old Israel is inherited by Christianity and Israel and Islam.

In 1448 Vasco de Gama reached Calicut. Followed Portuguese, Spaniard, English, French, Danes and others. India under Mughal had stabilized its security. But at the time of Aurangzeb it got weakened. The Western nations had developed weapons with the help of technology and now India could not face the challenge of European's might and machinations and the country fell to the European traders. After 1857 the British became masters. The British quit India in 1947. The work of some of the Christian missionaries has improved the life of some Indians.

Jesus' life shows that future is because of the past, death is followed by birth then, death. Contemplation of cross is the contemplation of symbol of life's mystery.

ISLAM

Islam, a monotheistic religion based on teachings of Prophet Mohammed, originated in Arabia. Literally, Islam means submission to God, Allah. Islam's body of law is contained in the Kuran and Sunna. Followers of Islam are known as Muslims. The modernized Muslims equate Islam with peace. Such an equation does not convince others because Islamic history is submerged in voilence and terrorism though there is much to applaud Islamic contribution to the progress of humanity. As for the present they have gone astray. Suicide bombing is the most inhuman and nefarious thing one can think of.

Islam, Christianity and Judaism came often in conflict in the past, Muslims term the conflict civilizational clashes. The Muslim clerics analyze their weaknesses and failures and find fault in their deviation from the religious teachings and they stress the necessity of revival of the golden age of Prophet Mohammed.

Muslims and their religion have been immensely influenced by the Prophet's life and they are very sensitive even to a minor critical reference to Mohammed by non-Muslims. Muslims like Rushdie fear for their life and dare make no more comments. Mohammed's life serves as a role model and ups and downs in the prophet's life bear influence on their own course of action in varied situations.

Mohammed was born posthumous son of Abdullah and Amina around 570 CE in the Quraish tribe at Mecca in Saudi Arabia. Mother Amina died when the child was only six days old. Then it fell on grandfather to bring up the child. But misfortune did not spare and the grand father died when Mohammed was six years old. The responsibility now fell on uncle Abu Talib, head of Hashmite Quraishi clan who was also responsible for the shrine at Mecca. Under the circumstances Mohammed could not receive formal education. However, he managed a job connected with carvans for a lady, Kahadija, whom he later married at the age of 25.

In the 6th Century people in Arabia practiced an animistic – naturalistic religion. They worshipped as many as 50 gods and goddesses, stone idols and trees, and thought the world was peopled by Jinn, elves. Important among their deities were Minat, El Lot, Havlas, El Mukun, Athan, Rahat, Chan ul Kaun. Tribes had idols of Wad, Sowa, Yughul,

Yank, Nasr (vulture), El Yazza, Kareshis, Kozah, Isaf and Nala. Intra-tribal rivalries fouled the atmosphere. This affected Mohammed, and to avoid these he frequented caves of Mt. Hira to meditate. In 610 he had a vision of Angel Gabriel, "Recite in the name of the Lord who created man of a blood-clot." (Kuran, it may be mentioned, is the final word of Allah for Muslims.) The command was followed by revelations which Mohammed codified but the Meccans paid no hreed to these, although visitors from nearby places, including Yathrib (Medina) became Mohammed's followers.

Disturbed by the people of Mecca, Mohammed went to Medina in 622. This visit is called Hijra and from it began Muslim calendar. At Medina, Mohammed became the ruler of a spiritual and temporal movement and consolidated the community. In 634 he won a victory over the Meccans at Badr. Even so the Meccans did not accept the authority of Mohammed, and a conflict developed with Abu Sufiyan, who got aid from local Jews. In 628 Mohammed and his opponents made a truce (treaty of Huday Biyyah) but it did not last long as the Muslims demolished their opponent's idols and shrines. Mohammed returned to Medina where he promulgated a constitution to regulate relations amongst Muslim communities. Then by treaties and threats and force, he extended his control over Arabia. After his last pilgrimage, he died on June 8, 632 without nominating his successor.

Islam is based on five main pillars, namely Shahada, Salah, Zakat, Sawn, and Hajj (from Mecca to Mt. Mercy (On Arafat), Muzdalifa, Mina ti Mecca.) Shahada – There is no god but God and Mohammed is his prophet.

In addition to these pillars, Muslims believe in Jihad which means that Shahada : a holy war can take forms like learning, good work and self control. But it appears the term had been misinterpreted to cover violence against injustice done by non-Muslims. One Sura 9:29 says, "Fight against those who believe not in God and the Last Day and do not forbid what God and his Messenger have forbidden – such men as practice not the religion of truth, being of those who have been given the Book – until they pay tribute out of hand and have been humbled." Two, Sura 9:36 prescribes, "Fight the unbelievers totally even as they fight you totally; and know that God is with the God-fearing." Three, Sura 2 Verse 216 prescribes Jihad as every adult Muslim's duty to fight in the cause of truth. Add to this the Muslim belief that dar-ul-Islam (i.e. territory of Islam) is dar-ul-harb (i.e. territory of war). Mohammed said, "I am commanded to fight until men bear witness" to Shahada. (There is no god but Got and Mohammed is his prophet.) From this it is inferred that Mohammed gave his seal to Jihad in his campaign to gain control over Mecca. This creates problems because to extract such a realization from non-Muslims, a Muslim ruler had to undertake a campaign against them. 2 Salah : to say five prayers a day facing towards Mecca – at dawn, noon, mid afternoon, evening and night – on all days including Friday – preceded by wudud (purity of body). 3 Zakat (or Sadqa) – giving alms voluntarily from personal income. 4 Sawn (to foster) obedience to God and unity among Muslims. All adults except pregnant women should fast during Ramadan (29/30 days) and during the period they should recite Kuran every day. (Lailat ul Qadr – the night of power – when Kuran was revealed to Mohammed is important). Ramadan ends with Id-ul-Fitr, the first day of Sawwal (new 10th month) when fast is broken. Muslims exchange presents, visit friends and relatives and say special praiyers at the mosque. 5 Hajj : Every Muslim who can afford expects to go on pilgrimage to Mecca once in his/her life time. The pilgrim walks around Kaaba anti-clock wise seven times. Its foundation was laid by Adam and it was restored by Abraham. Around the Kaaba are buried many prophets. It was a polytheistic shrine and had innumerable statues of gods, it was said.

The pilgrim starts from Mecca goes to Mt. Mercy on the plain of Arafat and meditates there from noon until sunset. Then he returns to Mecca via Muzdalifa and Mina. The drill consists of (i) Going around Kaaba seven times, (ii) Running between al-Sufa-al Mas seven times. (Abraham left his wife Hagar and son Ismael at Maus. She ran up for water until she discovered the well of Zamzam). (iii) Five mile walk to Mina. (iv) Ten - mile journey to the plain Arafat. Spends day in meditation and searches for 49 stones. (v) Five - mile hike to Muzdailfa. (vi) Return to Mina and throw stones at three pillars. Isamael had stoned Shaitan who tempted him to disobey Abraham. (vii) Return to Mecca. Pilgrimage ends with Eid-ul-Huda when an animal is sacrificed in rememberance of Abraham's faith in God's advice to sacrifice son Ismael (not Isaac, as some non-Muslims say) who was substituted by a sheep. In the end have a final walk of Kaaba lead one campaign against "infidels" and Muslims believe that martyrs to the cause of Islam go to heaven directly. In the recent past in stead of fighting against injustice, the Jihadists have inflicted injustice in the name of jihad against innocent men, women and children and all those who differed from them. Practically every Muslim country has been plagued with Jihadists. The incidents of 9/11 of 2001 were caused by Jihadists. They destroyed World Trade Center and affected Pentagon buildings, besides killing 3000 people by hijacking and hitting aeroplanes.

Nothing would approve such a ghastly act. Neither the Islamic way of war (as revealed in Kuran) nor the Hadith encompass total destruction of the enemy. History provides such ghastly acts by the Mongols of Changez Khan in the 13th century who rampaged through Iran, Iraq and Afghanistan, destroyed the water systems, rendering Central Asia into a desert. Afterwards Tamerlane visited destruction to the area. In 1522 Babur's conquests followed the same bloody template of his ancestors. Likewise the Bedouins carried out desert war – a series of raids for livestock's, booty or women.

The 9/11 incident erases from our mind that ethnically and culturally Arabs were different from the Mongols. They donot differ from the descendants of Changez Khan who indulged in barbarity.

Judaism, Christianity and Islam, originated in Middle East and claim to be revealed, through part of Old and New Testament and Koran, respectively the revelations were made to prophets. Angels guard the gates of heaven and hell. Shaitan is the chief of fallen angels. Angels record thoughts and actions of individuals. Angels Munkar and Nakir interrogate individuals and place a book on the right hand of the righteous who go to paradise guarded by Rizwan. Malik is in charge of hell. Every one will be judged on The Day of Judgment.

Arabs claim to be from the seed of Abraham Mohammed had welded the desperate Arab tribes into unity. With religious inspiration, aggressive ideology and military discipline, they – the Arabs – developed into a famidable force and within two decades they defeated the strongest rulers of the times – the Byzantines and the Sassanids.

Kuran for Muslims is the completion of God's message and the culmination of sacred scriptures. It regulates all aspects of Muslim life. Divided into Suras (chapters), it addresses subjects like oneness of God, need for man to thank God and obey him, God's role (part) in history – from creation to the end of the world and Day of Judgement. The revelations exist in heaven and were piecemeal revealed to Mohammed in Mecca and Medina but the Kuran was not finalized by the time of Mohammed's death in 632. On the prophet's death dispute of succession arose. Abu Bakr had begun the work of collecting revelations and the collection work continued under Caliph Umar. Collection at different periods resulted in divergent versions. Finally caliph Usman ruled what was authentic or otherwise. To Usman goes the credit of finalizing the scripture.

Muslims believe that whatever is in Kuran is revelation by Allah and is true. Mohammed had stressed the authority of Sunna consensus but after a few centuries it cracked down. The revelations clash with the scientific view about creation of world and creator. The Muslim Koranic view led to a stand still of Islamic science from 11th century. Many myths have been created about symbols. To cite one. Aralha, an Abyssynian general swore to demolish Kaaba. But his elephant would not budge. Ultimately his army left and the soldiers were hotly pursued by birds throwing stones on the fleeing soldiers. Mecca and Medina are two sacred places and their glory has been described in two epics. Muslim hero's exploits figure therein.

After Mohammed's death in 632,, the question of his succession arose. The Quraish installed Abu Baker, Mohammed's father-in-law as Caliph. He called himself Commander of the Faithful and reigned for two years (632-634). He quelled discontent among Muslims and extended the frontiers to Syria Egypt and Iran. He was assassinated by a Persian slave. He was succeeded by Usman of the Ummayyad clan or election by six companions of Mohammed. He founded the first Islmic dynasty of Ummayyads. Usman was authoritarian and was accused of misappropriation. He was assassinated by Muslims of Iraqi and Egyptians garrisons. This caused violence and Shia-Sunni division. Usman was succeeded by Ali. Aisha opposed his succession. He exiled her to Medina and moved the Caliphate to Kufr in Iraq. Ali won the battle of Suffir but agreed to put his claim to Caliphate to arbitration. This angered Ali's supporters who formed their command as Khajites. They conspired and assassinated Ali in 661. (Succession amongst Muslim is full of violence. After Mohammed's death, three Caliphs were successively assassinated).

After Ali Mawaiya became Caliph (from 661-680). He reigned from Damascus and established his own dynasty. (Hasan and Hussain (of Ali's family) staged a revolution but they were defeated at Karbala). The Muwaiyas expanded their power westward to Spain. They routed Zorostrian and Byzantine forces and annexed Libya, Egypt, Palestine, Syria, Iraq, most of Persia, Morocco and Spain. In 717 they captured Armenia but failed to take Constantinople in their effects between 717-778. In the east they marched across Caucacus, captured Sindh (an Indian province) and marched upto borders of China. The Islamic army fell short manpower. This shortage was met after 700 by converts from Persians, Berbers and Turkish people though they allowed Christians and Jews to retain their religion, subject to the payment of Jizya (Poll tax). The Islamic Army had committed several cruelties on people. To assuage their feelings they revived arts and poetry.

The last Umayyad caliph, Marwan II was assassinated by the Abbasids who stressed more on religion than race. They ruled for 500 years. The army was more mixed and Islam was open to non-Arab philosophy, literature and architecture. Khalifa al Mamun opened a House of Knowledge in Baghdad and built observatories. Al Azhar university was set up in Cairo in 970. Harun al Rashid set up inquisitional tribunals to enforce orthodoxy and Jihad and stressed Caliph's spiritual authority. The Abbasid reign produced great thinkers like Ibn Sina, Ibn Rashid. The disintegration of the empire started by military coups by Turkish troops who deposed Caliphs one after the other and it came to an end in 1258. A rival military-based Buyid dynasty came up. They too did not last long and were replaced by Seljuks, who established an Islamic state which lasted 150 years.

Elsewhere too, rival Caliphates came up in Tunisia and Egypt. The Sevener Ismails ruled, one of whom developed a sect, known as Assassins in Syria. Their downfall came at the hands of Mongols in 13th century. There arose other dynasties – Charmarthians (central and eastern Arabia). Ghazanvids (Turkish led), Almomids, Berbers, Almahadas (in Morocco), Umayads (Spain). Mongols assailed the Islamic empire. In 1258 Halagu sacked Baghdad. The Mamluks of Syria ruled Egypt. From the Mongols arose Khamid dynasty (1162-1227). Halagu's great grandson Mahmud Ghazani (1295-1304) was the first Il Khan (ruler) to covnert to Islam. Tamerlane built a vast empire.

Ibn Batuta, a Moroccan traveller mentions that Muslims were living in Central Asia (14th century). This region was annexed in Russian empire. Only in early 1990s Muslim States of Uzbekistan, Kazakistan, Tajakistan, Kirgizia, Turkmenistan and Azerbeijan have emerged. Islam came as a victor armed with swords. Monotheism was not unknown to India.

The Mughal forces under Babur defeated the Indian forces of Ibrahim Lodi in 1526 and carved out an empire in northern India. The downfall of Mughal empire came because of Aurangzeb's intolerance. The Muslims found themselves as cosufferers with Hindus. By policy of divide rule, the British who took over ruled upto 1947 when they left after partition of the country carving out a Muslim State of Pakistan. Not only that they bolstered religions fanaticism in Pakistan.

Muslims are divided into two main sects – Sunnis and Shiyas. Both believe in Kuran and Hadith but differ in their interpretation of Kuran, history and authority. Sunnis deny succession by progeny (e.g. of Ali son-in-law of Mohammed).

Today about one fifth population of the world follows Islam. Of this one-third is in Bangladesh, India and Pakistan, another third in Middle East and Africa, and the rest one-third is in South East Asia and Central Asia. There are racial differences among Muslims. North Africa has Berbers, Turkey and Asian Republics have Turk Muslims, the Muslims of India, Africa, Chinese, Turkistan, Afghanistan and Pakistan are of Indo-Aryan descent.

Technological advancement has raised a dilemma for Islam - whether or not to embrace these advancements which pose threat to their traditional cultures. Should they come to terms with these or impose a total Islamic way of life on people? There are instances where countries adopted what soever suited them. For instance, Turkey and Tunisia separated religion from politics. Saudi Arabia and Gulf States supported Islamic institutions though they have alliances with west. (The 9/11 episode in USA has exposed the hollowness of Muslim communities in US and Western Europe. The British Muslims demonstrated against

Salman Rushdie for his secular writings *The Satanic Verses* and showed how difficult it is for Islam to coexist with liberal and secular societies).

Afghanistan and Iran experienced religious turmoil and highly charged rhetoric against West. The last three decades of 20th century showed that moderation is alien to most of the Muslim world. Radical fundamentalist groups are now active wherever there are Muslims. Immigrant Muslims are influenced by customs and values of their homelands, though they feel the need of democracy and secularism.

Of the Muslim countries, Indonesia has the largest Muslim population. Islam was brought to Indonesia in the 11th century by Indian traders. In 15th century Java was the first state to adopt Islam. By the end of 20th century 90% of Indonesian population is Muslim. Surprisingly Java has even today a Hindu minority. From Indonesia, Islam spread to Malaysia. In Indonesia and Malaysia Islam was combined with native cultures but terrorism has changed the cultural complexion as also the liberal attitude of their people.

Turkey under Ottoman rule developed in the second half of 15th century into a great power. Sub Sahara Africa has a number of Muslim nations like Mauritania, Senegal, Mali, Nigeria, Sudan, Ethiopia, Tanzania, Dgibouti, Somalia, etc. Arab and Persian traders reached China in 8th century and gradually they became integrated into the Chinese way of life through intermarriages. Muslim influence grew in China when Mongols opened routes from Central Asia. They settled in Yunan and Gansu. Upto 18th century they lived peacefully but in the 19th century Muslim insurrections incited (or inspired) by the Naksbandis occurred. The government has no alternative but to quell through force. Muslims in Xinxiang province of China are creating a problem for China.

Surah 5:48 of Kuran says, "To every one we have given a law and a way. And, if God was pleased, he would have made you all one people. But he has done otherwise, that he might try you in that which he hath severally given unto you, where fore press forward in good works. Unto God shall ye return, and he will tell you that concerning which ye disagree."

In 10th century India was fragmented in to kingdoms which indulged in internal strife. They failed, because of lack of unity, to meet the onslaught of Turks and Mongols who tried to convert Hindus to Islam. But despite temptation and force they could convert only a small section number of people.

Crusades :

The Muslims had differences with Christians and tried to settle these by arms. The Seljuk Turks defeated the Byzentine force at Manjikot in 1071.

The Byzentine emperor appealed to the Pope and the other West European Christian rulers for help leading to crusades beginning 1096. (4th Crusade took place in 1204). The crusades continued for two centuries. Though Muslims were defeated, they gradually regained all lost land. In 1291 crusading States fell to Muslims. Islam spread to Central Asia. When Mongols advanced, Seljuks could not stand upto them and were defeated. But the Alhmounds were forced to withdraw from Spain in 1225 and Christians subjugated all Muslim kingdoms. By the edict of 1614 Islamic Spain come to an end.

Eight forms of Padmasambhava who built the first Buddhist monastery in Tibet. Earlier effort to erect buildings there had failed as the demons would tear down the building under construction.

PARSI

Some historians say that the people of Aryan stock emigrated from central/eastern Europe. One of their groups found their way towards Greece. Another found its way to Parse (Iran) and some continued moving on till they reached Indus.

Those Aryans who stayed over in Parse became known as Parsis. The Persian kings created a vast empire and fought battles with the Greeks on the west and with Hindus (Indians) on the east. The Parsis followed Zorostrian religion, so known after the Parsi Chief Priest, Zoroster who was opposed to Devas and worshipped Asuras, Devil gods.

Zoroster at 13 begged Ahur Mazda to educate him how a man could practice righteousness for his pure existence. Then a miracle happened. The Wise Lord appeared to Ahur Mazda and told him what they had to do to purify mankind before the end of the time of long dominion. Ahur Mazda lit with fire the way of Truth man must follow if he does not succumb to Lie. So Zorastrians light the sacred fire in a dark place, while the men chanted, "When all men become of one voice and praise the Wise Lord with a loud voice and at the same time he will have brought the creation to its consummation, and there will be no further work he need do."

When the father of Darius Kshatrap of Bactria was on way to Susa (Iran's capital), the Turanians invaded. They slaughtered people while Zoroster was saying his last prayer :

> This I ask Thee, O Lord, answer me truly
>
> Who among these whom I speak is righteous and who is wicked
>
> Which of the two? Am I evil myself or is he the evil one who would wickedly keep me far from the salvation? How should I not think him the wicked one.?

As Zorster bowed, the Turanians assassinated him. Of course they were in no time taken captives and impaled on sharpened stakes.

Zoroster said at the beginning there was fire and all creation seemed to be aflame. He drank Hoama (soma) and the world looked ethereal and as luminous as the fire itself that blazed the altar. Iranian history describes that Zorastrianism was founded 3000 years ago. It was followed by the Achaeminian, Parthian and Sassanian kings. A winged disk represents Ahur Mazda. The Parsis believe in Amesha, Spentax (which with Mainyu – holy spirit – are linked with God's creation.) Ahur Mazda heaven and hell (reached after crossing bridge), coming of a saviour, resurrection of the dead, last judgement of the soul, after life. Zoroster told Ahirman – neither our thoughts nor deeds nor conscience or soul agree. In the end Zoroster will defeat Ahirman.

The zorastrian teachings were first written during the Sassanian times (224-651 CE) in 21 books in an inverted alphabet-different from Avesta. These books except Avesta were destroyed during the Arab, Turkish and Mongol invasions. Some literature in Pallavi was saved. This is mostly anonymous. The gathas are short inspired utterances and philosophic works.

Iranian power was ancient. They were great fighters. Cyrus the great conquered the Medes at the battle of Pasargade in 549 BC. Two years later he led his subjects to victory, at Sardis over Croesus, King of Lydia. After a long siege, in 539 BC, Babylon capitulated. In 530 BC he died in a battle against Sythians. Alexander defeated Darius III at Gangamela in 331 BC.

The Aryans of Persia followed the mythology of Ahur Mazda, the creator. But Angra Mainyu, an evil power of darkness and deception infused evils into it. Consequently there is a continuing conflict in the powers of light and darkness, truth and deception. These are cosmic powers and each individual will align with one of these. He would contribute his thoughts, words and deeds to restore the world to perfection. There will in the end be ways when Saviour Sao Shyant will come. Angra Mainyu will lose and the purified will be released and peace will prevail for ever.

The Parsis who came to India brought their faith with them. That is a story worth telling. The Arabs invaded Persia and they supplanted Islam in place of Zorostrianism. Those who resisted conversion were put to sword. A small group of Zorostrians escaped in boats and landed at Sanjana, near Bombay. At Sanjana they asked the ruler for permission to settle down there. In reply the ruler sent a bowl of water, which the Parsis returned after symbolically mixing some sugar. The ruler took it in right spirit which was that the Parsis will mix with Indians like a sweetener, and would practice their religion without creating any problem for local people. The Parsis have ever kept their words. For sometime they maintained contact with Iran's Parsis and their replies to quarries, including rituals, are recorded in Rivayats.

Initially the immigrant Parsis began life as farmers and traders. Later they took to business and prospered. After the advent of Europeans they developed into a wealthy community, and the Tatas, one of them, were the wealthiest family of India.

Parsis keep fire burning in their hearth and wear Kusti (cord) like the Janeoo Hindus do. The legend is that fire represents ash i.e. truth and righteousness. They pray before their hearth fire on which they could focus with the help of sun or moon. They avoid pollution and pray before a light only after ablution and only thereafter conduct religious ceremony. They untie and retie Kusti. It is passed three times around the waist over a shirt. The Parsi priests perform Yasna etc. (rituals) and recite gathas or other texts. (The priests go to retreat for nine days for purification before engaging in rites). Outdoor rituals can be performed in any clean place. When the ceremony is over, people partake Malido and Darun, and fruits.

Parsis have seven days which are obligatory. There are other holidays – one for water, one for fire when they offer sandalwood to temple fire. Earlier, women used to segregate during menstruation and child birth for 40 days.

Parsis expose their dead to birds of prey in *dakhmas* (i.e. towers of silence).

Worship of fire is common amongst Parsis and Hindus. The very first Shloka in Rig-Veda is devoted to Agni (i.e. fire) and sacred fire symbolizes Zorastrianism. Parsis (and Medes) had hereditary priests known as Magis, just as the Brahmins are the hereditary priests of Hindus. (Brahmin is a caste). The Magians workshipped Devas – Anahita and Mitra – and drank Hoama (soama). Zoraster defied the Magians and Zoroastrians were victors over devil worshippers.

The Parsis are a small community of a hundred thousand people and inner breeding among them is causing serious genetic as well as social problems. They are conscious of these problems as their aim has always been to live a good life. Many have migrated to USA. US Parsis are building a temple near Washington.

BABRI MOSQUE
RAM JANAM BHUMI

> "If I were a Muslim, I would tell my brethren: A certain group believes, and genuinely believes, that its God was born at this particular spot. I may not agree with that belief. If no saint of mine, nor my God was born at that spot, I would say give the land to them."
>
> -Fali Nariman M.P.

SIKH

The basic tenets of Sikhism are : There is only one God and one humanity. Sikhs do not believe in casteist division of society. Search for God within yourself. Good deeds give you freedom from rebirth. Guru Granth Sahib is the cornerstone of Sikh faith.

The Sikh faith was founded by Nanak (1469-1539). His spiritual message had three aspects : meditation, honest toil, and alms-giving. Meditation in Sikhism means chanting hymns; it is not a yogic step. Guru Nanak preached his message widely – beyond the confines of India. He was concerned about social injustic and condemned Mughal emperor Babur for sacking the town of Saidpur.

Sikhs had 10 gurus. The first was Guru Nank and the tenth was Guru Govind Singh (1666-1708). While Guru Nanak was peaceful, Gobind Singh took to arms in the defense of religion. He armed his followers to fight against the injustice of Mughal emperor Aurangzeb. He taught them to use force against assailants for defense purposes and never against non-combatants. It should be a *dharma-ydha*. The Mughal had treated Guru Teg Bahdur and other gurus barbarously and cruelly. Guru Tegh Bahadur and his two sons were hooked alive. Guru Arjan Singh (1563-1606) compiled guru granth sahib and the community was to live by its teachings.

Guru Gobind Singh was the tenth guru. He conferred guruship on the Guru Granth Sahib and community and declared there would be no more human guru to lead the Sikhs. The Panth was to live by their teachings. He had in view that God is the Guru of Gurus – truth lies in his voice in the message, not in human personality of any of the 10 historical gurus. Sikhs bow to the granth Sahib because of the word it contains. There have been temporal Gurus, the most important of them was Maharaja Ranjit Singh (1780-1839) who established a large state of Punjab. (Guru Granth Sahib is essential in naming, marriage and initiation of ceremonies, as well as in worship. It is recited reverentially before weddings, funerals, *Grah Pravesh* etc.

Two important movements viz. Nirankari and Namdhari have emerged from Sikhism.

BOOK V

13

SELECTED MYTHS

CASTE SYSTEM : A Necessary Disgrace

'Aap Ka Nam'?, 'Aap Kaun Jat?' (What is your name? What is your caste?). These questions posed to a stranger evoke responses that convey personal information about the respondent. His replies to the question consist of proper name, father's name and end name (also known as 'Sir' name). For instance, Mohandas Karamchand Gandhi. Mohandas was proper name, Karamchand father's name and Gandhi, the last name is caste name. There are regional variations. In Maharashtra the last name, say Punekar stands for the native place. Punekar indicates he originally hailed from Pune. In South India, Aiyer/Ayangar etc. the last part of the name indicates the caste. In the Hindi belt and eastern-India end name such as Sharma/Singh/Gupta/Verma/Banerjee/Sinha indicates the caste. In some cases the end name may tell the person's vocation like Saraf, Manihar, Soni, Patel.

The second querry 'Aap kaun jat?' is responded by a title or caste that shows the person's social standing or place in the hierarchy. Sometime this serves a useful purpose. May be the questioner and respondent belong to the same caste and the two might find some existing relationship between them.

Independence of the country and improvement in people's financial conditions have made no difference in the rigidity of caste system. At best in metropolitan and big cities intracaste and interstate (provincial) marriages in small number do take place. People of Punjab and some army men have shown more flexibility in negotiating martial relations. But caste system prevails over suitability for the boy and girl. The first preference of even advanced and literal people is to find a match from their own caste.

In the Vedic times professions and occupations decided the caste of human beings. Perhaps this system had some logic behind it. Proficiency and skilled workmanship were appreciated by persons engaged in the same type of work which brought them closer. The Purusha Sukta of Rig Veda divided the society in four parts, but the division was on equal basis and without any differentiation. It did not accord them lower or higher social status. Brahmins, Kshatriyas, Vaishyas and Shudras could intermarry /interdine with each other. Social changes crept in between them later, which the Dwijas exploited to their advantage. They did not distinguish between manual and menial. Manual workers were treated as menial. At the bottom of the Hindu society was the vast mass of people who evolved their own sub castes on the basis of occupation/profession they pursued. The lower limbs of the Purusha were further divided. The society was one but its divisions were many. "One 'I' became many" and the Dwijas assigned them hierarchy. The thread system – upanayan - that segregated the Dwijas from the non-Dwijas became a mark of superior status. The worst affect was to push down the Shudras and create fissures and divisions among them. Initiation of the Dwijas and creating hierarchy in the mythical whole went together gradually. Manual work as the source of livelihood came to be thought of poorly – it was rated inferior and even the backward among Dwijas were classified as Shudras.

The backward castes developed their own myths of creation from Brahmin or Kshatriya caste. The one time rulers, Yadavas and Ahirs mostly agriculturists were pushed to Shudra status, and as in-fighting became predominant, Kurmi, Lodhi, Lodh, Jats, Gadariyas, Kori, Kachhi, Rangrej, Dheemar, Teli, Tamoli claimed to be called Kshatriyas. The Nais (barbers) claimed their descent from Maurya and became Thakur/Sen. The Kumhar (potmaker), Barhai (carpenter), Lohar (iron-smith), originally Brahmin or Kshatriya were categorised Shudras. Prajapati had descended from Brahma, Barhai from Rishi Bharadwaj, Lohar from implement and weapon-maker Kshatriyas. The Soni said they were Kshatriyas but because of extermination efforts by Parashuram took to smithy for a disguise. To bracket the most enlightened people, the Kayasthas as Shudras was atrocious. The effort to downgrade the Vaishyas as Shudras did not succeed because of their control over purse strings and cleverness. In Bihar 'Guptas' were classed as Shudras. Similar was the Jati hierarchy evolved by the Brahmanic form of Dharma that had developed. This was Varna-Vyavastha.

This was denunciated by the Jain Trithankars and Buddha in ancient times, and by enlightened Dwijas like Dayananda in recent times. Their efforts failed. The recent political intervention, a democratic effort, has not only failed but has rolled the ball back and it is a conscious effort to perpetuate the Varna-Vyavastha by creating a further class of 'Backward Castes'. The backwards differ from 'Scheduled Castes', again on the basis of manual work. The philosophic myth of a discourse of Shankaracharya and sweeper is well known. The great soul Acharya did not hesitate in accepting the sweeper as guru as he was convinced on seeing the truth in sweeper's arguments. But so sweeping is the effect of casteism that efforts of the Brahmins themselves are unable to make any major dent in the system.

The Hindu caste system resembles 'slavery', the order of the ancient Greek civilization. Like Hindu Shudras, it was manual work that categorised the working Greek as 'slaves'. Organizationally Shudras were at the mercy of Dwijas who controlled Hindu religion. The slaves in Greece were at the mercy of the higher strata of gods and goddesses. The slaves were mostly captives in campaigns in foreign lands. The Greek agriculture, business and commerce prospered because of the physical and mental exertions of serfs and that was the reason why every Greek who could afford acquired one or more slaves for work. Even so, a large number of Greeks were always on the edge of marginal subsitence and the slaves could not look forward to economic advancement as a reward for their labour. They took pride in their craftsmanship but not in the virtue of labour. Xenophone, an economist of Greece in 350 BCE put forward a scheme before the Athenian Council whereby every citizen would be maintained by the state chiefly from revenue to accrue from publice owned slaves working in the mines. Slaves could be employed as clerks, policemen and attendants but not to public office nor could they join as warriors in battles. According to the author of Oceanomica a slave's life consisted of work, punishment, food, floggings and torture. This enabled a Greek citizen to lead an aristocratic life - with the help of slaves !

The talk of improving the lot of slaves was a hollow academic and intellectual exercise. Sometime there was demand to cancel debits and to redistribute the land so as to help slaves. But the citizens never talked of freeing the poor. The demos (common people) had power for namesake. Slaves provided help in rowing in the fleet and they were given free admission to theatre and minor doles. But no demagogue ever suggested anything of interest for working class or anti-slavery. Nor did the poor make a common cause. To the contrary after the Peloponnesian war, Athens and Sparta concluded a treaty that should the slaves rebel the Athenians would assist the Spartans to suppress rebellion. Some slaves were freed but the institution of slavery survived and remained in tact. In 1885 an ex-US slave, Frederick Dauglas wrote "Beat and cut off your slaves. Keep them hungry and spiritless and he will follow the chain of his master like a dog, but feed and clothe him with physical comfort, dreams of freedom (will) intrude. Give him a good master, and he wishes to become his own master". The difference is that the Westerners have done away with slavery, the Hindus have not done away with the degrading caste system.

A Roman Jurist, Florentinus stated, "Slavery is an institution of Jus Jentium (law of all nations) whereby someone is subject to the dominion of another country or nature" or, "there is demographic law that no slave population ever reproduces itself, that they must always be replenished from outside". Many were thrown in cages of wild animals in the arena and they were incapacitated from regeneration of themselves.

Tulsidas, the renowned poet of Ramacharitamanas (Ramayana) echoes Greek poets Homer and Hesiod who casually talked of cattle and slaves that 'came' (were brought) as captives from the Black Sea region. Slaves were both male and female, besides there were slaves born in Greece or Rome also. Some slaves were conditionally manumitted as an act of charity. Later the supply of foreign captives declined. Increasing influence of Christianity also reduced the hardships of slaves. Despite, slavery continued for long in Europe and U.S. and Islamic countries. Till 19th century slaves worked as domestic servants in U.S.

In India slavery never took roots, though the system of servants (Das or Bhratya) existed, and it was feudalism that maltreated them. Yet it cannot be denied that they suffered from the Brahmanic fad of purity, rituals, caste distinctions. Shudras and women could not use Sanskrit for expression because that was the language of cultured people and of gods. Yet because of the scriptures the institution of Shudra was considered morally tolerable. Saint poets all over India softened peoples' attitude towards the Shudras. Tulsidas was the other extreme. One of his *chaupais* reads, "Drums, rustics, Shudras, cattle and female should be kept under control and reprimanded, if necessary". (The middle-East was the worst place for slaves. The condition has improved, we were informed. Surprisingly, the Central Asia, South Asia and South East Asian regions had plain rules. Compared to slaves in Western society, the condition of Shudras was better. While food and potable water from a Brahmin's household was acceptable, to all castes, pucca food and water from other Dwija and some Shudra houses was acceptable to all, including Brahmins. The pucca and kuchcha food and drinking water considerations were applicable to Muslims and Christians also. During the Second World War there were pios for drinking water, separate for Hindus and Muslims.

In India much of the manual work was done by Shudras, and the menial work by the lowly among Shudras and the condition of the latter category was almost inhuman. Even today, they remove the night soil (faeces) from houses in remote rural areas for which they are niggardly paid in the form of left overs. Even Shudras of upper crust practiced casteism with the lower crust of Shudras. Bhangi, Chamar, Khatik and many others suffered at all hands. The Brahmins had appropriated to themselves the right of placement of manual workers in the Vaishya or Shudra category, though most of them claimed to have been forced out or diverted from Brahmin or Kshatriya caste. The myth was that when Parashuram began exterminating Kshatriyas en mass (and for fear of curse no one protested), the latter took to manufacturing and agricultural jobs.

And, once a person or family was branded doing a specific manual job, come what may, he suffered from the caste stigma. Their matrimonial alliance was separated. This narrow mindedness precipitated downfall of Hindus. Since Muslim rulers governed, and later Christians offered them casteless society, there were conversions, much to the chagrin of Hindus.

While the world over slavery has been discarded, Hindus continue to cling to the caste system. Much against expectations the condition of Shudras after independence has hardly improved, the upper castes have managed to improve their financial conditions. (Like the Shudras, women too continue to suffer, Caste women versus Shudra women. The same condition prevails, though caste women are better educated, not employment-wise. Politicians have desultorily treated caste divisions, women politicians are no way different from their male counterparts. However Shudra or otherwise, the women Chief Ministers of States have shown their guts. Mayawati, Rabri Devi, and J. Jayalalitha are matchless, though sometime their actions betray and lack tact.

Not all but some do feel the need of uncovering the evil, the goodness or moral neutrality and indifference of the class system. Nietzche refers to both labour and slavery and castigated them as a necessary disgrace. Today, as earlier, Shudra as a labour is a necessity.

In the 19th century when slavery was being heatedly discussed, a question was posed; Did slavery come in the domain of law of people or in the domain of law of nature? We may revise this and ask: should Shudras he treated as a concern of society or of nature? We may also pose one more question: Was the concept of Shudra taken from chattel slavery?

The occupation-based caste system of the Vedic times turned during Brahmanic time exploitative of the Shudras. This was a political reality. After many centuries the political reality turned into economic reality. It is a matter of despondency. What is of material importance is that human degradation must stop. The East-India Company had desolved slavery by an Act V of 1843. The constitution of Indian Sovereign Republic is against all sorts of exploitation, and this objective requires elimination of caste system.

The hymns of the Rig-Veda carry no trace of rigidity of caste system. Then inter-caste marriage or change of occupation was no taboo. Brahmins married Parjanya women. Shudra women were not detested by Brahmins and families were not wedded to professions.

The Indian Constitution is based on moral perceptions and it has incorporated the best from other constitutions. But implementation of its provisions has faced many obstructions at the hands of politicians, bureaucracy and business. Fixing of percentage for employment of SC/ST candidates in public service has not helped the poor nor improved services. Amendments to the Constitution have been resented. Sometime back when former Prime Minister, VP Singh raised caste as an economic issue, the higher castes made hue and cry and opposed the proposal tooth and nail. They insinuated that Singh was raising the issue for political aggrandizement. But which politician does not do so? They forgot the economic aspect and the whole matter became controversial – a vote catching device. The offshoots later created problems.

Compare the weaker sections of people of India and Greece- Indian Shudras and Greek slaves. Except for vote the Shudras donot count for BJP, Congress, Communists, Socialists, Janata and even Dalits and Bahujan. It is difficult to say whether the society can emancipate itself from the despotism of extremes - or extravagant, moral, intellectual and political pressures. It is difficult to conclude that like the slave who was a basic element in Greek civilization, caste was ever considered as a basic element of Hindu civilization.

Was slavery the cause of the decline of Greek science or was it the loose sexual mortality or unemployment that precipitated the decline of Greece? The pseudo scientific approach and Kantian idealism demanded a systematic investigation into the functioning of slavery, and ultimately they found slavery was a curse. People in India have been living in a casteist society and like slavery it has affected society badly. A study is called for how to do away with the scourge of casteism. (This requires doing away with the deep rooted beliefs, practices, rituals and customs and also the gimmicks and sermons of the godmen and godwomen). This is necessary in the present day industrial and commercial society, where vocational castes have become irreverent, and instead the principles and policies of equality and fundamental rights spelled out in India's constitution provided in Articles 12,14,15 and 16 must be pursued. In bringing about these changes the Acharyas and others must extend their helping hand. Another method is to abolish caste system, like the untouchability, by making it an offence under the constitution. It will take very long but it is better to begin somewhere.

The division of the society in castes/varnas is thousands of years old. During this long period, all civilizations, except the Hindu, have disappeared from the scene. If Hindu civilization could survive inspite of its casteist division, it was because of its inherent system of adjustment with the environment. It did not, rather it avoided coming into clash with others, and was assimilative. It absorbed all those who came to the land and its scriptures proved helpful in this.

Hindu scriptures (Rig Veda X.90, YV XXX1.5.22, AV 196) divided the Purusha in four parts each of which worked according to its capacity to work, and without setting any superiority on any one of them. The Brahmins, the Kshatriyas, the Vaishyas and the Shudras performed different functions necessary for the whole Purusha (allegorically Purusha could be society as a whole or Bhagwan). There was no Varna Vyavastha, which could not be thought of without Avarna Vyavastha, which the Purusha did not provide. The partition was consensual. Equality, fratemity and justicc were not lacking.

Hindu civilization offered a psychological swap - that in the historical perspective poverty was not man-made. If there was starvation it was not because of poverty, it was self-imposed. Individuals had prospects, only if they endeavoured to improve their lot in this as well as in the next world by acting together. This vision offered great satisfaction. Different parts of the society offered services to each other. Was it for this reason that there were less conflicts and there was cohesion in the society? As a whole this was versified for living together.

Sah Nau Bhavatu, Sah Nau Bhunaktu
Sah Viryam karvavahe.

There was plenty for each and adversity in a unit was manageable. But as prosperity grew, feeling of getting less remuneration created dissatisfaction. Purusha had lost the grip and the matter for existence's sake, had to be settled by force both against inside pulses and pressures and outside tyrrannous attacks. The Brahmins used their knowledge and the Kshatriyas applied their muscle power to settle the issue but failed. The myth of Vishwamitra and Trishanku exemplifies this conflict. Parashuram thought he had settled the issue by exterminating the Kshatriyas many of whom took to other vocations: Parasuram was deified as an evatar of Vishnu. What other quality did that matricide possess? Brahmins were strategists and finding purse strings in the hands of vaishyas, the three joined together as Dwijas and settled the score with the Shudras by creating the myth of thread - Yagyopavit. The thread gave rebirth that is what it meant. The Dwijas pushed down the 'Ekaj' (once born). The powers of intellect, muscle and purse prevailed over "service" and the manual work was declared derogatory. The symbolic division affected real division. Four castes became reality. Yet another myth was created "unity in diversity". No such class (Shudra) was created by Persian Aryans who too wore thread. Nor did Christians for whom baptism serves the purpose of thread.

Hinduism admits multiplicity of deities and it is for an individual to choose one or more or see divine power in every thing. There are various ways of finding the truth. "Truth is one, call it by any name". Also there are various ways like Gyan, Bhakti, Karma (knowledge, devotion, action) to reach it. This too unfortunately created discrimination. Discriminatory treatment of Shudras who are immersed in poverty continues to degrade humanity.

There have been ample explanations in justification of the system. One of them is birth which they say is ordained by God and is not accidental. An individual is born in a caste because of his past karma and God's pleasure and nothing can change God's vidhan (system). If one is born a Brahmin, it is because of his virtuous deeds in the past life, and if someone is born a Shudra that was because of his past evil deeds. God's will and individual's past karma settles the issue and seals his place (positioning) in the society. Neither a Brahmin could be relegated nor a Shudra upgraded. The theory of karma proved both beneficial and lawful to the society. Innovation of the theory of rebirth squared up with the theory of karma. The Varna Vyavastha was sanctioned by religious authorities. Manu did it. Bhagvat Gita did it. Thus Hindu society was polemicized. How could the Hindu Dharma pivoted by the Brahmanic culture survive? Undoubtedly, Hinduism had its inherent capacity to effect changes to suit the circumstantial needs. How and why the low caste did not revolt? Why did they not quit for social benefits offered by Christianity and Islam? The law of averages worked here as well. Few amongst the converts could improve their lot.

One drawback of Hinduism is lack of organized corrective measures (like the Christian Council, Muslim congregation, Buddhist Assembly). The Shankaracharyas, piths and priests work more for preserving what the religion and society provide, than keeping in step with developments scientific, technological etc. Do myths meet every situation? We had no reply to our Indian Christian missionary friend who taunted whether it was God who had delegated the Hindu/Brahman priests authority to bar Shudra entry in temples. Our quick mental search to find suitable words of Buddha, Tirthankars, Basavas, Nanak, Dayanand and Vivekananda failed us. Diffusion of prosperity too has failed to undo psychological barriers.

One shudders to think of human conditions in the past in alien lands. In his critical study on Myths titled "Myths to Live By", Josef Campbell mentions that one of the best preserved graves was of a woman named "Shub-ad" with her count of 25 attendants directly above the male entombment of a male personage named "A-bar-go" with whom 65 or so had been laid to rest. The animals and human beings had been buried alive in the monstrous grave. In Egypt and China tombs have been discovered containing as many as eight hundred or more entombed ! One unfortunate human being (woman) burning on her husband's pyre in the name of Sati is enough to cause shivering, think of tens or hundreds!

The Romans behaved savagely when they attended and witnessed prisoners/slaves being thrown to wild animals in the arena for punishment as also for entertainment. In 1960 the late Dr. Radhakrishnan, former President of India, referred to finding solution to the problem of racial conflict viz. extermination, subordination, identification or harmonization. Destruction or enslavement of the weak and unfit is not a good solution. Every race and society should have opportunity to develop. The backwards should be enabled to utilize opportunities to grow. (At the same time it has to be recognized that racial fusion at a large scale is an impossibility).

In dealing with the problem of social conflict Hinduism adopted the only safe course of democracy viz each social group be let to develop without impeding others' progress. "Caste is the affirmation of the diversity of human group", Dr Radhakrishnan said. Those who brought races together are worshipped as makers of Hindu society (Rama, Krishna and Buddha brought Aryans and tribals together). The rules of food and marriage of communities were maintained. The lower castes developed their own customs, laws and beliefs. "Caste is really custom". Yet there has been a general fusion of foreign blood and a small but steady flow of blood from the higher to the lower castes by Anuloma and Pratiloma marriages. Is this a solution? Such indiscriminate crossings created untouchable castes. Such a genetic solution to formation of caste system is unconvincing. The second step of marriage in caste has been in vogue. Stress on savarna marriage is retrogressive. It is unbelievable that an eminent philosopher, Dr. Radha Krishnan, would say "savarna marriage is not unsound". This sounds like a justification of superiority of upper castes. Can the savarna Jati Vyavastha he changed to Avarna Jati Vyavastha?

Aliens had sensed that caste divisions play a divisive role in the society. Lord Lamingdon had observed, "The real guarantee of our stay in India will remain as strong as ever, viz. The caste system, the diversity of national ties and creed and the lack of confidence and trust of one native for other" (Creative Mind by Howard Gardener 1993, p.324).

Casteism was given a seal of approval by Samkhya, Bhagvat Gita, Shankarcharya, Dr. Radha Krishnan, Mahatma Gandhi and many other eminent Indians. This does not, however, mean that casteism has the sanctity of the entire Hindu scriptures, certainly not of the Vedas. Casteism is not Vedic. It was born of a threat to Ritu. It is a product of Brahmanic influence. It is the result of interpolations in scriptures. It continues in Sanatan (Hindu) Dharma. Casteism is a fortification of rights of some which is now psychologically ingrained. But the higher castes treat it as a divine grace – man is born in a caste because of divine design. Birth in a caste is a gift of God. Birth may be an accident of genetics which is responsible for varied traits.

In fact the genes give man/woman traits – not birth in a specific caste. Parasar's son, Vyasa Vardarayana was born of a Shudra woman, sage Vishwamitra was a Kshatriya, who attained Brahminhood, Ekalavya was a Shudra. They proved that birth had nothing to do with caste. There are innumerable instances. They respond to the querry of "Aap kaun Jat".

The symbolism of Purusha can be applied to a polity, apart from society or individual. The Sukta of the Rig-Veda can explain the partition of the country (India) in an artificial manner, first into India and Pakistan, and later Pakistan's division into Pakistan and Bangladesh, yet is not the loss being realized by fundamentalists. If the partition of the country is abhored, so should the artificial partition of the Purusha be, logic dectates.

War between gods and demons in air, on land and sea as visualized by Malvika (10) and Rishab (7)

INDIA THAT IS BHARAT

The name-game 'India That is Bharat' tells an interesting anecdote embedded with a couple of interludes. The name was formalised by the Constitution of India in 1950. Bharat is an Aryan word (name) and 'India' derives its origin from the Western people.

In the heyday of Aryan purity, Fuhrer Hitler claimed Aryan descent for his flock, the Germans. Other tyrants stood up to be counted amongst the pure. German scholars proficient in Sanskrit traced Aryan descent for Indians on the basis of philology and literature and aligned them with the Caucasians. Coincidentally, a Rig-Veda deity Aryaman and classical Sanskrit word Aryavarta had 'Arya' common, of course Aryavarta referred to a smaller land.

Prior to this, the land with slightly extended geographical boundary was referred to as Saptasindhavah. That was not for reason of common ancestry. 'Sindhu' happened to be a mighty river that separated the land to the south from lands to the north. The southward land had prospered because of its protective boundaries, river systems and herdsman, nomads and travellers who had criss-crossed and enriched it with legends. (A legend called it a land of rivers flowing with milk and honey.) Saptasindhavah means of 'Seven Rivers" of which Sindhu was the mightiest. The Iranians could not pronounce 'S' of Sindhu, instead they pronounced it as Hindu, not Sindhu, and its people Hindu not Sindhu. That is how Sindh became Hind, and Sindhu became Hindu.

The Iranians and Greeks were great warriors and fought for supremacy. Initially Iranians had an upper hand but later Greeks succeeded in defeating Iranians. When they proceeded on, Hindus shattered the Greek dream of world conquest. The Greeks, too suffered from linguistic handicap. They could not pronounce 'H' and instead pronounced it 'I', and called the river Sindhu as 'Indos' and the people living on its banks as Indicos. The Greek army turned back on boats. Alexander died in his return journey.

The country was also known as Bharatavarsha, perhaps after its king Bharat or a tribe known as Bharat who inhabited it. (We cannot say whether the name went after the king or tribe). However, it is a fact that for centuries the land was called Bharatavarsha, with defined boundaries.

The Vishnu Purana says, Bharatvarsha is the land that lies north of the ocean and south of the snowy mountains and its progeny is Bharati.

Bharat, the abbreviation of Bharatavarsha the prosperous land with rivers of milk and honey attracted several predators such as Pallavas, Scythians, Arabs. The last named Arabs, invaded Bharat in 7th century and called it 'el Hind'. Muslim rulers called it Hindustan. Seven centuries later the Portuguese, who came in search of commerce and trade changed its name from 'Indos' to 'India' which has stuck up. The British confined the Portuguese to Goa, Daman and Diu and conquered the whole country by their policy of divide and rule. The British like the Portuguese called it India. (The French called it 'l' Inde').

Indians learnt the lesson 'United we stand, divided we fall'. Their spirit of nationalism and the economic crisis the British faced after the second world war forced the British to quit India. But before they quit, they partitioned the country into - India and Pakistan - on the basis of religion. Either because the Muslims pressed unbearably hard or the British with their future imperial perspectives gave the minority Muslims the Muslim majority western provinces (Punjab, Sindh, NWFP and Baluchistan). Princely India had a different experience. They could not be partitioned because of the large number of states (561 in all) spread over their large domains. The princes had liberty to join either India or Pakistan. In this respect Pakistan played a predatory role in Kashmir. The Indians had now an opportunity to draft their constitution and to give name to their country. They drafted the Constitution and after considering various aspects in 1949 reconciled all differences and named the country 'India that is Bharat'. India celebrated January 26, as its Republic Day. That in brief is the story of "India that is Bharat".

We may narrate an interesting experience about the name. In 1977 we were in Paris. One early morning we were to take a bus to Callais wherefrom we were to board a hovercraft for London. A lady atop a multi storied building amused at Amrit's flowing sari waved her hand and accosted 'l Inde!'. The friendly gesture from a stranger made us happy to be recognized in a foreign land.

A friend narrated us his personal experience during his pilgrimage to Mecca. The tent city in Saudi Arabia the section marked 'Hindi' accommodated both Indian and Pakistani pilgrims. There was no protest from anyone. That was in 50s.

To revert to Aryan immigration. In order to prove that the Aryans were not original inhabitants but were conquerors (like the British themselves) who had pushed down the original inhabitants, Dravidians, the British historian created several myths, which served their imperial purpose of divide and rule. According to them the northern Indians were of the Aryan blood and the South Indians were Dravidians. Though the British left in 1947, their mischief to divide people worked. Provoked by the myth, Dravidian leaders opposed one-language formula for the country and threatened to carve out a Tamil country. Fortunately the Tamil people ignored the call. The country 'India is alive today.' Agitation against Hindi, resulted in giving preference to English as lingua franca.

Besides, European scholars propounded other theories and doctrines. They stated that the Aryans had migrated from 'dark, damp and squib' Siberia, Eastern Europe or Central Asia for change to a favourable climate of India. To support their thesis they tore apart Suktas (hymns) from the Rig-Veda. One such prayer which Hindus have said for thousands of years is:

Lead me from non-being to being
Lead me from darkness to light
Lead me from mortality to immortality

This is a simple innocent prayer. But a British historian finds in this simple prayer it a hidden message. A man wishing to escape the dark, damp and squib surroundings. The God granted their wish and they trudged down to India to lead comfortable life in its warm climate. He said:

Na tatra Suryobhati no Chandratarkannama
Vidyohhati kutoyamagnih
Tamaye bhantamanurbhati sarvam
Tastya bhasha sarvamidam vihhati

There the sun shines not
Nor the Moon nor the stars
Nor the height not to speak of Yama's fire
It is refulgence which makes all things shine

Further, the critic imagines the Gayatri mantra (prayer to Sun) is directed towards the same object. The Gayatri mantra:

Om bhurbhuvah swah tatsaviturvarenyam
Bhargodevasya dhimahidhiyo yo nah prachodayat.

The mightiest and the most brilliant, Sun, may your auspicious light purify our intellect and illumine the path to auspicious deeds. As fire (i.e. Agni) also gives warmth – the critic adds shlokas addressed to Agni for giving them warmth, heat and energy and the very word Yajur of 'Yajurveda' stands for conservation.

B.G. Tilak, an Indian scholar-politician preferred the Arctic region for the original Aryan home. He based his view on astrological perceptions, Vedic Usha (Dawn) Vedic cows, astronomical data and religious and literary sources, which made good ground for propagation of myths. This did not go unchallenged. AC Das asserted that the Punjab and adjoining areas were the cradle of Vedic Aryans. Prior to Das, Elphinstone too had opposed the theory of immigration of Aryans. In fact he was the first (Governor) from the ruling class who had forcefully propounded that they (Aryans) were the original inhabitants of the land (India). (Elphinstone was a scholar in a true sense. He declined a short Governor–General ship and instead preferred to remain Governor of Bombay to compete his pursuits).

The controversy persists even today. A group of leftists (of whom Promila Thapar is one) and another group of BJP historians (who are criticised for their Hindutva) continue to engage in the controversy. We fail to understand why those renowned people should stoop down to malign each other at personal level. It does not behove well to use cheap expressions like 'Sangh Parivar' or 'leftist' in support of their stand. Serious thoughts can't be expressed in slang. The communists were certainly not rational when they called Jawaharlal Nehru as 'the running dog of imperialism'. That did not win over Indians to their (Chinese) views. The contents can be explained in a polite, decent and gentle way. We wish such myths are thrown out without giving them a second thought.

Another myth about Aryans is that the Rig-Veda is a hymnal of an early, primitive and barbarous society, and from Vedic revelation originated Hinduism. (Inferentially Hinduism has to be barbaric.) Further, Hinduism was accused of being devoid of a centralised authority and of being 'Crude in its moral and religious conceptious, rude in the outlook upon the world that envisioned'. 'Then, Hinduism became fragmented into movements and sects'. But it goes to its credit that it could create a holistic unity !

Sayana, the commentator of the Vedas, had accepted rituals as part of divine knowledge, which was endowed with a mysterious efficiency. Western scholars thought this was an eleboration of old propitiatory sacrifice offered to imaginary superhuman personages who could be benevolent or malevolent. The Vedic gods were identified in their external aspects with nature powers and lesser powers with primitive myth-making. They divided Vedic hymnology as half superstitious, half poetic allegory of nature with an astronomical element. For them the rest was superstitious rituals and history.

Thus arose the theory that the Aryan races were northern barbarians who broke from their colder climates and from the civilizations of the Mediterranean Europe which could be identified from the Sanskrit and Greek terminology used by people. Thus there are myths within myths, mostly created by scholars and imperialists.

From antiquity to modernity and now a combination of the two – India and Bharat – India that is Bharat – is accommodative for everyone ancient or modern. More than one billion people owe allegiance to their country. Besides there are 20 million people of Indian origin (PIOs) in other countries. So what is the wrong? One can use either – India or Bharat – so long it precisely conveys India that is Bharat.

GOD

The latest form of swearing by God with flamboyant Americans ladies is "Oh my Gosh". Why such an endearment to God? God always had his votaries and opponents. Indian Community Service Center (ICSC)'s creative persona Chandrashekhara says he is dead set on eradicating 'stupid God'. This has earned him voluble epithet from other members of the ICSC of Santa Clara. They hit back–God is capable of taking care of himself and he will survive this venomous onslaught. The forecasts of god's doom by great thinkers like Charvak, Nietizche, Marx, Freud buried but God continues to visit the minds and hearts of his devotees. Charvaka had boldly prescribed his dose : Don't worry God nor worry about him, Live on well is what matters, enjoy yourself even if you have to live on borrowed money.

Nietczche in his work 'Joyful Wisdom' pronounced, 'God is dead'. He took the clue of God's fate from Ludwig Feurbeck who was absolutely clear about God in his head and posed : the qualities of compassion, benevolence, mercy, etc. attributed to God are nothing but a figment of man's imagination.

Marx had no compunction of any sort. He boldly pronounced that religion was a product of opium and that God was a lotus eater who would one day die with the end of capitalism. But curses like 'He is dead as Dodo' could not touch his fringe and God went about scot-free.

The French sociologist Emile Durkheim, joined the fray. He said God was a product of society, and when we worship God we worship the society. Secondly, God is a ritual imbued with its binding beliefs and symbols. He is eternal. Durkheim's point of view benefited God. Another revolutionary thinker, Freud thought religion gave impetus and made civilization possible. He assigned religion two poles – cognitive and practical. Cognitive denoted "making world intelligible" and its ability to understand nature of the society, its involvement in ideas, faith, dogms, theology. But he opines that science and philosophy have displaced or are displacing religion's ability to explain every day life, while the society ignores the practical aspect of religion. Energy released by rituals gives the followers security, happiness, and inner strength, besides belongingness. Rituals bring those people together who have a common set of ideas, norms of behaviour. However, today it is more of technology and reason that is deemed to give support to economy, politics, education and law than belief in God. Religion and nationalism foster cohesion and unity in parts of the world. However, it cannot be denied that religion divides communities while serving its links with the past.

The organizers of temples, mosques and churches (and religious institutions) claim that religion helps their followers in improving their lives (both outer and inner), identities, inner strength, meaning and purpose of life. It can also mediate between minority communities and State by offering protection to beliefs and practices of minorities from the State which wields sweeping powers.

Religion and God are not dead. What future do they have? Serious students think that the idea of a transcendent God beyond human existence is meaningless. They also assert that God has himself withdrawn to allow people the space and scope to exercise responsibility in such matters in their lives.

The jurists too have something to say – we mean juridical minded religious people. One such enlightened soul, Bishop John Robinson (in *Harvest of God,* 1964) advised people to stop thinking of God and not to treat him like an old man in heaven who at times intervenes in matters on earth. T.S. Eliot was sarcastic when he said, "Men have left God for no God", which never happened before : only some have left. There are people who believe in Jesus as the son of God who resurrected.

Most of the people regard their own religion and civilization alone as true, and this is what has led and may continue to lead to "clashes of civilizations". What happened in the USA on 9/11, has become myth 9/11. It was horrible. It was all consequence of closed minds, "men of madrasas." By killing men, they don't realize, they are not propounding or proving the truthfulness of their religion or of God or Prophet. They are in stead killing the creation of God. Political maneuvers over – powered and threw aside the leadership of Deen (religion) and took to violence, instead of compassion, which was the result of thinking theirs as the only 'truth'. It is not improbable that Truth is one but can be reached by various methods/paths. Not that we profess or believe in superstitious tenets of any religion, but we do find a ray of hope in the saying of the Rig-Veda: "Ekosad Viprah Bahudha Vadanti". Truth is one, sages explain in different ways. Let religions explain the sanctity of human life, which should be the truth acceptable to every one. Saint poets preached the message in "Dark Ages". It appears darkness continues returning from time to time. We often wonder – can we treat myths as constructive. But soon flashes the message – Are there destruction myths?

Fortunately more people want to find new ways of understanding God and they are prepared to experiment in religion to suit the present situation. But are now people less dogmatic and are they ready to accept belief and traditions of others. New movements open new vistas but they too after a time become moribund. May be some movement is eclectic enough for all. There, fortunately, is a view that in future religion may be the concern of self identity and personal well being of humanity as a whole.

It is noteworthy that for sometime past there is great religious fervor in mystical direction in US. It is not certain whom the gurus from India, Mullahs from Islamic countries, monks from Japan and lamas from Tibet serve. Disturbing news comes from educational institutions (Madrasas e.g.) which instead of preaching God preach hatred and violence. Organized religion and sweet preachings disarm doubts and suspicions about these great men.

Majority of people believe in a Supreme Deity because of their lack of understanding of the laws and forces of nature which are automatic and operate independent of value systems. They apprehend that such forces will overwhelm and hope that worship and prayer would fetch them relief in helpless situation, which may be the main cause of their belief in miracles and myths. The propagation of such fears and hopes has given rise to religious fervor and faiths.

Religion (with God, the creator) has been a great sheet anchor for humanity because it believes that it brings to man comfort and peace in moments of fear and anguish. This blind faith is exploited by professional practitioners of such faiths, who preach that religion harmonizes man's conduct with natural laws, religiosity is commitment to truth, and god is the embodiment of cosmic phenomena and origin of man. This gives place to dogma and superstition. To the Hindu guru, God is the universal spirit that pervades the universe.

Brihadaranyakopanishad approaches God in a rational way : (or is it realistic?) People say, "Worship this God, worship that God". This is his creation. He himself is all the gods. People do not see him. When breathing, He becomes breath, when speaking he becomes voice, when seeing he is the eye, when hearing he is the ear, when thinking he is the mind. But all these are names of his acts. Whoever worships one of these, he knows not, and whosoever worships a divinity, knows not for his own self is divinity and the deities are productions and projections of his psyche. Are there any gods or have there been any gods who were not creations of man's imagination?

Then is god alive or dead? When was it certain that God was alive or there was God. One can at best say that not God but symbols are dead. Formerly people had horizons and mythologized God. These horizons have dissolved. Surprisingly humanism and democracy are bloodying the world. Dissolution and flooding do convey one aspect of the story, as narrated above in creation. Mythology and religion, like poems, have permeated everywhere and mystic traditions go well with them.

REBIRTH

What after death? Man is aware that death is a mystery. It has eluded man's efforts to find what death is? Its approximate definition is : Death is the mystery, which converts Being into non-Being. Since it cannot be replaced into lab conditions – it has slipped from the sight of the spectator, irrespective of his status may be his *swajan* (parents, siblings, wife, progeny) or doctor whose fingers have missed thc border line between life and non-life–death. That separating point is the mystery – and the measure of period of conversion is immeasurable. The dead – no more alive – is unconcerned about the surroundings – it knows nothing about his past or present or future. An inference is drawn that it is a mysterious phenomenon (calling it 'phenomenon' is in itself imprecise, inaccurate, unauthentic).. The poet terms it 'breach in thread'. All attempts of religion and philosophy keep their gazes fixed this side of the sore but they have not been able to fathom the depth to say if there is another shore or coast.

Since that mystery disappeared at an indefinable period, the scientists also is not helpful.

The failures of religion, philosophy, science have given Death a cloak of indescribability. It differs from God in that he may or may not be. Death was – it converted Being into non-Being. To atheists God is not. But even to them Death is but not 'Neti' – it occurred. Death is occurrence and nothing more nor less. It is an irreversible process. Biologist may say it is a natural phenomenon, beyond human control, but it (death) having every Being under its control is inevitable.

The Kathopanishad narrative precisely is : A young boy named Nachiketa, inquisitive and full of enthusiasm enquires of his father what death is. Unable to satisfy Nachiketa the father tells him better he finds it from Yama. The young lad knocks at Yama's door but finds he is out. He patiently waits for him. His determination makes him oblivious of his hunger and thirst,. He stays at Yama's doorsteps.

The god of death expressed his regret to the young man for keeping him waiting and encourages him to come out how he could help. Nachiketa asked, "Some say he is, some say is He not". The 'He' refers to Ishwar, God. Atman's relationship to Ishwar is that of part and whole. Body without Atman is inconceivable. Then on death body is there, what happens to Atman? But first what happens on death? On death, all of body's elements wither away and join their namesake.

Yama enlightened the persistent enquirer about the secret of life. The very kernel of human body is Atman (self), he said, "It is the owner and passenger of the chariot of the body". It controls, the various refractory senses of body. But when it departs, all that remains are elements which wither away. Although the Yama did not elaborate but an inference is drawn that the Atman merged with the Brahman (Ishwar).

The probing mind was not satisfied. Yama offered Nachiketa very many temptations but the lad remained unmoved. The explanation unable to satisfy developed into the mythology of the Brahmanical system of rebirth. This did not, however, go unrepudiated.

Those who opposed rebirth included hermits, sages, ascetics, and other materialists who propounded heterodox doctrines such as non-violence, libeation (release from cycle of birth and death). What did they offer in return?

What after death? Where does the Atman (if there be one) proceed to? If to heaven or hell, according to his Karmas, would the Atman be transitory there too? Is there one death or are there many deaths? If more, then need he prepare not only for earthly death but also for indeterminate number of deaths? Could the great divinity, Bhagwan, help it to escape the clutches of death and birth in the after life? Are there any other solutions or escape routes? Asceticism was one. But before we go to ascetic aversion to transmigration, let us just probe about the Vedic and later Bramanic approach to brith and death.

The Brahmanic literature talks of one death and one great divinity who could be propitiated by uttering 'Swaha' (i.e. hail) and death could be avoided in the after life. This Brahmanic solution was not very convincing.

Ascetic practices were offered as another solution. They give man magical and superior powers. These practices could be fasting, celibacy, yogic exercises, psychopathic forms of self torture such as lying on bed of thorns, hanging upside down from trees (as Alexander and his Greek army saw) and such practices could be helpful in expunging effects of sin and instead providing securities. They developed the doctrines of Sansar and Karma which they linked with forms of life – gods, demi gods, human beings, animals, worms. The constant passage of soul from one body to another body life passing from one body to another, according to karma – deeds done in the past-is sansar. As he did, so would he reap in the next birth. For instance, a glutton could be reborn, as a pig, or a man of violence as tiger or some other wild animal. And, as is known sinners allegedly suffer in purgatory unless their sins are expunged and the sinner is given another chance on earth. On the other hand the virtuous enjoys bliss in heaven before retiring to earth for a new life.

These were not the views of the Vedas. Vedas make no clear reference to transmigration of soul i.e. passage of soul from one body into another. The situation changed in upanishadic times, as is evident from Nachiketa - Yama episode above. The *Chhandogyopanishad* (5.10.7-8) went a step forward and supported the varna system. It described that those who please gods by their conduct would be reborn as Dvijas.

Discrimination can also play a role in avoiding rebirth. He who lacks discrimination and is unmindful and impure will not reach the highest state of liberation – no rebirth. Thus transmigration is a fact of life. However, the process is still a mystery and that mystery hecame an open mind and by Buddah's time the doctrine of transmigration of soul had become acceptable.

About the same time Pathogorus (born 570 BCE) had also developed the idea of rebirth. In India the materialists like Ajit Keshakambali were opposed to the idea of life after death. Charvaka, Lokayats and Nastiks too sailed in the same boat. They were against the doctrine of transmigration.

An episode almost parellel to Nachiketa and Yama's is one that relates to Yajnavalkya, one of the greatest thinkers of his time (in our view of all times). He was questioned by another rishi, Artabhaga about life after death. The last question he posed is interesting :

Yagnavalkya, when a man dies, his voice enters fire, his breath enters the wind, his eyes the sun, his mind the moon, his ears the quarters, his body the earth, his atman space, the hair of his body the plants, the hair of his head the trees, and his blood and semen repose in the waters. Where is the man then?

Yajnavalkya's reply was:

To whatever his mind and character is attached, to that a man goes with his works. He reaps the reward of the deeds he does on earth and comes back again to the world of action. (But) he who is free from desire…., being Brahman itself, goes to Brahman. When all desires in the heart are released, then the mortal becomes immortal and he attains Brahman. (Brihadaranyakopanishad 4.4.5)

Two other episodes resemble the Yajnalvalkya – Avtabhaga dialogue. One involves Uddalaka Aruni, Svetaketu, and Pravahana – Jaivali; and the other relates to Uddalaka and Chitra Gangeyayani. The messages, in dramatic forms, are almost the same as in the case of Nachiketa – Yama. These could be summarized :

The Atman is eternal, it neither dies nor decays, whilst it passes through a cycle of births and deaths, bondage and emancipation. There is continuity of lfie. Man's expected life is one hundred years – 100 autumns/winters. *(Pashyem Sharadah Satam, Jeevem Sharadhah Satam).*

A man who commits sin has to face its consequences, and he has to extricate himself from it.. One's struggle is itself atonement. Sin leads to bondage which leads to liberation. Bondage finally becomes a reward and liberation is the purpose of life.

Rigveda, Yajurveda and Atharvaveda refer to rebirth after death. The rebirth is either in human life or animal life in which case it may be forest or domesticated animal life. Animal life could be any one of 609 types of animal life.

Ved and Vedanta deal with God as the source of knowledge. Vedas' message is perennial for all time. It is empirical and transcendent. Vedas enumerate Dharma – coduct of life – Avidya, Asambhuti, Apar. They also import knowledge of Brahman – Vidya, Sambhuti, Nishreyas, para for higher stage.

About one fourth of West European people believe in resurrection i.e. life after death. In India it is believed that spirits gone astray are born as Bhuta, Preta, Pishacha. Mr. Arya Bhushan, an American of Indian descent, an expert on the subject cited Dr. Browman's experiences of past life that affect people's lives. "Past life memories sound, look, act and feel distinctly different from fantasies because they issue from a different source. Fantasies are the mind at play. Past life memories, on the other hand are full bodied images of real events". She describes four signs of children's past life memories viz. 1. Matter of fact tour, 2. Consistency over time, 3. Knowledge beyond experience, 4. Corresponding behavior and traits and adds, "Reincarnation is not as many people in our culture think a belief tied down to India or to any religion or culture. It has been an ending spiritual belief for billions of people for thousands of years all over the world". As for Christianity in 553 a decree was passed against reincarnation by Church. Still people continued to believe in it. Then in 13th century a crusade was launched against Catholics, a sect of Christians who had continued belief in reincarnation. Half a million people were massacred.

Elsewhere also there are myths around death and rebirth. People of Hokkaidi and Sakhalin Islands near Japan practice a strange bear cult. They kill the animal, remove and eat the meat and ceremonially bid the released visitors bon voyage, but invite the little divinity to return to earth. It appears Ainu faces no such thing as death, which thought is expressed in burial. The beast has to be broken to release him for return to his other world home. Plants also get similar treatment. The murdered beasts and consumed beasts are thought to be willing victims. In Ainu rites fire goddess FUJI is invited to participate in eating and drinking in the Neanderthal chapel.

In India a custom just the reverse of the Ainu is observed at the time of weddings. A few days before the date of wedding, the ladies sing songs in melodious tune inviting gods and goddesses, including local devatas, to participate in the wedding – actually come and bless so that the occasion gets over happily. In the same song are invited – oral invitations are sent out to ancestors– Purkhas - to join the same way as the devatas are. The occasion is both happy and somber. It sounds as if the family is expressing its heart felt feelings, how good it would have been if the ancestors were alive and graced the occasion.

A legend of the Black Foot tribe of North America tells us through the character of a Bull that "there is no such thing as death." The other characters are a girl, a father and a bird. (told by Campbell). A myth of another tropical tribe tells, "Death is the giver of life." (Men have secret societies where women are not allowed. Different customs are observed about sacrifice in different tribes. Some observe rite.of animal sacrifice, while others worship animals. Some observe sacrifice in a different way – they offer sacrifice of the first fruits of the field, of the first born, of widow (on husband's funereal pyre, and entire counts). The Islamic suicidal bombers have contributed to the myth of Jihad. The mythic theme of the willing victims has become associated with the image of primordial being that in the beginning offered itself to be slain, disemembered and buried, from whose buried parts arose food plants.

The Cook Islands (Polynesia) have a myth that tells the sacrifice of human head through a comparable material – coconut. (In India coconut is offered to a deity in the temple or house). The story is quite interesting. Hima (=Moon) a maiden bathed in a pond. One day a big eel named Le Tuna swam past and touched her. Then one day she turned into a youth and started visiting her daily. One day he announced that he was leaving for good and asked her to cut off his head. As announced he turned up and as asked she cut off his head next day. She buried his head from which a shroud appeared and in course of time it produced fruits. These are the first coconuts and every nut after husking shows face and eyes of Hima's lover. (Campbell in Masks of God – abridged). Pythagoras forbade eating beans because they contained, in his view, transmigrating human souls.

Socrates also believed in rebirth. He said, "We believe that all souls are created at the beginning. In due course these souls are born once, and once only. (This concept differs from the Indian concept which is that a soul is born and leaves, and is born again thousands of times in different forms.)

Zoroster raised the question : Men die but what happens to the mind that inhabits their flesh? Once free of the body, the soul returns to the Supreme Lord. But first the soul must cross the redeemer. There who have followed in life the Truth will go to the house of good mind and happiness. Those who followed the Lie will go to the house of Lie, and suffer torment. Eventually when the wise lord overwhelms evil, all souls will be at one.

Miscellany

JANTRA-TANTRA-MANTRA

The ancient concept of three worlds (loks) – Prithvi, Akash and Patal – involved three types of inhabitants. Human beings, who were mortal, inhabited the Prithvi (i.e. Earth), gods lived in heaven (Akash) and demons in Patal (under the earth). Their respective inhabitations defined their standing. Gods were immortal, privileged and came down on earth floating to reach their destinations. When propitiated, they blessed the person seeking help and saved him from suffering. But if god was annoyed he could curse, even for a flimsy reason, and unsettled the man (or woman) physically, materially and mentally. Man enjoyed or suffered – he was destined to – depending on God's pleasure and the man's good or evil past deeds. After death the human being was carried away by Yama, the Lord of Death, to heaven or hell according to his deeds. Even so, there was scope for divine dispensation – by the deity himself or his agent who had earned power to change the course of destiny and to undo or reduce his suffering.

The demons and devils of the underworld – were impetuous and uncontrollable and could disturb both the divines and humans. Some individuals by their penance secured power to control the evil spirits and by their mystic power warded them off. Some could cure or dispel their affect by black magic (Jadu-Tona). All religions have such individuals – priests, maulvis, clerics – who by their intervention mitigate human suffering on account of health, enmity, family or socio-economic problems. Some magicians too claimed to change the curse of adversity by unraveling the mysteries of life. Experts however ridiculed the idea and said, "Magic is only in our mind. Like ghost it has an ephemeral existence, such a tool is neither good nor bad." It is like the gun or nature that defines morality. Magic too defines its morality. The magic, some claim, is a forerunner of science.

While the Jadu-Tona (or magic) is a process to secure control over a super natural power, Tantra has psychological and extra sensory implications. The tantrics and astrologers calculate and suggest propitation measures to mitigate evil affects. They advise time for going on journey, offer Sagun that wards off evil effects. Some people ridicule existence of super natural power. "Is it that God created man or man's mind created God?'

In his stage of food-gathering and herding, man learnt making fire and used it to move out of darkness and since fire helped him, he worshipped Fire, which became Fire God. But when he saw shadows of figures moving in the darkness of night, he was frightened of the shadows and called them Bhuta-Pret (ghosts). To get over fear, and provide security for himself, he evolved charms and amulates, and evolved recitations that helped him. Besides, he started inviting ancestors, particularly on family functions like weddings. Occult experts criticized charms and amulates and castigated them as nothing but scraps of paper or metal pieces with numerals, syllables, diagrams. Unfortunately, no religion is untouched by such charms.

A man in trouble curses his fate and seeks help from a spiritual healer. The healer's hocus-pocus sometime work, at others they fail causing further frustration. He thinks, he has been duped.

The other course is Gurukripa – the grace of the teachers (or men of god) who give their disciples mantras such as Om, Gayatri, Hari, Ram, Krishna, Shivaya Namah which, it is claimed, possess supernatural powers and if properly pronounced in proper circumstances they place the individual in harmony with the universe. By the effects of sound, rhythm, texture and meaning the mantra proves effective in helping the man. The gurukripa secures the disciple the bliss of a mystical quietude. Those who believe in guru say that without his grace nothing is possible, thus opined Umapati in his Tamil work. (Its English translation is "The Fruit of Divine Grace.")

The devout say man is like an impure metal, whose impurity can be removed only by mercury. The gurukripa removes the disciple's ignorance (impurity). That is why guru is to be treated as a venerable preceptor. He is embodied god and brings the disciple nearer to liberation. The guru initiates the disciple into mystery and helps him loosen ignorance. Divine grace assumes the form of guru. But non-believers cite queer instances like that of Ekalavya who believe in guru's fairness.

Om Namasshivay (or Om Shivay) is the substance of all truth, according to the Shaivites. The chant consists of five syllables which are grace of Shiva and Shakti and a guard against the bond of finite ignorance, darkness and delusion (Maya) of soul. The five graces are concentrated in the mantra. The Mana (mind) consisting of Ma and Na represents impurity, which needs to be purified by the mantra, representing guru's grace. The devotees explain the syllables – Shi is shiva, Va is grace, and Ya is soul. The proper chant is Shivay Namah – not Namah Shivay.

Om is the source of Trayi Vidya, that is Gyan (knowledge), Bhakti (devotion), and Karma (action), in the Vedas (Rig III 62.10). The Upanishads elaborated it. Om, as a part of Shruti, is its own proof *(Swatah pramanam).*

The *Prashnopanishad* refers to OM as the comprehension of Vedas and cosmic reality. According to the Mandukya OM is Akshara, i.e. imperishable, indestructible. The past, the present, the future – all that was and will be is and all else that may exist beyond the bounds of time is OM. The Chhandogya says the Udgeet (i.e. OM of the Vedas) is formed of three parts Ud, Gi, Ta. Ud refers to Samaveda, Gi to Yajurveda and Ta to Rgiveda. From the recitation of the three Vedas emerges the sound OM. Prajapti said that when he uttered OM, he found refuge in this fearless, imperishable sound. When he repeated OM, it produced Agni, atmosphere affected by OM produced Vayu, and Chants of Soma caused Dhyan, from celestial space came Aditya. Further exerted efforts produced the Gayatri mantra: "Om bhurbhuvah tatasaviturvarenyam, Bhargo Devasya Dheemahi Dhiyo Yo nah Prachodayat Swaha." The Gayatri mantra is devoted to Sun God – the principle that causes Sun to thrive. It exercizes its magical power for the reciter.

Shri Krishna in the Bhagvat Gita identfies himself with OM. He says "I am the taste in water, thought and moon in the Sun, the secret syllable OM in the Vedas, the sound in OM." Yajurveda considers OM as a religious symbol for prayer and meditation. It illuminates atmosphere between self and the immediate hearing. It refers to degrees of consciousness.

Om consists of A, U, M, each of which possesses its own quality. (Some say OM has one more sound which is not heard). Silence surrounds it – it rises from silence and falls back into it. The A resounds from the back of the mouth and represents working consciousness; U is the sound mass that moves forward and fills the whole mouth. It is dream consciousness, Man closes the cavity of the mouth at lips. The subject and object in A are expressed separately; in U the subject – object (the dreamer and the dream) are separate, at the back. M has no subject-object. The three make different affects. The teacher told Satyakam, "The syllable OM is both Nirguna and Saguna Brahman. On meditation of OM he comes to reach after death and the Rig verda leads him to the world of man where austerity, chastity and faith whereby he experiences greatness on earth.

Myths appear to have been concocted about importance of the mantra "OM". Unity of a and u leads to the Antariksha, the world of moon and retires still higher. If he meditates on a, u, m he is united with brilliance of the Sun. When freed from the Sun, chants of Soma lead him to the world of Brahman. With OM he supports the truth. The knower reaches Tat which is peaceful, imaging immortal, fearless and supreme. The gods and seers who know OM as the nature of Brahman will become immortal.

Psychological and physiological studies of the mantras and tantras have been made. In the ancient times human body was said to have six charkas (also called Padmas) – psychological centers. Some thought there was one more center that was invisible and silent. These centers are located in the Sushumna Nadi which runs from head down with the back bone. The nerve is coiled like a sleeping serpent and can be awakened by kundalini yoga. Repeatedly activated, the Nadi generates consciousness and helps the yogi to realize bliss.

When two objects clink, they generally produce a sound in the time space frame. The sound comes when breath strikes the vocal cord. But there is one sound that comes out without a clink. That is the sound of primal energy of which the universe is a manifestation for instance the interior humming sound of protons and neutrons of an atom is not heard.

About knowledge, figuratively it was said that the Vedas are the limbs of the Lord. Yajur is the belly, Sun the head, and Rig his form. Yonder is the Brahman. The Brahma Vidya was transferred from teacher to taught, father to son. Brahma transferred the Brahma vidya to his son Prajapati, who gave it to Angiras, who gave it to Bharadwaj. Bharadwaj transferred it to Satyavah/Angiras.

The charkas mentioned above have their proper name, location, colour, petal and element as below:

No.	Center's Name	Location	Colour	Petals	Element
1.	Mooladhar	Between lung & anus	Crimson	4	Earth
2.	Swadisthan	Level of genitals	Vermilion	6	Water
3.	Manipur	Navel (Nabhi)	Cloudy Dark	10	Fire
4.	Anahat (not hit)	Level of heart	Orange-crimson	12	Air
5.	Vishuddha	Larynx	Smoky Purple	2	-
6.	Agya	Mind (between Brows)	White	2	-
7	Sahsrar	Crown of the head	- -	1000	-

VIMAN AND MISSILES

Fantasies sometime turn into reality and boon to human civilization. Mythology provides many such instances, and imaginary as well as fictitious characters. Children are (or were?) kept spell bound by 'Hogworth', 'Magic' 'Harry Potter'. Half a century ago Hindi journalism had thrown up an interesting fellow with equally weird name – Lal Bujhakkad (a know all man). Science fiction is another source for children as well as dults. The television programs became so popular that children got "glued to the idiot box and ignoring that some of them were of educative value they asserted their authority by prohibiting cartblanc these to children.

In epic stories such fantasies have soared into sky. In Ramayana 'Pushpak Viman' changes hands from Kubera to Ravana. The viman could fly you according to your wish. Kubera, the prosperous king enjoyed that pleasure. His cousin Ravana was too greedy and in stead of enjoying Kubera's hospitability he grabbed it and flew to Lanka. He too was deprived of it by his assassin. Temporarily and, to the surprise of people Ram with his favourites landed at the capital Ayodhya.

Iracus and Dedalus are known for their air craflmanship in the western world. They fixed wings with wax and tried to fly like birds. So temping it was for the younger flier that his wings gave way from the Sun's heat and he met his end in the sea. Threads of the ingenuity were picked up later and the tenacity of experiments finally achieved success. All inventions consume time. In our life time we saw queer things like 'drone', and miraculous things like satellite etc. And, so are missiles. Their present breed owes much to slings, arrows and scientific approach. War strategies and innovations have contributed to move on and on. The landmarks command respect. People are familiar with 'Surs' (gods), Asurs (demons), 'Rakshasas' (giants), 'Pishachas', 'Bhoots' (ghosts and devils), 'Nags' (snakes), 'Gandharvas', 'Apsaras' (nymphs residing in water and on tree and sky), 'Bhrigus' and Matriswans. Some of them are beneficiaries and some evil for the human beings.

'If wishes were horses' sounds queer. What looked absurd once turned out time. In our dreams we find ourselves soaring up in the sky, fulfill self wish to fly while asleep. It leaves delightful sensations. The Late Jawaharlal Nehru, Prime Minister of India has mentioned about his dream fantasies in his autobiography.

Dreams are dreams, a dreamer forgets. Myths are myths, yet not all myths are false or imaginary. The latest mythic 'e-mail' is fascinating. Telephone with self picture is another mythic that is waiting in wings to appear and become public. Miniature watches tied to the wrist would remind the wearer that he is being remembered by some one some where. Think of the grand child with his charming smile reporting his thrill. His smile is the reward that thrills us.

Vigorous efforts to fly had been made in 19th century. In July 1900 count Zeppelin of Germany made his first flight in his own constructed aircraft. Crowds had lined the shores of Lake Constance as the cylinder shaped vehicle, 420 ft long flew for 18 minutes over the water. The count became a world celebrity. (During World War I the Zeppelins used it for spying on enemy territory and even dropped bombs on London. Soon thereafter the airship was used as a passenger air service. Two zeppelins Graf and Hindenburg made round trips from Germany to Rio de Juneiro and to Lakehurst (Germany).

The airship was an interesting carrier. It was three times of jumbo jet in length and as tall as 1-13-storey building. As for passenger amenity, a passenger had a cabin with a bed and washing facilities. He could stay in his cabin or wander through the lounge or look out of the windows which could be opened. Fifty passengers ate meals in the dining room seated at tables. After all it was built for comfort, not speed. It had a crushing speed of 80 miles an hour and an altitude of 650 feet and crossed Atlantic in 43 hours.

Earlier in 1929 the Graf flew around the world in 21 days landing at Tokyo, San Fransisco and Los Angeles. Other countries envisioned a great future for rigid airships. Britain planned a fleet of sliver giants to India and Australia. A US airship (known as Shenandoah) was the first rigid airship to use helium instead of inflammable hydrogen. But the flights faced weather difficulties. In 1933 the Akron and in 1935 Macon crashed which heralded the end of America's era of giant rigid airships. Britain's R101 could not fly beyond France. In 1937 the Hindenburg met with an accident that killed 36 people. The era of the giant airstrip came to an end. (India too made a mark when Tata flew from Bombay to London).

Great strides have since been made. Moon and Mars have been reached and partly explored. US astronaughts have shown courage and spirit of adventure. All because of fantasy of flight and attempt to go to the unexplored!

JYOTISHA

Predictions based on correct data and correct calculations turn out correct. It is a matter of faith, says our friend Balasubramanian. (The matter for section on Jyotisha has been contributed by him, we gratefully acknowledge.) Jyotisha is not a myth, he says.

The Vedic Astrology, which is five millennia old, is a natural cosmic science based on astronomy. The accuracy of its predictions is complete and unique.

The Vedic astrology recognizes heavenly bodies in our solar system. They take the rest of the galaxies and constellations as reference points in relation to planets based on the constellation they are moving against. However, it is true that the science of Astrology is a sign of indication.

Planets play an influential role in our personal life and man's activities. The nine planets, the number is so well known, are Ravi , Som, Mangal, Budh, Brahaspati or Guru, Shukra, Shani, Rahu and Ketu. The week days have derived their names from planets. (Rahu and Ketu are not planets. They are descending and ascending modes of the Moon). Sometimes Ketu is depicted as the personification of comets and meteors.

Shani, Rahu and Ketu are not auspicious. Hence believers propitiate them. It is not always so, because, if Shani is pleased it can prove extremely beneficent.

The horoscope (birth chart) cast on the Indian system is unique since it makes adjustments for the dynamic Zodiac/universe which is moving and is not static. It takes into account that zodiac is epileptic and not circular due to which 12 houses in the birth chart are not exactly 30 degrees each but vary according to the time of birth. Due to this difficulty the horoscope cast on the Indian system comes out in a different form. Indian horoscope is more accurate, however.

The birth chart is a symbolic interpretations in the form of a table for the placement of planets in the Zodiac for a particular place at a particular time and day. It is a snap shot of the sky at the specified time of birth. For the purpose of uniformity we fix the point rising on east-called Ascendant – lagna and to read the charts.

The horoscope analyses are made – a statistical, mathematical permutation combination of planets, their occupant houses – with the exact strength of planets. Strengths of friendly and enemy planets are considered. Saturn, Mars, Rahu (serpent head), Ketu (serpent body) are known for their evil effects.

The evil effect of Saturn for a period of 7½ years is well written about in Indian mythology. Nala and Harish Chandra, though mighty rulers, could not avert tragedies predicted because of Saturn's influence.

The Indian system, provides for match making compatibility for marriage. Some principles are prescribed taking the effect of Mars in view.

	(PISCES)	**(ARIES)**	**(TAURUS)**	**(GEMINI)**	
	12 MEENA/ JUPITER	1 Mesha/ ARIES MARS/ OWNER ASWANI BHARANI KRITHIGAI-¼ = ASCENDANT/LAGNA	2 RBRISHABH RISHABA/ VENUS KRITHIGAI-¾ ROHINI–1 MRIGA	3 MITHUNA/ MERCURY	
AOUARIUS	11 KUMBHA/ SATURN			4 KATAKA/ MOON	CANCER
CAPRICOR	0 MKARA/ SATURN			5 SIMHA/SU N	LEO
SAGITTARIUS	9 DANUS/ JUPITER	8 VARUCHIKA/MARS	7 THULA/VENUS	6 KHANYA/ MERCURY	
		SCORPIO	LIBRA	VIRGO	

12 Months – 12 HOUSES/ OR BHAVA/OR RASI

1 HOUSE - 2¼ Stars/ Star 1, Star 2 & 3rd Star ¼ - 1st Padam.

Each Star – Divided into 4 Padhas

360° – for 12 HOUSES, Each House 30 °

Ascendant is calculated on the base of Sun rise time of birth date

Rasi is based on moon.

Ascendant is the exact degree of Sun in Zodiac/Rasi

Every 4 minutes the degree changes, so it is very important to know the exact time of birth. Even a few seconds make difference in calculations.

1st House	:	Behaviour, health affairs
2	:	Finance – gains and losses
3	:	Mental aptitude, sibling, early education
4	:	Home, Parent, Brothers and Sisters
5	:	Love, marriage, children
6	:	Work, employer – employee, Health, Life
7	:	Marriage, partner, husiness
8	:	Life, death, sex
9	:	Higher learning
10	:	Social status, regulation
11	:	goal, hopes and wishes, organization
12	:	Social responsibility

The people of the Vedic times explored the realms of inner self and secured insight into some of the fundamental mysteries of the inner-most realms of psychic and spiritual world as also of Brahman and his realization. Several verses of the Arya Bhamiya Sukta of Rig-Veda refer to astronomical observations, each going round the sun. "The sun having three mothers and three fathers stood on high chariot; the 12 spoked wheel of the sun revolves round the heaven and never tends to decay. 720 children in pairs, Agni, abide in it". The Vedic verse kept 21 days in each cycle of four years restricting the number of days in a year to 360. The three quarter days of the consecutive solar years in each cycle of four years are also termed as the steps of Vishnu. The 1st of the four is called Kali, the 2nd is Dwapar, the 3rd is the Treta and the 4th is Krit.. or Satyug.

The Yajuveda measures are : 10000 – Ayut

10 Ayut	=	1 Night
10 Niyut	=	1 prayut
10 Praynt	=	Arbud
10 Arbud	=	1 Nyarbud
10 Nyarbuds	=	1 Samidra
10 Samidras	=	1 Madhya
10 Madhya	=	1 Put
10 Aut	=	1 Parad
10 1 Parad	=	10^{12} (or one English billion)

The planets are found depicted in temples – Sun in Center, facing east with other grahas fixed around it. His chariot of one wheel is drawn by seven horses with Arun (the deity of dawn) as his charioteer. Shukra sits in a golden chariot drawn by eight horses (or in silver chariot drawn by 10 horses). Shani rides an iron chariot drawn by eight horses. Rahu rides a black lion or is seated on a throne or on a silver chariot drawn by eight horses. Ketu rides a vulture. The other eight face him.

There are eight Dikapalas (deities) who rule over eight quarters of the universe. Indra, Yama, Varuna and Kubera rule over the east, south, west and north, respectively. Agni deals with south-east, Nirrti with West, Vayu with north-west and Ishan with east.

Kshetrapla, an aspect of Bhairava, is chief guardian of the temple. He is naked and inspires awe. A Dwarpal is the guard.